IMAGES
of Rail

SAN FRANCISCO'S INTERURBAN TO SAN MATEO

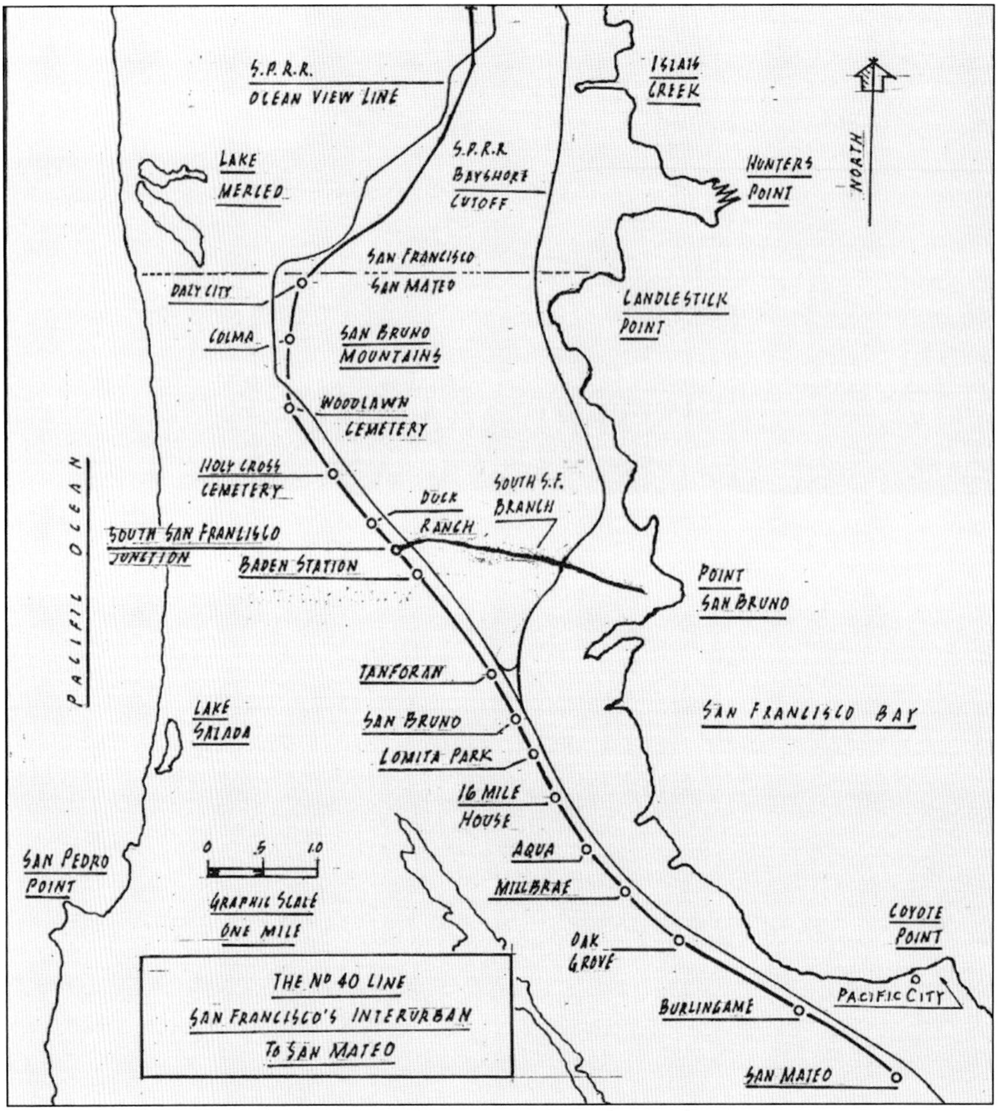

Above is the basic route of the 40 line. (Courtesy Don Holmgren.)

ON THE COVER: Car No. 1225 is southbound at Orange Avenue Station. (Courtesy Walter Vielbaum.)

IMAGES
of Rail

SAN FRANCISCO'S INTERURBAN TO SAN MATEO

Walter Vielbaum, Robert Townley, Walter Rice,
Emiliano Echeverria, and Don Holmgren

ARCADIA
PUBLISHING

ISBN 978-0-7385-3008-6

Published by Arcadia Publishing
Charleston, South Carolina

Printed in the United States of America

Library of Congress Catalog Card Number: 2005928087

For all general information contact Arcadia Publishing at:
Telephone 843-853-2070
Fax 843-853-0044
E-mail sales@arcadiapublishing.com
For customer service and orders:
Toll-Free 1-888-313-2665

Visit us on the Internet at www.arcadiapublishing.com

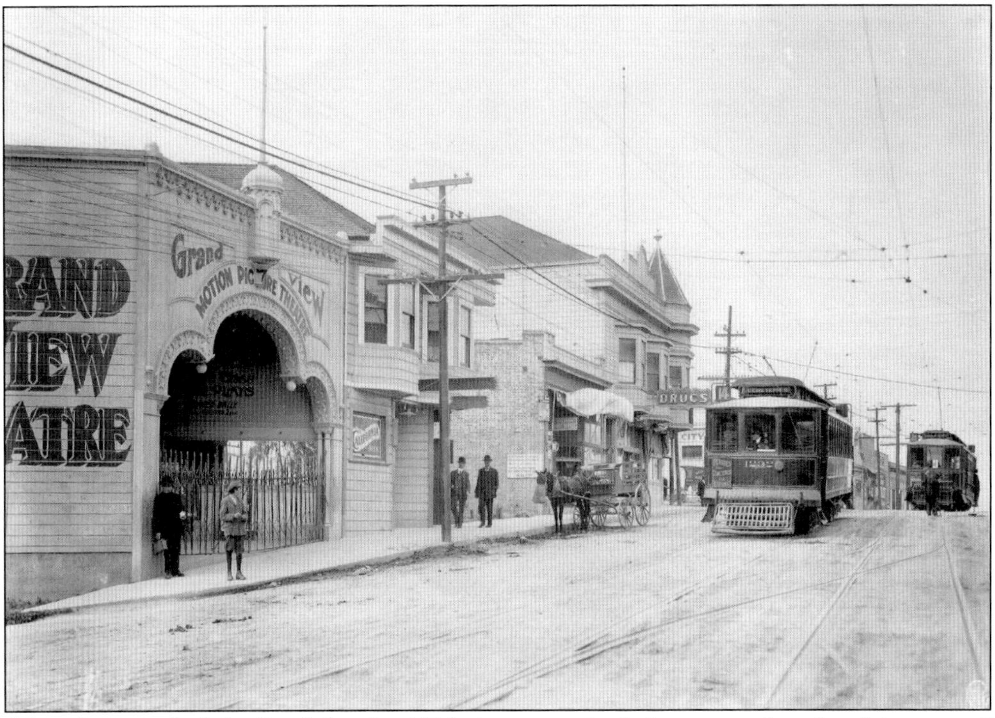

After the arrival of the Big Subs, the 1225-class series Lacledes were reduced to "city status," mostly operating on the Mission Street lines to either the beach or cemeteries. During peak hours, some Lacledes were used in "tripper" service. This photograph was taken at the Top-of-the-Hill in Daly City, looking north. In the background is a 1300-class car at the No. 26 line terminal. (Courtesy Rudy Brandt.)

Contents

ACKNOWLEDGMENTS

Twenty-eight months before the last 40-line car left San Mateo in the early morning hours of January 16, 1949, the Bay Area Electric Railroaders Association (BAERA) was born. It was in September 1946 that a group of Bay Area railfans gathered to save from the scrapper's torch Key System streetcar No. 271. Since none of the group wanted to personally own No. 271, it was decided to create the BAERA.

Two of the authors—Bob Townley and Walt Vielbaum—were part of that original group that in December 1946 formally organized the BAERA. During the mid-1950s, authors Townley and Vielbaum served as BAERA president and board member respectively. A third author, Walter Rice, is today a director of the BAERA. Most of the individuals who contributed to this volume are association members.

The streetcar era presented by the 40 line has long since passed. Today at the BAERA's Western Railway Museum, the ambience of this period is faithfully presented. The museum has over 100 city streetcars, including car No. 271, as well as interurbans, locomotives, and mainline passenger equipment. Three pieces of the collection ran on the tracks of the 40 line: rail grinder No. 0109, crane car No. 0130, and the party and school car "San Francisco." The museum also has a fine archives department that houses the corporate records and photographic collections for a variety of Northern California rail properties.

In recognition of the importance of the Western Railway Museum as a link between the past and present, the authors are donating all of the proceeds from this volume to the BAERA's car house No. 3 project.

As all realize, a project of this scope is a collaboration of many persons, some of whom are unknown. The photographs are credited to their respect photographer or collection. Three photographers deserve a special mention. Authors Townley and Vielbaum walked the entire 40 line private right-of-way prior to abandonment. Wilbur Whittaker has a record that spans over three-quarters of a century of creatively photographing Bay Area streetcar operations. His images are legendary. Through the lenses of these and the other photographers we are able to provide the 21st-century reader with the most complete pictorial history of the 40 line ever published. Emiliano Echeverria, who has spent a lifetime researching San Francisco's rich transportation past, enriched the pre–Market Street Railway photographic record. Grant Ute's research was responsible for discovering the 1905 essays about the then newly built line to San Mateo (Chapter 2).

A very special thank you goes to Don Holmgren who researched, designed, and drew the maps. Don's maps are the most comprehensive 40 line maps ever printed. A BAERA member since 1952, Don was in charge of the organization's equipment division in the mid-1950s. Don has also continued his tradition of providing vignettes that have both enlivened and enriched the text.

We also want to acknowledge the motormen, conductors, and other 40-line operating personnel who made the trip from the heart of San Francisco to downtown San Mateo a memorable experience, for those fortunate to have ridden the No. 40 car. To the civil engineers who designed the route and the entrepreneurs who built and ran San Francisco's only interurban line we say "thank you." Even the often reviled United Railroads president Patrick Calhoun merits special praise. Calhoun extended the line to San Mateo and purchased both 1225-class cars and the Big Subs.

Lastly we want thank Arcadia Publishing for bringing our efforts to reality. Our appreciation goes to Arcadia's John Poultney for his support and encouragement.

INTRODUCTION

San Mateo Interurban Car—Minimum Fare 10¢

The night was chilly, but the mood was festive—for a funeral. On Saturday, January 15, 1949, scores gathered across from the Southern Pacific Railroad's San Mateo station at Third Avenue and B Street to either witness or ride along to San Francisco with the last cars of San Francisco Municipal Railway's (Muni) route No. 40 streetcar, the 21-mile-long San Mateo Interurban.

The funeral cortege consisted of the last revenue car No. 1241 in Muni's blue and yellow paint scheme that the railway had introduced in 1939. Car No. 1235, a "railfan special" painted in Muni's postwar green and cream wings design, followed.

The No. 40, which was to become one of San Francisco's most successful streetcar lines, had its beginnings on April 27, 1892. On that date, San Francisco's pioneering electric railway, the San Francisco & San Mateo Railway Company (SF&SM) began service. Like many contemporary companies, its corporate title was more ambitious than the reality of its operation. The farthest south the SF&SM reached was Baden (South San Francisco), 13 miles north of San Mateo. This destination was reached by a circuitous San Francisco routing (other companies had the franchises on major streets) and a change of cars at Thirtieth Street. Nevertheless, the SF&SM was the first phase of the 40 line.

On May 12, 1901, what was now the San Francisco & San Mateo Electric Railway was purchased for $1.6 million by the "Baltimore Syndicate." It was rumored the new owners were looking for other San Francisco street railway properties, and by March 1902, the "syndicate" had purchased Southern Pacific's Market Street Railway and the Sutter Street Railway and its subsidiary, the Sutro Railroad. The new amalgamated corporation became the United Railroads of San Francisco (URR).

The URR immediately rushed to complete the San Mateo extension. The first car to arrive in San Mateo was line car No. 0301 on December 26, 1902. Service commenced as a roughly 40-minute shuttle operation between Baden and San Mateo on New Year's Day 1903. Single-truck dinky No. 572, built by Hammond in 1896, had the distinction of making the first revenue trip.

At the same time, the Laclede plant in St. Louis was building 20 closed interurban cars. Measuring 45 feet and 9 inches in length, the cars were San Francisco's first interurbans, numbered 1225–1244. On April 18, 1903, the first Laclede interurban arrived. However, shuttle service, now with 1225-class cars, continued between Baden and San Mateo until August 1, 1903.

On that date, a 75-minute through service was inaugurated from San Francisco's Fifth and Market Streets to San Mateo. New San Francisco routing brought the line to the city's downtown via Mission Street. It was not, however, until after the 1906 earthquake and fire that electric service was operated on Mission Street between Onondaga and Daly City Hilltop. The interurbans until this time were routed via Onondaga, Ocean, and San Jose Road to and from Daly City Hilltop.

The once financially strapped SF&SM Railway Company was now evolving into the highly profitable San Mateo line of the URR and its successor, the Market Street Railway (MSR). During the 1920s, this was the MSR's most profitable route.

On April 18, 1906, the earth shook as the great San Francisco earthquake occurred. Buildings came tumbling down, and the city was soon ablaze. The quake damaged the San Mateo line at several locations, and the URR went rapidly to work reopening the line on May 6, 1906. Patrick

Calhoun, the URR president, seized the opportunity the destruction presented to eliminate most of the URR's vast and unwanted cable car system. San Francisco suddenly had an extraordinary demand for new streetcars.

Calhoun went on a buying spree in St. Louis for new cars, including 16 classic interubans, 12 motor cars, and 4 trailers, which had been rejected by the Philadelphia & Western. The St. Louis Car Company soon shipped all 16 cars to San Francisco. Calhoun sold the four trailers while in transit to the Northern Electric.

At the time, the new interurbans were San Francisco's largest electric vehicles at just over 52 feet in length (over buffers) and weighing 75,640 pounds. Their size earned them the nickname "Big Subs," a term applied to these mighty interurbans because the URR called the line the "San Mateo Suburban line." (It was the MSR that changed the line's name to San Mateo Interurban and assigned the number 40.) The Big Subs operated until 1923 when they were withdrawn. After more than a decade in storage, the last Big Sub was dismantled and burned in 1935.

The SF&SM started running funeral cars in 1892 to San Francisco's principal cemeteries at Colma, just across the county line in San Mateo County, from funeral homes throughout the city. Funeral cars transported the bereaved and deceased for many years over the inner part of the 40 line directly into Mount Olivet, Holy Cross, and Woodlawn Cemeteries via connections owned by the cemeteries. The SF&SM's successors, the URR and MSR, continued this service.

Typical of interurbans of the period was a distant amusement park as a destination, which bolstered ridership (ownership was separate). The short-lived Pacific City amusement park was located at San Mateo's Coyote Point on San Francisco Bay. While San Franciscans enjoyed the amusements, the extra cars were stored in a siding just north of the Burlingame's Southern Pacific station.

"Elephant trains" shuttled passengers to Pacific City from downtown Burlingame, the site of that city's Southern Pacific station. Elephant trains, originally called auto trains, were developed as sightseeing trains for the 1915 Panama-Pacific International Exposition. They consisted of open trailers with two outward facing benches each, while those traveling to Pacific City may have been equipped with cloth canopies. The trains were pulled by a tractor, typically with a Speedster body.

At Leipsic Junction, one mile south of the cemeteries, connections were made with the South San Francisco line (the previous transfer point was at Holy Cross Cemetery), which operated on Grand Avenue for just over three miles before crossing the Southern Pacific Railroad and terminating near Point San Bruno. This feeder was abandoned on December 31, 1938.

A real estate promoter's storage battery car met 40-line cars at Broadway, Burlingame between 1913 and 1917. This battery car constituted the entire fleet of the Burlingame Railway. Built in 1912 by Edison-Beach Company, the car featured a unique lightweight body built by the J. G. Brill Company. After the Burlingame Railway Company was abandoned in 1917, No. 1 was towed to the Elkton shops of the URR, where it was stored for a brief period. Its final disposition remains a mystery.

No. 1 spent its entire life on the street. At the end of the day, the company's one employee would park the car near the intersection of what is now California Drive and Broadway and cross the street to a nearby building where a battery charging station was located. Here he would unwind the charging cable and run it across the street and connect it to the car. Car No. 1 would then spend the night at this location, taking a full charge on its batteries. The employee would then return in the early morning and, after giving the car a cursory cleaning service, would begin the route anew.

More important to the line's success (or failure) was the establishment in 1915 of direct parallel bus competition by Peninsular Rapid Transit Company. This system became part of Pacific Greyhound lines. Greyhound slowly increased its market share until it was a major variable in the 40 line's abandonment decision.

In 1921, the Market Street Railway (MSR) inherited the operations of the URR. The 40 line was again the beneficiary of the new management. Track was re-ballasted and a new and faster alignment was opened between Colma and Cypress Lawn Cemetery. A decade later, the tracks in Daly City and on Mission Street were renewed. Power supply was improved with an additional rotary converter at the existing Millbrae substation. Improved shelters and waiting stations were constructed.

The retirement of the Big Subs returned the 1225s full-time to the San Mateo line. Several modifications were made to the 1225s because of their reassignment to interurban service. MSR lengthened the cars to just over 48 feet, enclosed the platforms to allow "Pay As You Enter" fare collection, installed electric heaters, cushioned leather seats, and air gongs, and enclosed the end smoking sections. In 1930, field-shunting was added to the 1225s. This increased their speed to the 50 mile per hour range and reduced the schedule by five minutes. They were removed in 1933 because of increased traffic congestion that slowed streetcar operation.

Cars left Fifth and Market Streets, San Francisco, from 6:10 a.m. to midnight except on Saturdays when the last car left at 1:20 a.m. because of the late theater crowd. Service from San Mateo operated from 5:20 a.m. to 1:05 a.m. Headways ranged from 10 to 20 minutes. Ten minute headways were common on Sundays when passenger counts of more than 200 per trip were experienced. In 1929, the 40 line required 16 cars to maintain its schedules, but by 1943, this number was reduced to 11.

By this date, deferred maintenance was becoming an increasing problem. The California State Railroad Commission held that the condition of the company had grown progressively worse and in 1943, declared that the standard of service had reached the lowest point in the company's history.

On February 23, 1943, service was significantly reduced despite strong and increasing ridership. Under an order from the Office of Defense Transportation, all evening service was discontinued except a one-man shuttle using 900-class California Comfort city cars between Daly City and San Bruno. As part of making 900-class cars adaptable for interurban service, several of the 900s assigned to the 40 line were equipped with Golden Glow interurban type headlights.

Effective August 16, 1943, off-peak service was cut to a shuttle on a 15-minute headway between Daly City and San Mateo, also using one-man 900-class cars. Through San Francisco, service using the 1225s ran only from 6:00 to 8:30 a.m. and 4:00 to 7:00 p.m. On Sundays, only a San Francisco to San Bruno shuttle ran. The alleged reasons for these service reductions were the wartime manpower shortage and car shortage.

At 5:00 a.m. on September 29, 1944, the MSR, including the San Mateo Interurban, became part of San Francisco's Municipal Railway (Muni). Although most of the 40 line was outside San Francisco, it nevertheless again benefited from new ownership. On December 24, Muni revived two-man through service and, on March 4, 1945, although evening service still operated only to San Bruno, through service was restored at all times from Fifth and Market Streets to San Mateo. To save between six and eight minutes by avoiding Mission Street congestion, service for 14 blocks was routed off Mission Street to Valencia Street. The car of choice was the 1225.

On July 26, 1946, Muni abandoned Valencia Street and returned the 40 line to congested Mission Street. There were short-lived plans to retain and rebuild former major MSR streetcar lines including Mission Street, but these were soon rejected.

Muni found it economically desirable to reduce service as postwar ridership declined. In August 1947, the 40 line resumed shuttle service from Daly City to San Mateo, except weekday and Saturday rush hours. At all other times, the dwindling numbers of through patrons were forced to transfer at Daly City. The two-man 1225-class was retained.

Two traditional extra operations continued until abandonment. "Racetrack Specials" were run during the horseracing season at San Bruno's Tanforan Racetrack. San Mateo and Burlingame high school students commuted to and from school on special "High School Trippers."

At the time of its abandonment, the 40 line was still covering its operating costs. However, track and overhead repair and new cars were badly needed. Muni's consulting engineer did "not believe that the necessary expenditure of $750,000 to $1,000,000 for such rehabilitation is economically sound." Part of the abandonment decision was linked to the belief that the City of

San Francisco should not operate its transit system beyond Daly City. Muni offered San Mateo County the 40 line. The offer was spurned.

Early Sunday morning January 16, 1949, with a cheer, No. 1235 became the last car (ironically No. 1235 was the first of its class to San Mateo) to depart San Mateo. The era of the San Mateo Interurban, which had begun as San Francisco's first trolley line, was over.

Authors' Note: At the time the Philadelphia & Western ordered the Big Subs, an order was placed for two baggage cars. One of these cars, No. 401 (originally No. 101), is still in existence. No. 401 had a long and productive career in work service, finally being retired by the Southeastern Pennsylvania Transportation Authority in 1990. The car is on display at the Electric City Trolley Museum in Scranton, Pennsylvania. This car can claim to be the last Big Sub.

One

In the Beginning

On February 2, 1888, Frank Julian Sprague successfully proved in Richmond, Virginia, that the electric streetcar was both technically and economically feasible. Horse cars, urban steam dummies, and cable cars were now obsolete. San Francisco's pioneer electric railway, the San Francisco & San Mateo Railway Company (SF&SM) was incorporated in 1890, only two years after Sprague's Richmond success.

The San Francisco Board of Supervisors granted the required franchise to operate in San Francisco on December 23, 1890. By July 29, 1891, track was completed to the San Mateo county line. San Mateo County granted franchises for the railway to build from the county line to Holy Cross Cemetery.

April 27, 1892, was opening day. The line ran from near the important Union Ferry building at the foot of Market Street via Stuart, Harrison, Fourteenth, Guerrero, and San Jose Avenue to Thirtieth Street. To avoid the steep grade on Harrison at Third Street, which electric cars could not reliably climb, the inbound route was via Harrison, Eighth, Bryant, and Stanley (later Sterling) to Harrison. At Thirtieth Street, passengers transferred to continue their journey via Thirtieth, Chenery, Diamond, and San Jose Avenue to the county line. From the county line, the railway followed the side of the old San Jose Road to Daly's Hill (Daly City) and then the side of the "Old Mission Road" to Holy Cross Cemetery. The explanation of the circuitous San Francisco routing was that rival companies already had the franchises on major thoroughfares, such as Valencia and Mission Streets. A second line known as Eighteenth and Park that connected the Mission District with Golden Gate Park opened on November 25, 1894.

The line's initial rolling stock consisted of California-type cars with very short open section at both ends and a center closed section. They featured deck roofs with Bombay windows on the ends.

Financial pressures, however, proved too much, and by the end of May 1894, the company went into receivership. On April 11, 1896, the bondholders sold the line. The reorganized company adopted the name San Francisco & San Mateo *Electric* Railway (SF&SMER). New cars were purchased, new rails laid, and a Romanesque office building with a rounded Queen Anne turret was built at Geneva and San Jose Avenues to store the company's equipment. This new building, known as the Geneva car house after September 16, 1909, was in use until closed by the Municipal Railway during September 1982. It still stands.

In 1897, the company began a successful lobbying campaign with the San Mateo County Board of Supervisors for the necessary franchises to complete the line to San Mateo. Surveys of the proposed route were conducted between 1899 and 1900. The final franchises for the City of San Mateo were granted on May 12, 1900. Construction of the extension to San Mateo began on January 25, 1901. The pace of the construction effort, however, was slow.

On May 12, 1901, the company was purchased by the Baltimore Syndicate. Its two lines soon would be incorporated into the United Railroads of San Francisco.

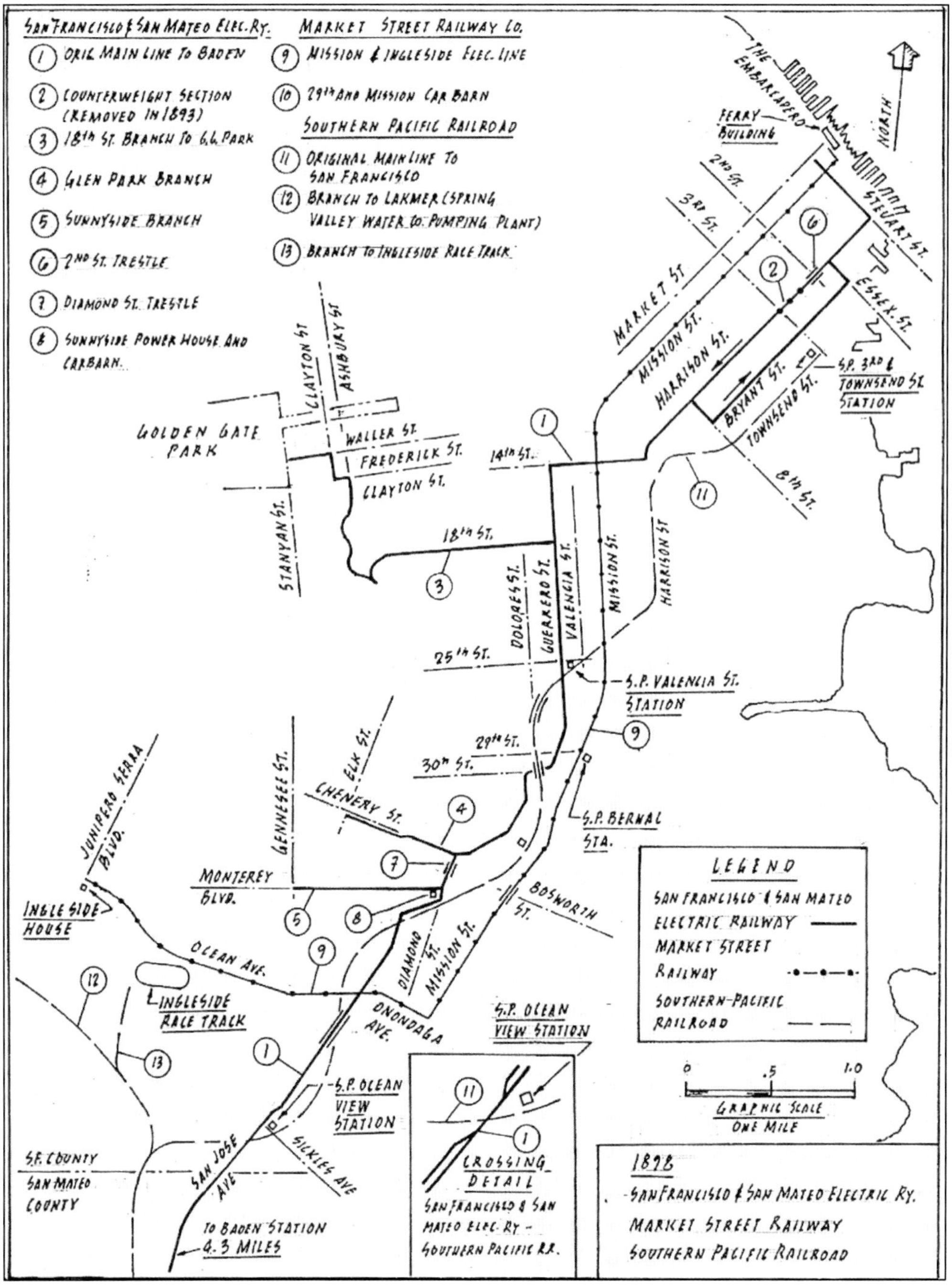

This is an 1898 map of the San Francisco & San Mateo Electric Railway, showing the Southern Pacific and Market Street Railway lines. (Courtesy Don Holmgren.)

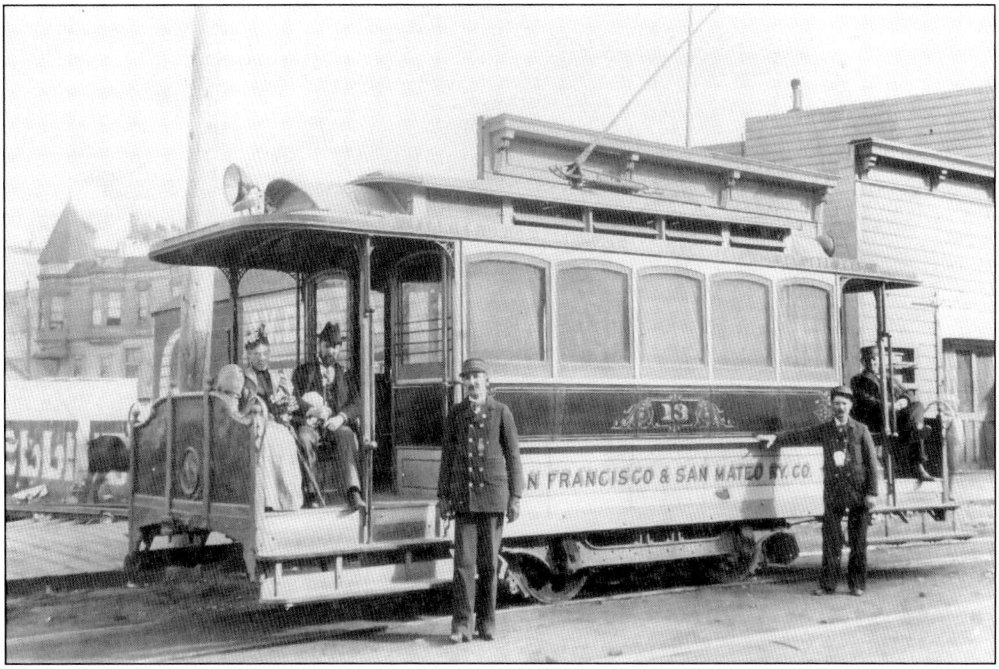

The crew and passengers of car No. 13 "watch the birdie" in 1892. The photograph was taken on Guerrero Street at the intersection of San Jose Avenue north of Twenty-ninth Street. The No. 13 was one of the original car types, which were single truck and operated between Thirtieth Street and San Jose Avenue and the ferries. (Courtesy Richard Schlaich.)

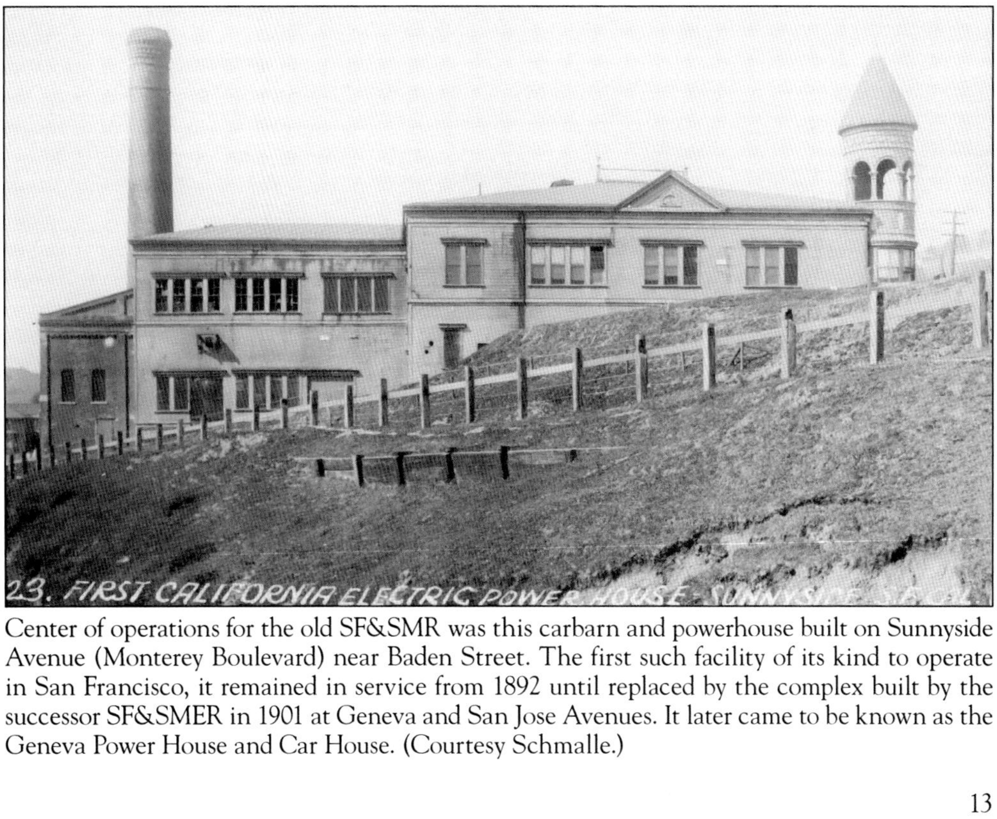

Center of operations for the old SF&SMR was this carbarn and powerhouse built on Sunnyside Avenue (Monterey Boulevard) near Baden Street. The first such facility of its kind to operate in San Francisco, it remained in service from 1892 until replaced by the complex built by the successor SF&SMER in 1901 at Geneva and San Jose Avenues. It later came to be known as the Geneva Power House and Car House. (Courtesy Schmalle.)

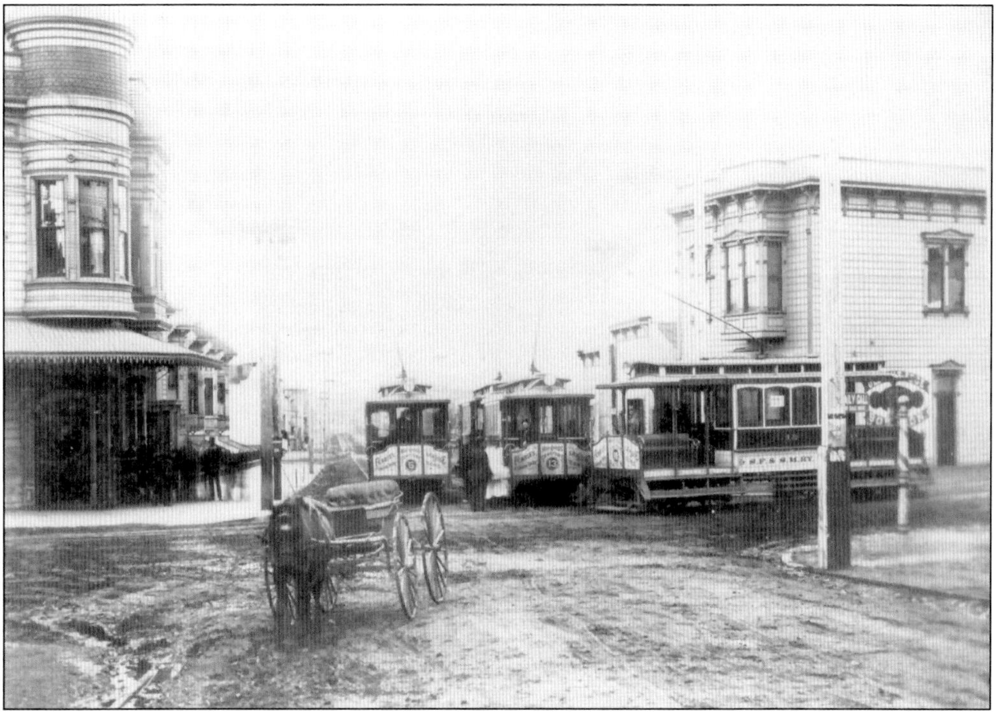

This is a view of the transfer point at Thirtieth and Guerrero Streets in 1892, shortly after the line opened. The building on the right still stands today. In the center are two single-truck "city cars," which terminated here. Passengers wishing to travel to points beyond were obliged to transfer to the double-truck car at right waiting to take them as far as Holy Cross Cemetery. (Courtesy Rudy Brandt.)

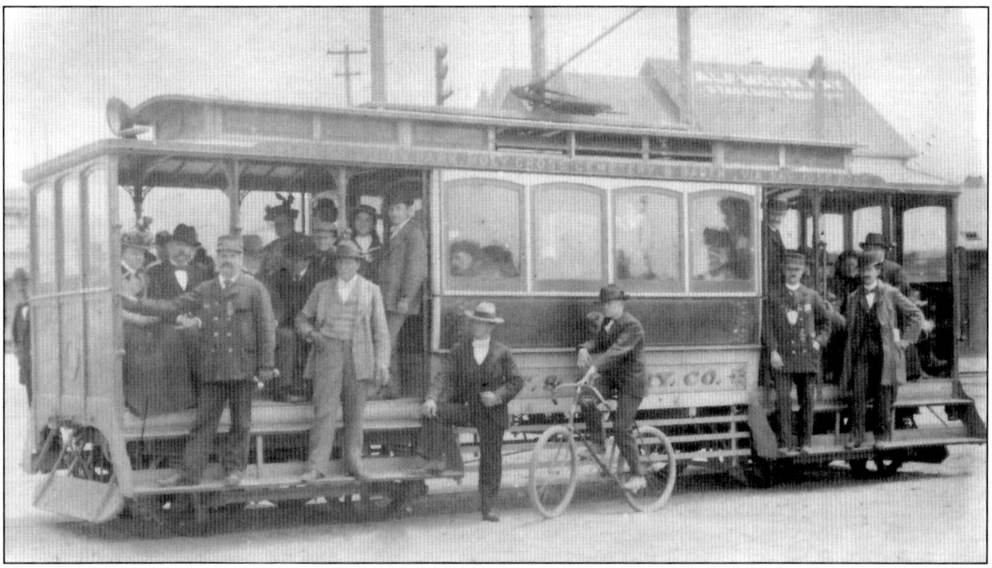

This 1895 photograph, taken at San Jose Avenue and Sickles, shows one of the original 1892 double-truck cars following installation of windows on the formerly open front. A year later, the cars would all be Tuscan red. (The photograph of car No. 25 on page 16 shows this later appearance.) (Courtesy Rudy Brandt.)

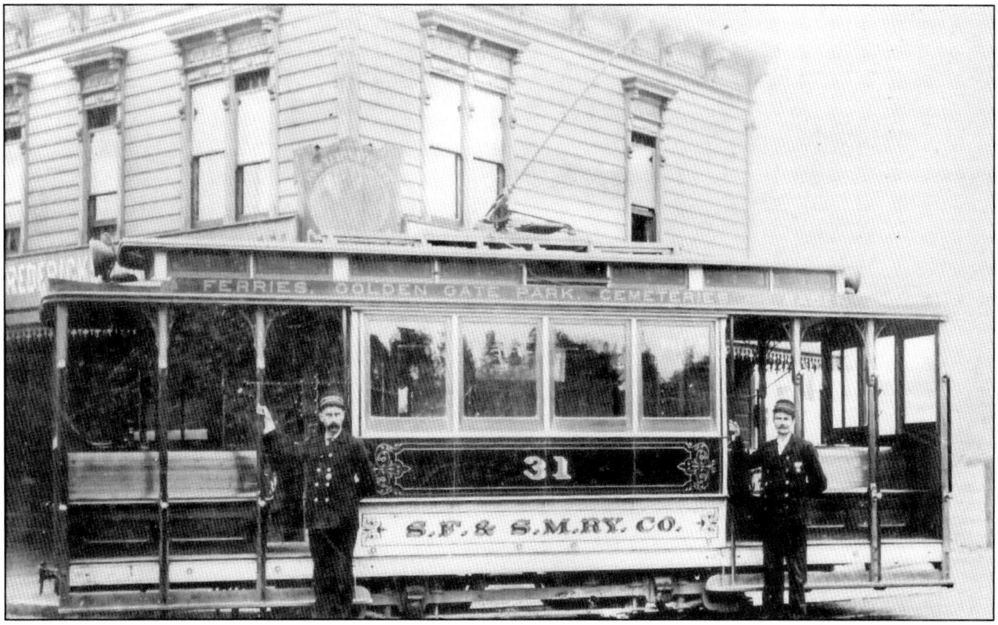

Car No. 31, one of a group of cars built in Newark, California, by Carter Brothers and numbered 31 to 36, was acquired in 1894 to supply sufficient cars for the company's new Park branch that opened in November 1894. This branch connected the Eureka Valley area with Golden Gate Park and was the first group of streetcars built for use in San Francisco to have windows on the ends of the cars. Up to this time, San Francisco's streetcars and cable cars offered little protection from the elements in inclement weather. (Courtesy Rudy Brandt.)

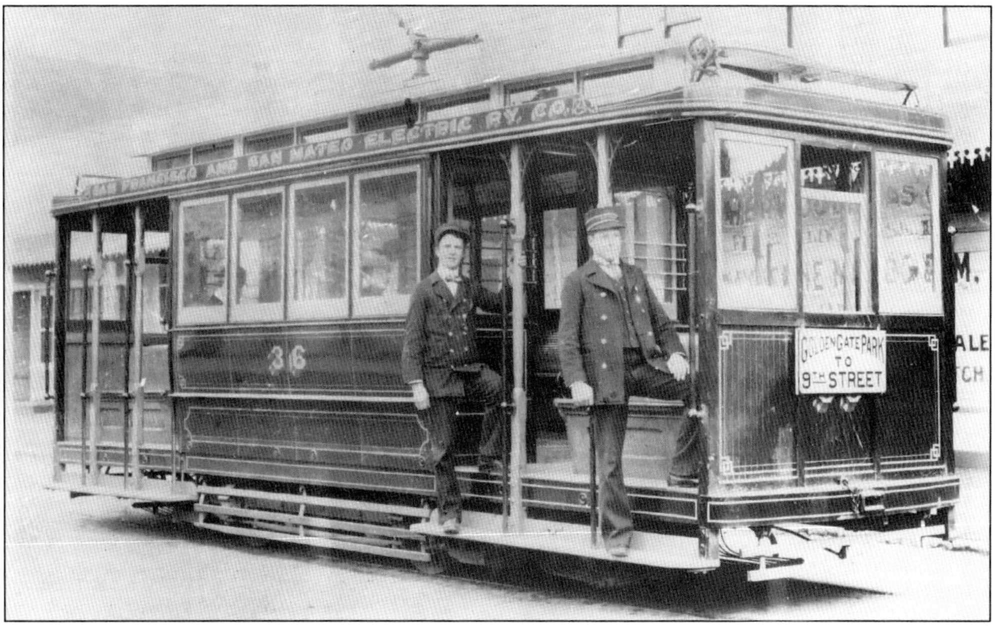

Car No. 36 models the paint scheme of the successor San Francisco and San Mateo Electric Railway, which was deep Tuscan red with gold striping. In 1898, another group of four similar cars numbered 37 to 40 was ordered and delivered from Carter. All 10 were sold by URR in 1905, with several going to San Jose. (Courtesy Rudy Brandt.)

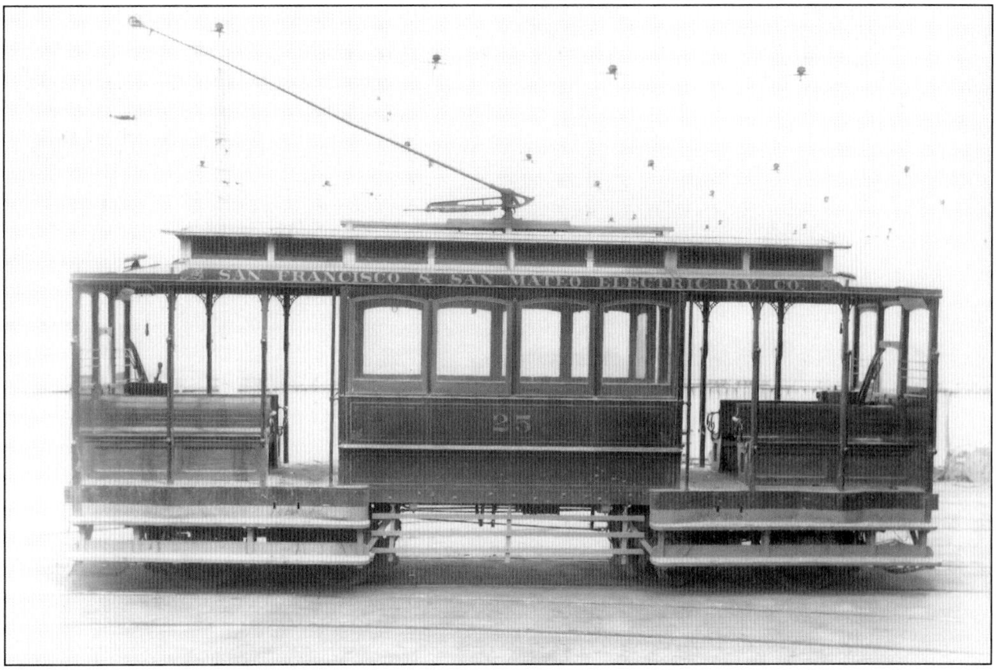

URR has bought the SF&SMER, and old car No. 25 poses on the Geneva ladder track in 1904 prior to it and its mates being offered for sale. These cars were scattered, with six running in Eureka and one each in San Jose and Richmond. (Courtesy Richard Schlaich.)

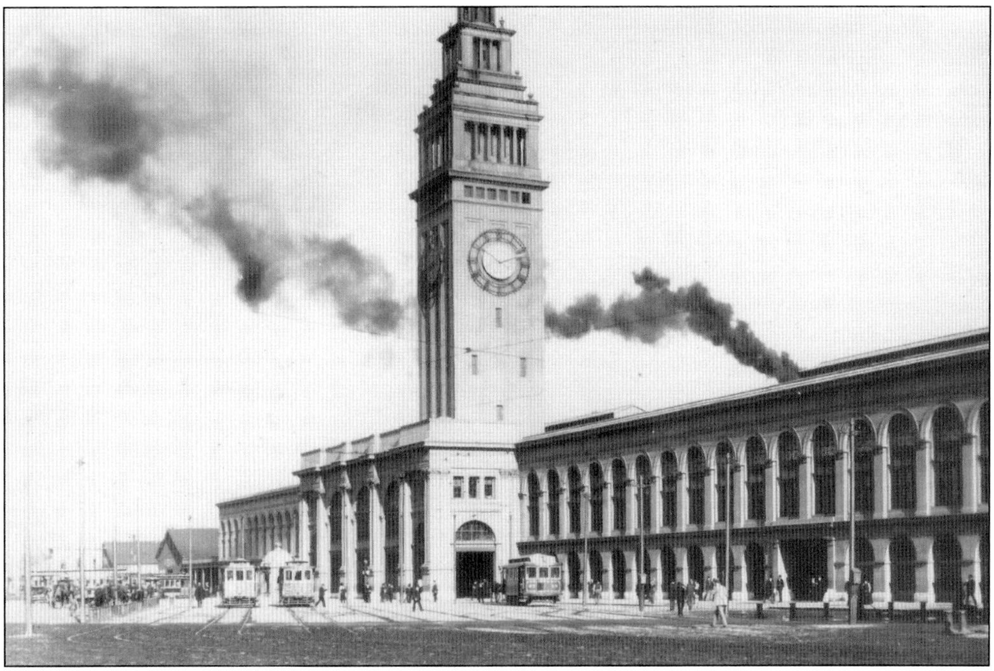

In 1898, the SF&SMER finally reached the ferries, being rerouted from Stuart north of Howard to a new routing via Stuart, Howard, and East Street to the new terminal at the front of the ferry building. Car No. 67 (St. Louis, 1900) was rebuilt into funeral car No. 2 in 1903 and into the party car "Sierra" in 1908. (Courtesy Charles D. Miller.)

Two

BIG SUB ERA

No better description of the newly built line to San Mateo can be found than those provided by URR riders themselves. An essay contest was held by URR in the spring of 1905 and the descriptions, reflecting 1905 spelling and language usage, by the first and second place winners are reprinted below:

A Trip to San Mateo (Winner of First Prize)

"In the West we live with a vim. Summer and winter do not lend themselves to inactivity, but work us with a rush. It is this very tirelessness that one day makes us yield to the temptation to slip away from the hurry and bustle of Market street for a few hours and ride down the peninsula to sunny, restful San Mateo, the city of homes.

"It is near the hour and the large, inviting car is waiting at Fifth street, and with a half-guilty feeling of neglected duty we sink back luxuriously into our seat. For a moment a street fakir absorbs our attention, and then as the car starts our glance falls on the old, historic Lincoln Grammar School, and with the picture of our own school days that it suggests, business is forgotten.

"On the northwest corner of mission and Fifth stands Uncle Sam's largest coning house, the stately U.S. Mint. The beautiful imposing new post office building is a block further on, and up Eighth street looms the city hall. The small, low houses down Mission street show that they belong to an older part of town, and yet right from their midst rise four great institutions of physical and mental upliftment—the San Francisco Nursery for Homeless Children, the Southern Pacific Hospital, the branch Public Library and the public school.

"Out here we catch our first glimpse of green hills, and the houses are new and modern. Further on more hills come in sight, with little cottages scattered over them.

"There is a quick turn on San Jose avenue and a momentary stop at the handsome red brick car house, and then we are right among the hills and the wild flowers and vegetable gardens of Ocean View. In a moment the county line is crossed, and San Francisco is behind us. A short ways on are the cemeteries, so beautiful with trees and grass and flowers and sunshine that they seem like living parks.

"And now the cars swing swiftly into the long stretch of level, poppy-bordered road, past the Southern Pacific depot and San Bruno, past Millbrae and on through the lily-hedges of handsome, fashionable Burlingame until we are right among the lawn- and rose-surrounded homes of San Mateo.

"There is one noticeable feature about this trip. The greatest beauty and development are along the tracks of this San Mateo suburban line. Inevitably this lovely country will develop in the future as it has in the past, and some day, instead of endless fields, it will be all lily hedges and lawn-surrounded homes, not crowded together city fashion, but nodding to each other over a reach of rose bushes. Back beyond them will be the orchard and vegetable gardens, a genuine Californian spot of fruit and flowers.

"In a city or a county or a State it has been the same—the railway first. It points the way and civilization and progress follow the tracks. The story is not new. In fact it is not a story—it is history.

A Trip to San Mateo (Winner of Second Prize)

"No better selection can be made for a car ride than a trip to San Mateo. Starting from Fifth and Market streets, the first point of interest is the United States Mint. The care turns here and runs out Mission street. On the right at Seventh street, you will see the new Postoffice building, at Eighth street the city hall and at Eleventh street the St. Ignatius church, at Twelfth street the Nursery for Homeless Children and at Fourteenth street the Southern Pacific Hospital. Going along, looking to the left is to be seen the Potrero Hills and on the right Twin Peaks, at Twenty-second street the new Mission Theatre, at Twenty-eighth street St. Luke's Hospital and on the left Bernal Heights. Next you pass the old St. Mary's College anon the right the new church. On the right, looking between the hills, is located Glen Park. The next point of interest is the Jewish Old People's Home. As you pass along you can get a good view of the vegetable gardens. You pass through the Excelsior Homestead to Onondago avenue. Here you see a large duck ranch where they raise on an average of 1,500 ducks per month. Then you see the House of Correction and the Sutro forest in the background. Then you pass the large new car house of the United Railroads.

"Crossing the steel bridge at Mount. Vernon Heights, look to the left and you will have a fine view of the Visitation Valley, with its vegetable gardens an dairy farms. Now we arrive at Ocean View, the city limits, where the next fare is collected. When you reach to top of Daly's Hill, look to the right and there a magnificent panoramic view is spread before you. See Lake Merced and the ocean, the Farallone Islands in the distance and white-sailed ships passing along. You are now in the San Mateo County. On the left are the San Bruno Mountains. Passing the Union Coursing Park on the right, now you arrive in Colma. Next you pass the cemeteries. There are the Servian, Italian, Japanese, the new Masonic, new Odd Fellows', Eternal Home, Mt. Olivet, Salem, Home of Peace, Cypress Lawn, Chinese and Holy Cross cemeteries, each one made most beautiful with plants and flowers. From here, on its private right-of-way, the cars run at a high rate of speed. The next stop is Baden station with its homes surrounded by trees. You get a glimpse of South city (South San Francisco). The Fuller Pint Works, the Steiger Pottery Works, the Pacific Jupiter Steel Works, the Western Meat Company's plants are located here. Next you pass the Tanforan race track and arrive at San Bruno. Here the new Southern Pacific Bay Shore cut-off will come in, and it is predicted that from South City to San Bruno there will be a great many new factories and plants erected within the next few years, and railroad shops and freight yards. There have been over 1,200 lots sole in San Bruno alone. Further along the line you pass Lomita Park, a new suburb, with its nicely shaded streets that have sold over 550 lots in the last few months, and many new buildings are going up. You pass the Sierra Morena range of mountains on the right. Looking to the left, you seen the bay with its marsh-lands, the home of the wild duck, and the oyster beds, the Oakland hills with Mt. Diablo in the distance, also Coyote Island. You pass the plant of the Spring Valley Water Company and arrive at Millbrae. You see the sub-station of the United Railroads. The homes are further back and cannot be seen for the wooded lands. Here is the Millbrae dairy with its herds of Holstein cattle, a most beautiful and clean place. Next the Black Hawk dairy, another large place with hundreds of stock. Now you reach Burlingame with its many beautiful residences, club houses and polo-fields. The equipages which are seen standing at the depot show the wealth of Burlingame.

"The run into San Mateo along its fine shaded streets does not show all of the fine homes, but gives one a good idea of what the place is like. Homes are covered with beautiful flowers, and tennis-courts and lawn abound. You pass along a few blocks of the business section of the town and arrive at the depot.

"The climate is simply incomparable, with no fogs or harsh winds. The bracing atmosphere of the bay mingles with the mild zephyrs of the valley, making it a most delightful temperature. Space will not permit for all that could be said of this beautiful place. The whole peninsula has a bright and prosperous future. When taking the trip, as the conductor to show the points of interest, and you will agree with me that it is the best trip that you can take for the money."

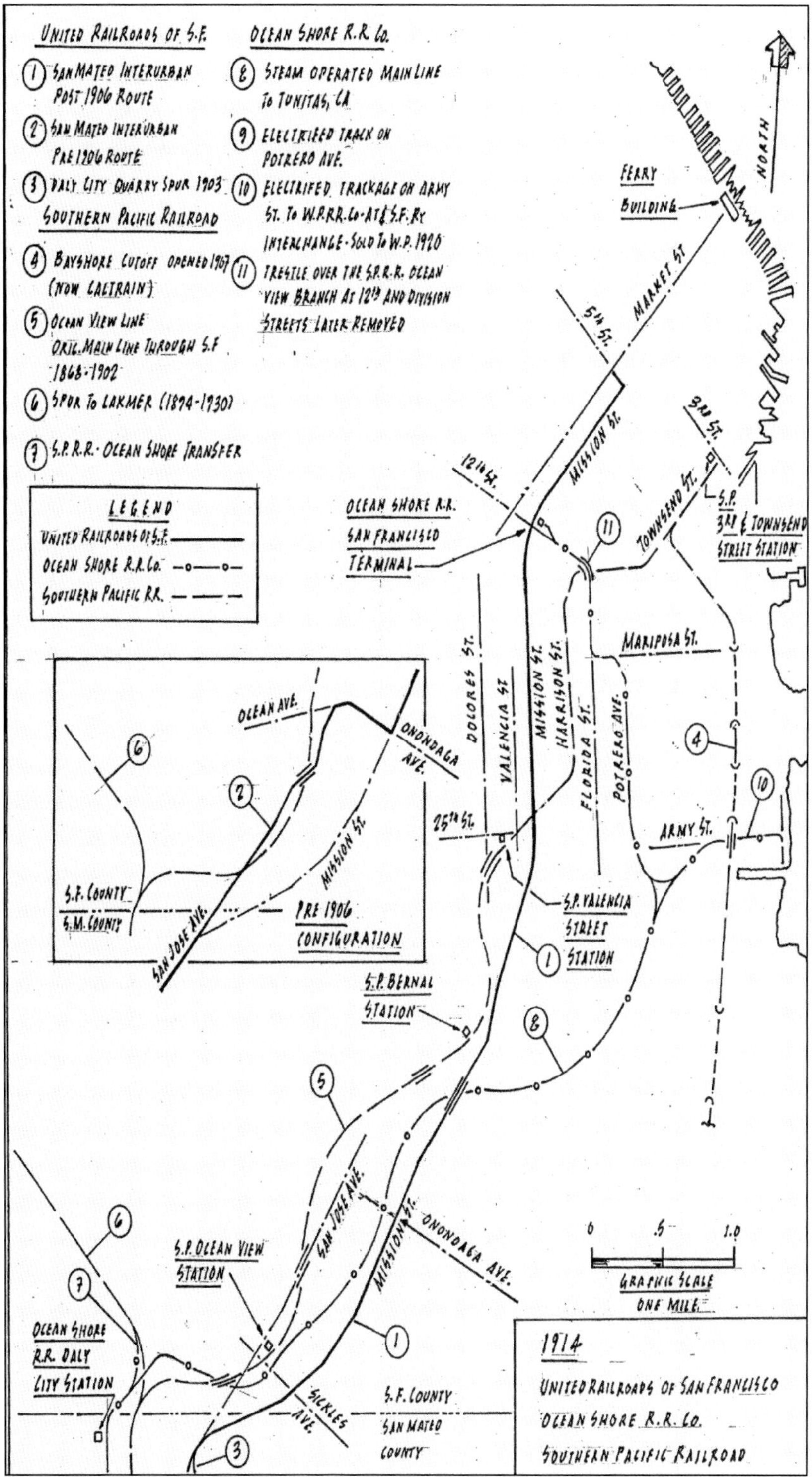

Here is the 1940 route of the 40 line, Ocean Shore Railroad, and Southern Pacific Railway in San Francisco County.

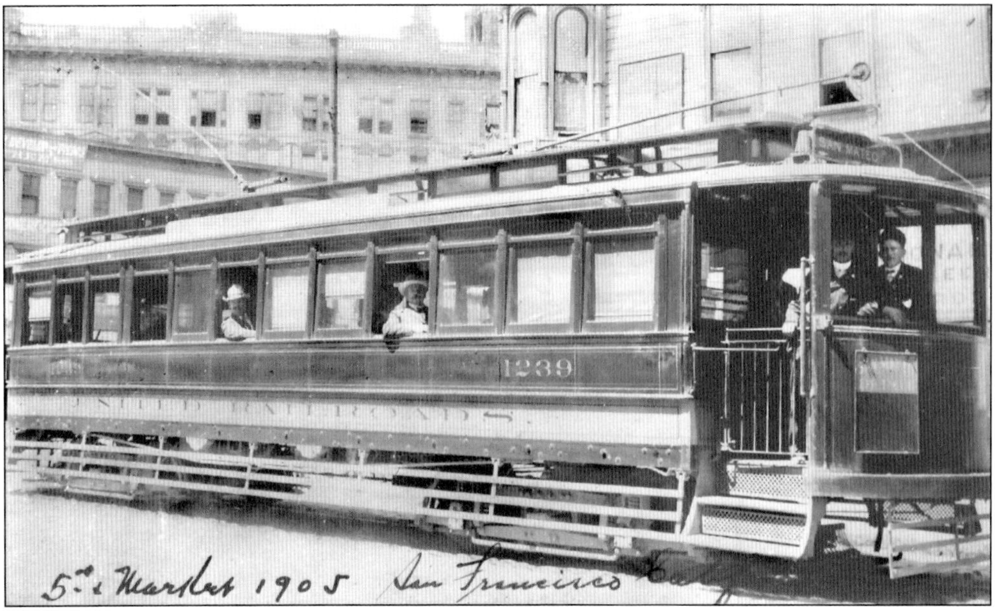

These brand-new 1225-class cars sport side slats over the running gear, end slats under the short flush platform, drop windows in the car body, drop widows in the ends, and gates at the steps. The side sign on the roofline and the flip-over front sign on the platform roof were standard on all cars of this period. It's hard to imagine why anyone would want drop windows on an open platform. Suburban car No. 1239 was photographed at its San Francisco terminal at Fifth and Market Streets in 1905. (Courtesy Emiliano Echeverria.)

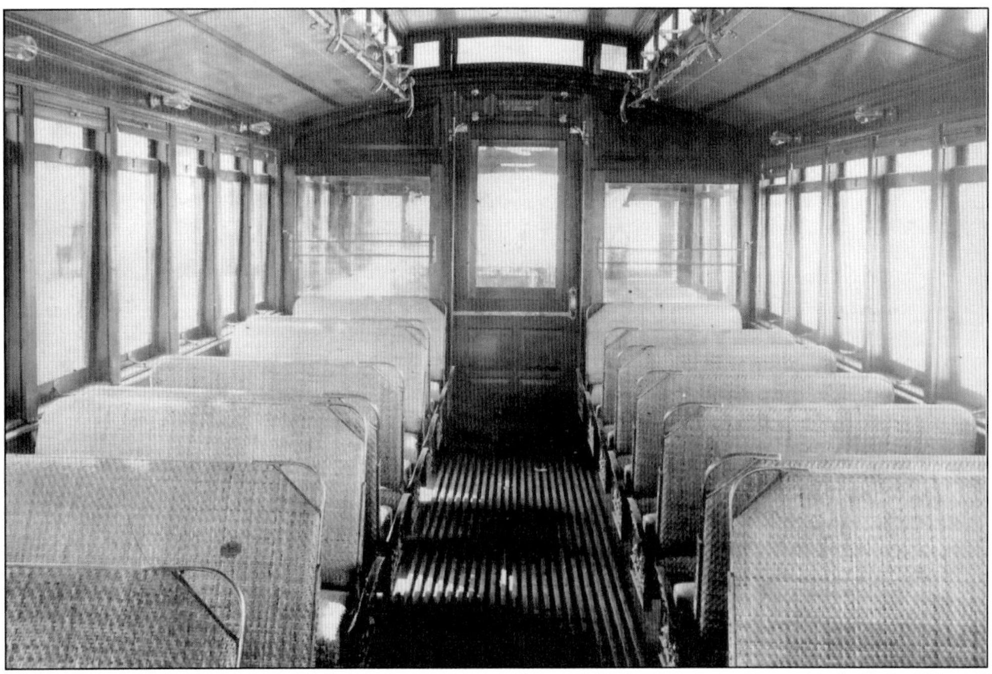

The interiors of the new Laclede cars upon arrival in 1903 had rattan seats, and the bulkhead above the door proudly proclaimed: Laclede Car Co., St. Louis, Mo. A major rebuilding in the early 1920s replaced the rattan seats. (Courtesy Charles Smallwood.)

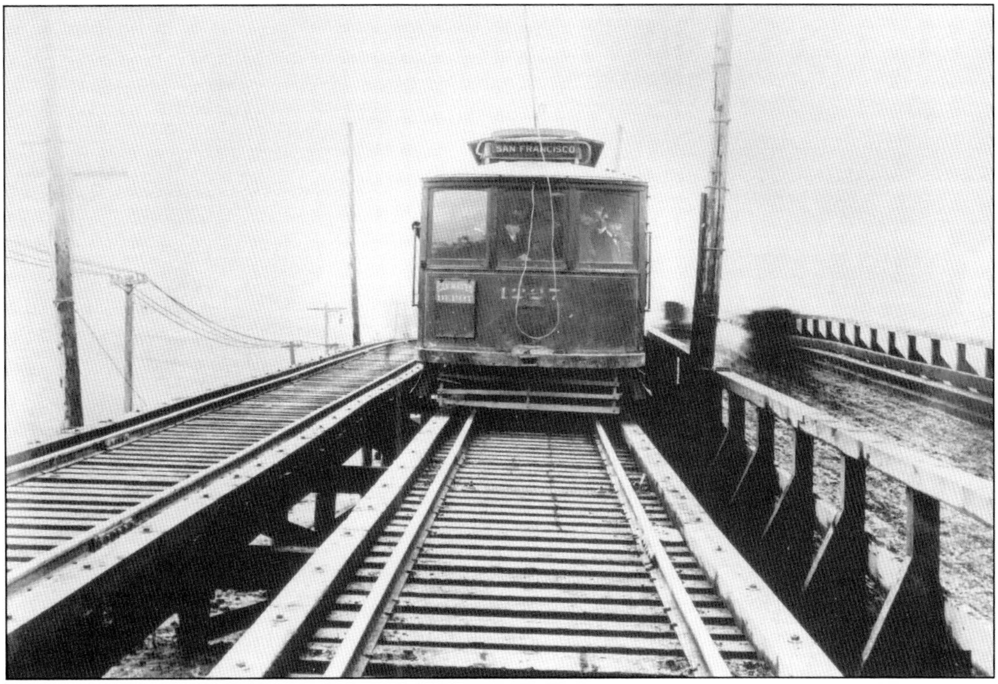

A 1903 test run prepares the Lacledes for service. Although these cars began to arrive on the property in April 1903, the full complement of 20 cars was not in service until August that year. (Courtesy Western Railroad Museum.)

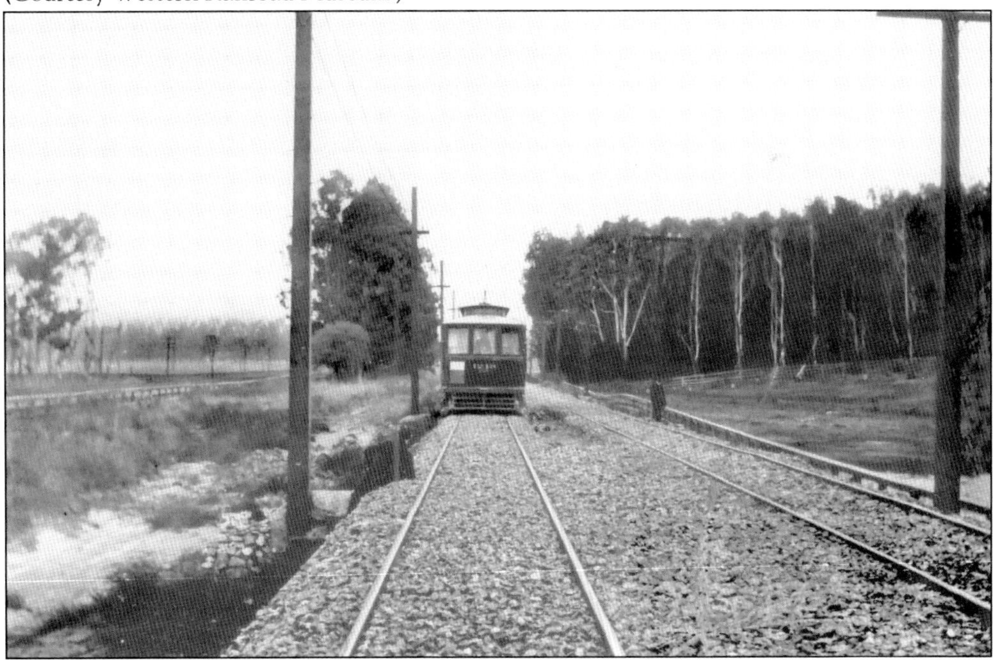

The year is 1903 and the Lacledes are new and being line tested. The Lacledes were the "last word" in suburban cars in terms of speed and comfort in 1903. In all, these durable cars lasted for over 45 years and were only beginning to show signs of age when they were removed from service. (Courtesy Western Railroad Museum.)

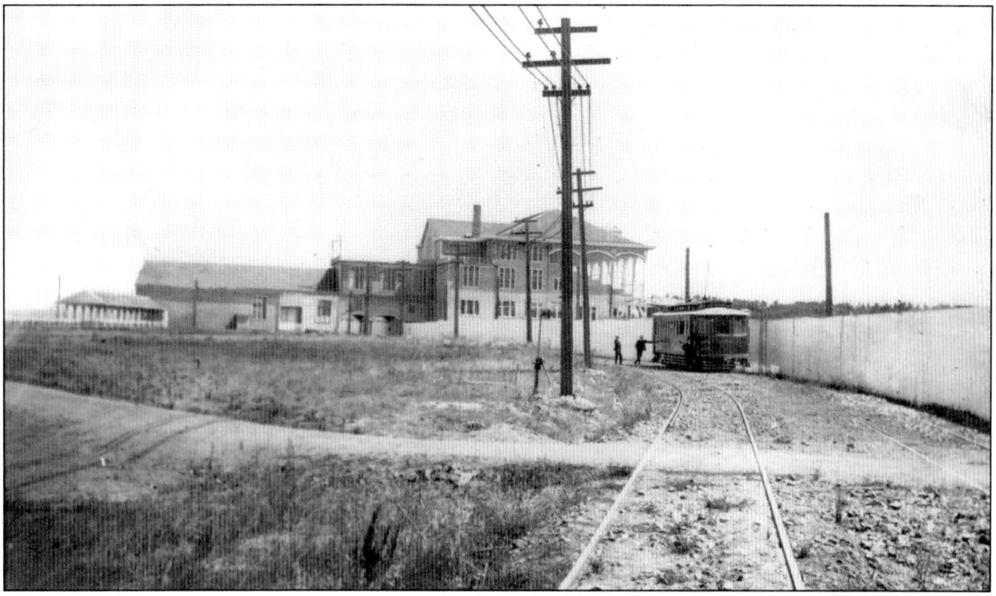

A northbound 1225-class car has been halted to pose for a photograph near the Tanforan Racetrack. The racetrack was built a few years before the San Mateo line but with the line in mind. This view gives a good idea of the locations of the racetrack proper, the San Mateo line, and the surrounding areas.

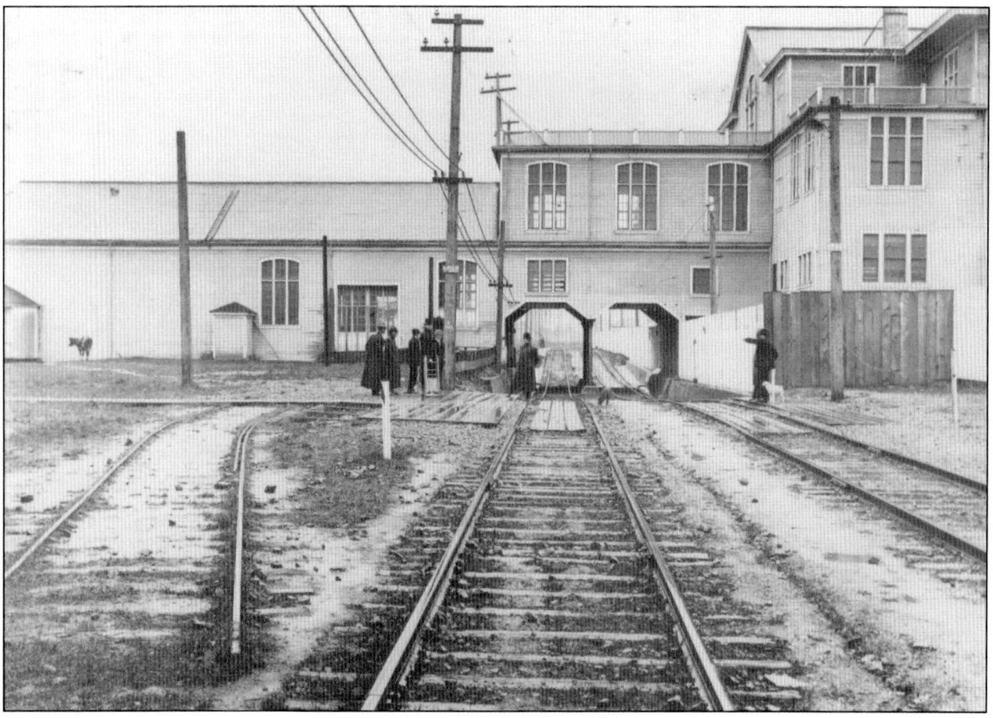

At Tanforan, the line dipped underneath a part of the racetrack structure. Note the disconnected siding running off to the left. This siding was where the horses were loaded and unloaded from the horse car, the specially built stable-on-wheels that shuttled horses from locations along the URR car lines to the racetrack. (Courtesy Rudy Brandt.)

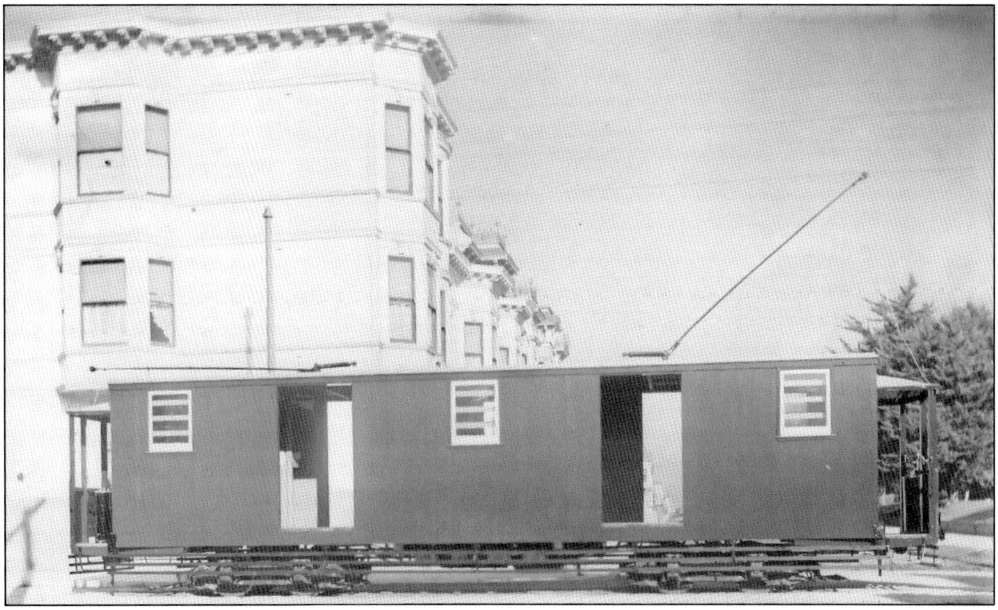

This car was built c. 1904 for the purpose of transporting horses to and from the Tanforan Racetrack. At that time, horses were often stabled in outlying parts of San Francisco or other points along the line. Also, horses from outside the area were transported from the ferries and the Southern Pacific depot as well. The car, while numbered 0910, was at one time known as "Mystery" and was used for transporting strikebreakers during the strikes of 1907 and 1917. After its horse transporting duties were taken over by motor vehicles, it became tool car No. 05 at the Twentieth Avenue sand pit. This photograph was taken in 1905 at Turk and Webster. (Courtesy Rudy Brandt.)

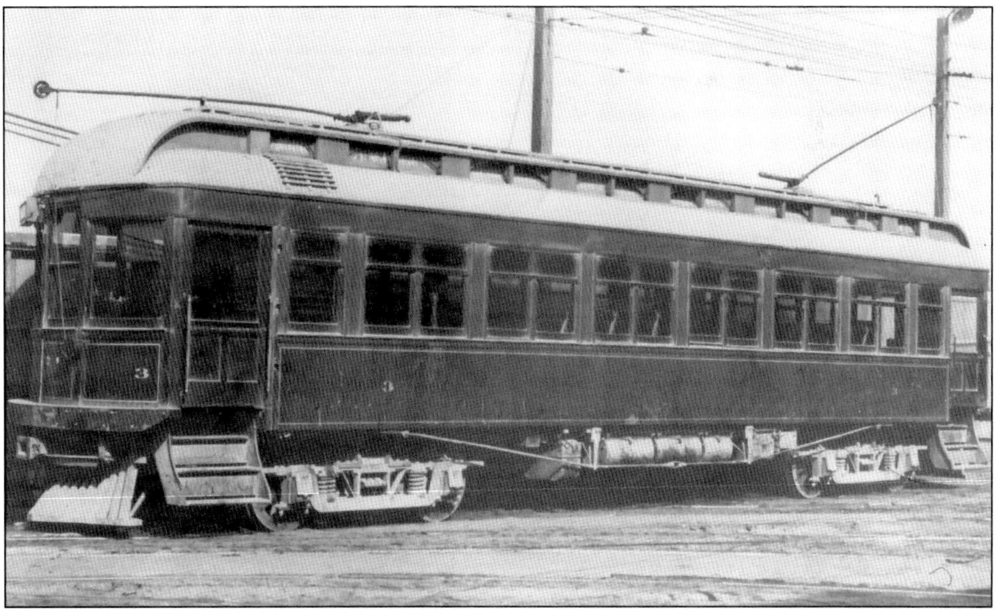

Fresh from the Factory! A newly arrived Big Sub shows off what it's got: spoked wheels, a pilot (cowcatcher) in front, with a lot of power and weight. Smaller wheels and the replacing of the pilots with eclipse fenders would later change the appearance of the Big Subs. (Courtesy Charles Smallwood.)

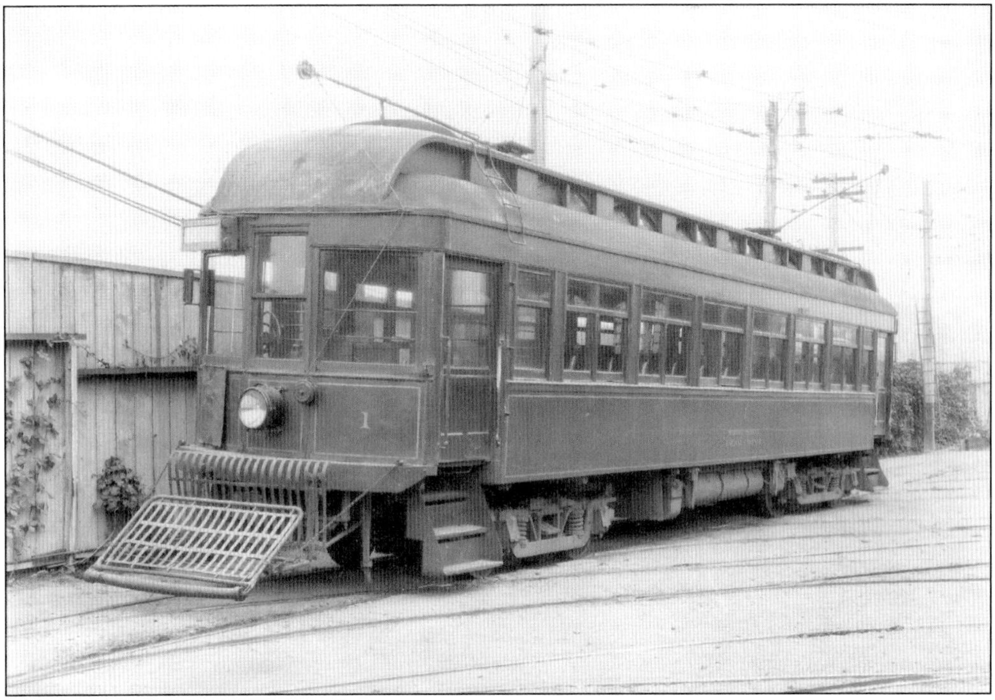

Here is a rare shot of Car No. 1 with a headlight. Usually the headlights were kept at the carbarn during the day and were thus seldom photographed. At this time, there were four No. 1 cars active in San Francisco transit: the URR Sub, Castro Cable, California Street Cable (an independent company), and Muni's still extant streetcar. (Courtesy Rudy Brandt.)

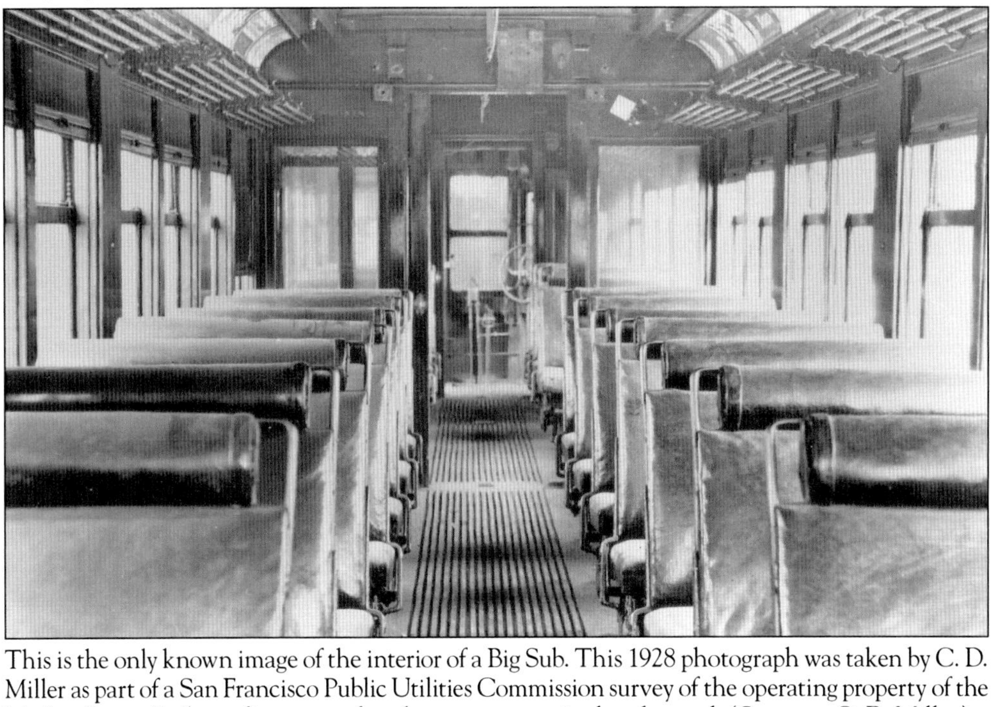

This is the only known image of the interior of a Big Sub. This 1928 photograph was taken by C. D. Miller as part of a San Francisco Public Utilities Commission survey of the operating property of the Market Street Railway, five years after the cars were retired and stored. (Courtesy C. D. Miller.)

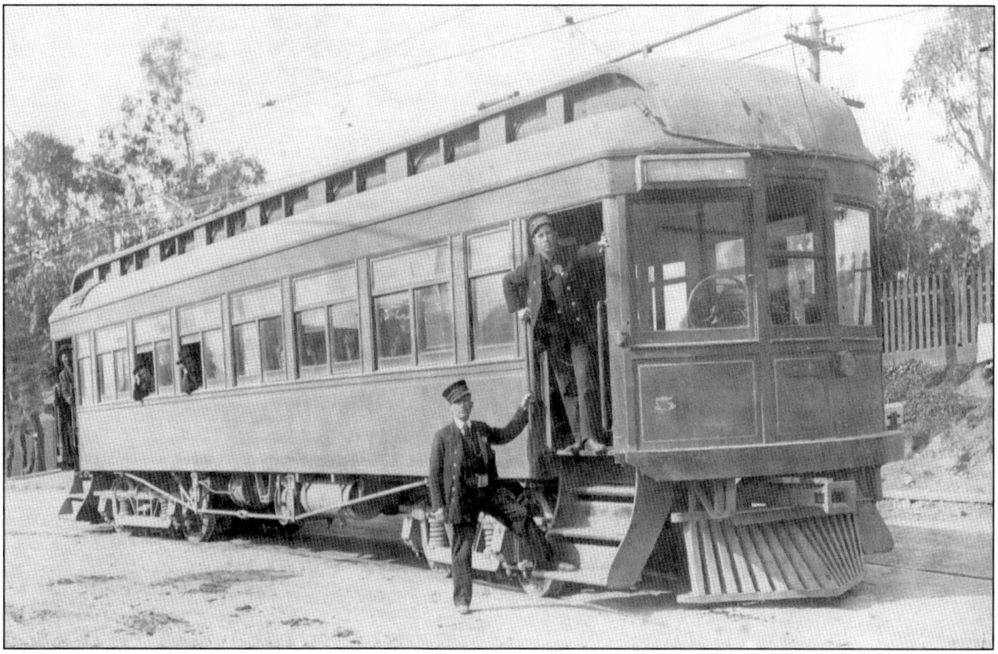

During the heyday of electric railroading, many itinerant photographers would drum up business by photographing car crews beside their cars. This was a nationwide phenomena and the result was many photographs of men and equipment for posterity. This photograph was taken near Holy Cross in 1907, showing off the original appearance of these cars. (Courtesy Charles Smallwood.)

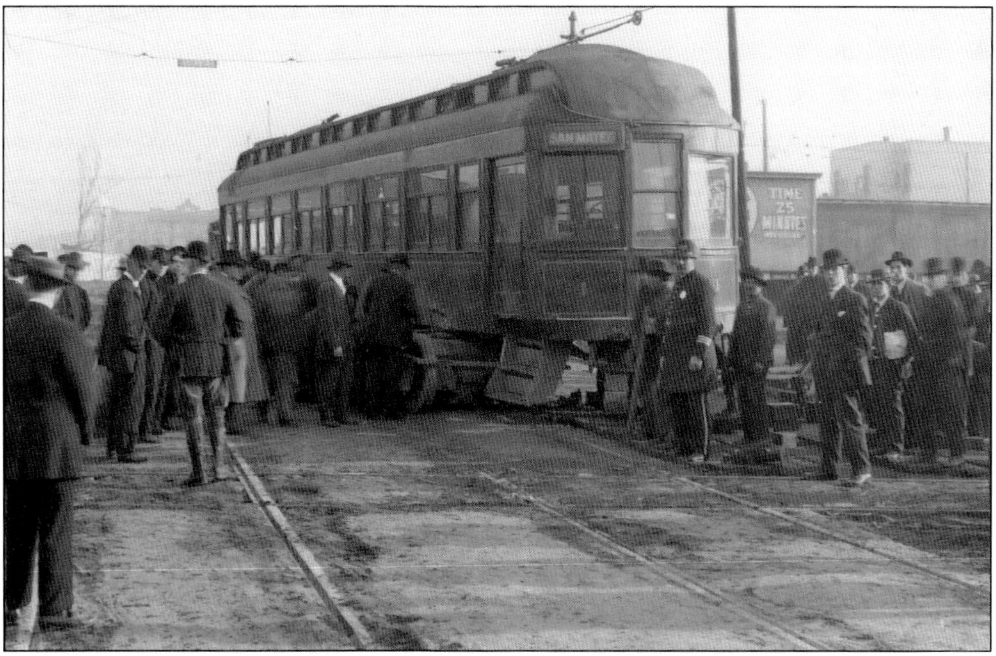

Ouch! In February 1911, an Ocean Shore freight train destined for the rock crushers on Otis Street knocked Big Sub No. 4 off its rails. Only the occasional freight used the OSRR trackage that crossed Mission Street, so the likelihood of accidents was rare, but in this instance somebody certainly goofed. (Courtesy Charles Smallwood.)

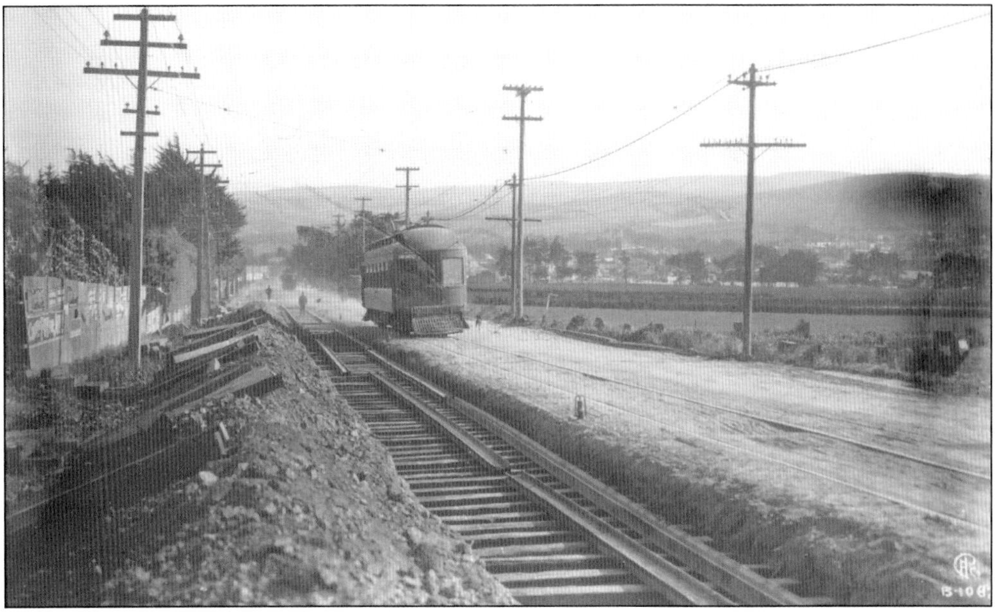

A Big Sub slowly creeps by track work being done on the Colma hill. The big cars were the heaviest cars on the system, and the rails constantly needed attention. As can be seen, much of the San Mateo line ran alongside the county roads. (Courtesy Western Railroad Museum.)

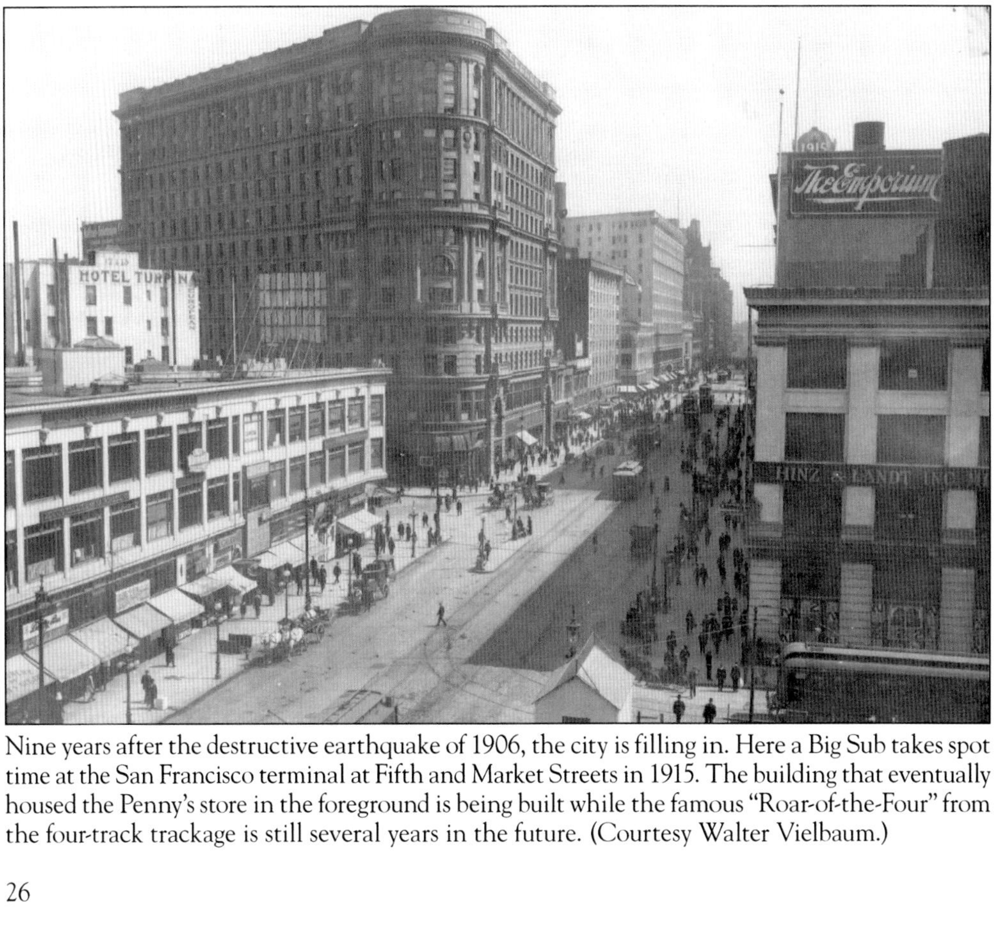

Nine years after the destructive earthquake of 1906, the city is filling in. Here a Big Sub takes spot time at the San Francisco terminal at Fifth and Market Streets in 1915. The building that eventually housed the Penny's store in the foreground is being built while the famous "Roar-of-the-Four" from the four-track trackage is still several years in the future. (Courtesy Walter Vielbaum.)

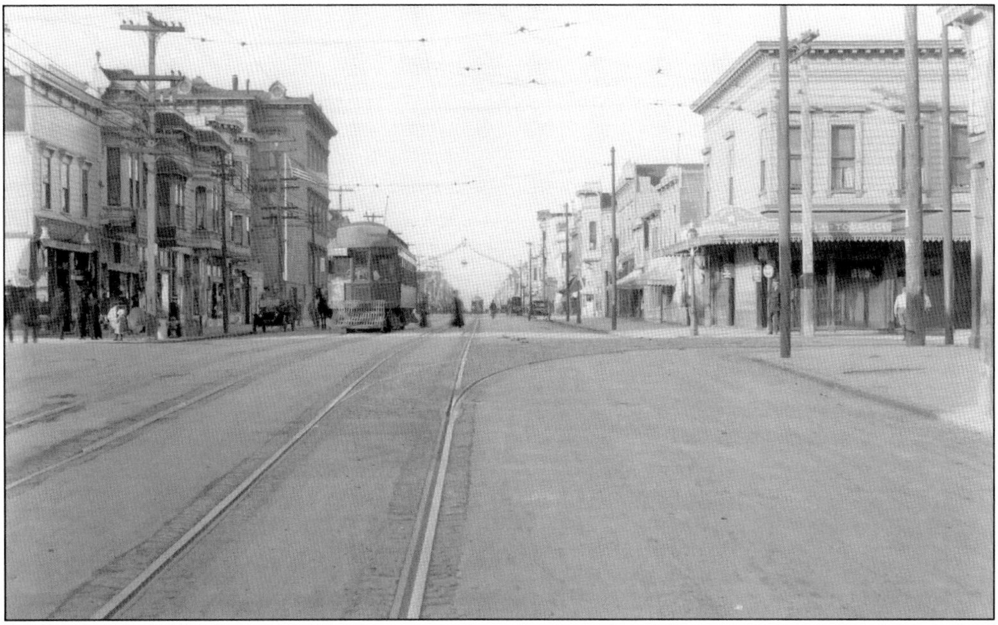

One of the downsides of the San Mateo line was its eight miles of street running in San Francisco along Mission Street. Seen at Twenty-sixth and Mission Streets looking north, a Big Sub approaches the camera. Note the street arch in the background at Twenty-fifth Street, similar to the ones built on Fillmore Street at the same time. The arch lasted until 1958.

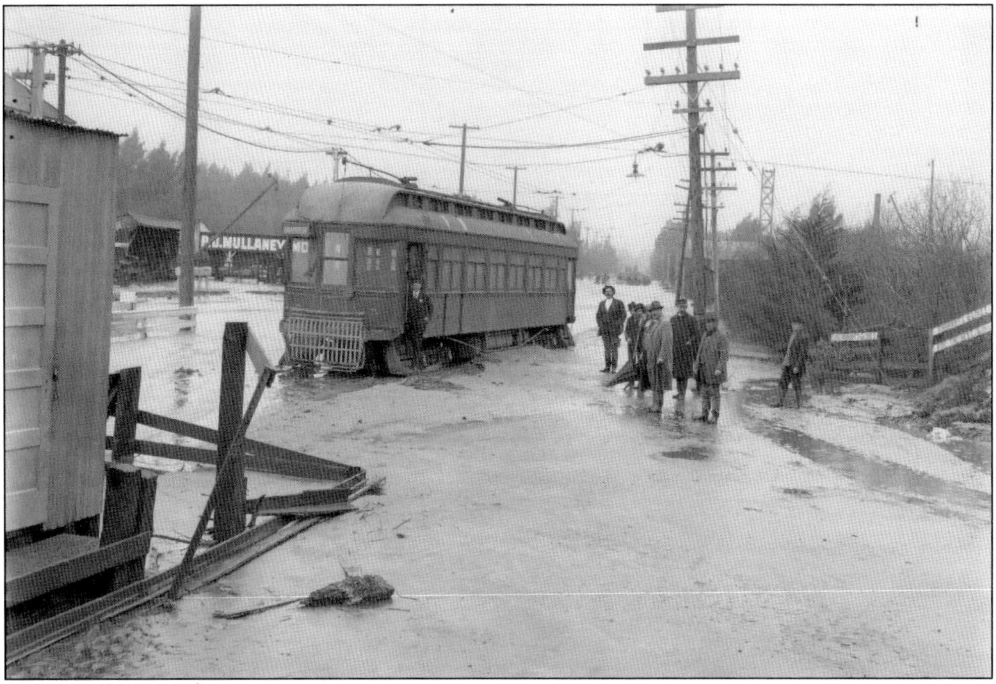

The San Mateo line ran through the low-lying area around Colma Creek. On occasion the creek became a small river with the San Mateo line somewhere along the bottom, especially near Holy Cross Cemetery and Molloy's Tavern. The cars were fairly high but when the motors got wet everything came to a halt. (Courtesy Rudy Brandt.)

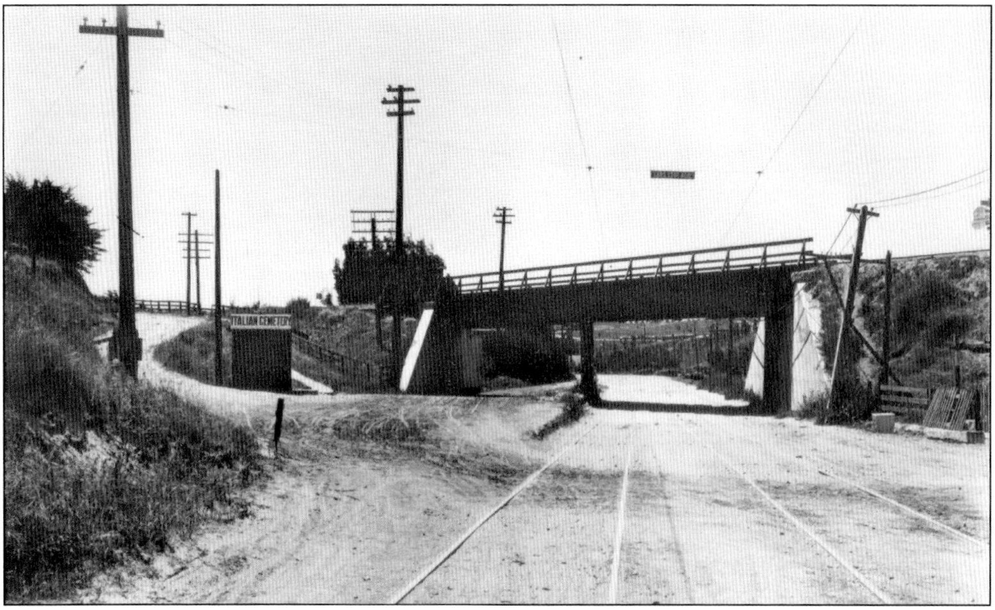

This 1908 photograph shows where the South Pacific crossed the San Mateo line at the overcrossing that separated the railroads from each other. This bridge was replaced in 1927, when the roadway was widened and the San Mateo line put in the divider. The bridge was demolished in the 1980s and has since been replaced with a new bridge at this location that carries BART passengers to the San Francisco Airport. (Courtesy Rudy Brandt.)

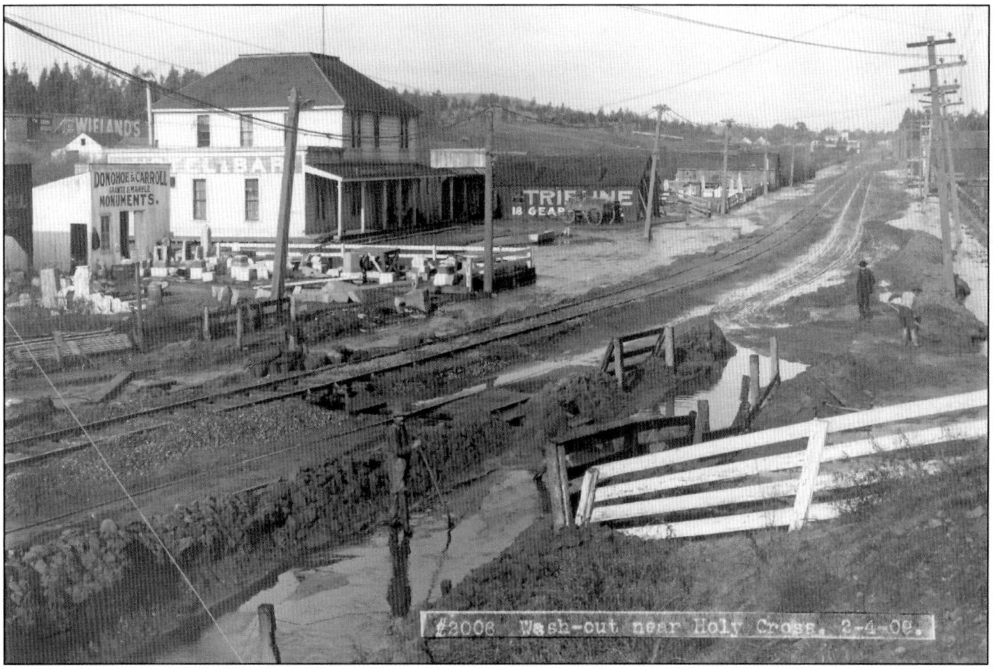

Although during the Prohibition years, Molloy's Tavern was a clandestine "wet" resort, Colma Creek took this meaning to extremes (again) in 1911, washing out a portion of the nearby track. Molloy's is still doing business at the old stand, with historical pictures of the San Mateo line displayed for the enjoyment of its customers. (Courtesy Rudy Brandt.)

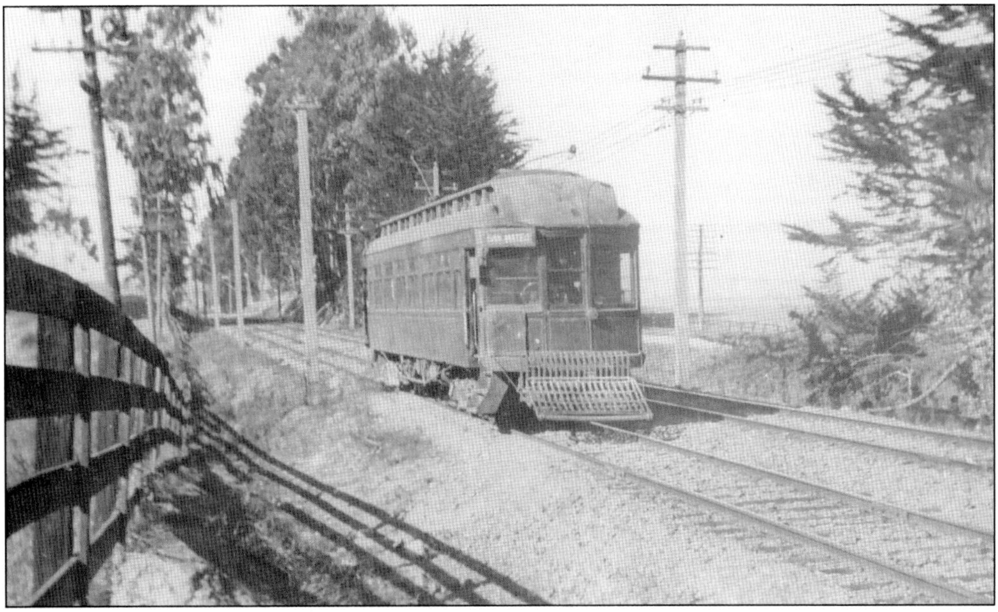

A Big Sub is caught at speed, south of Lomita Park. Near this spot in 1916, a nocturnal holdup took place on one of the cars with gunshots exchanged between the motorman and the highwayman. (Courtesy Lorin Silleman.)

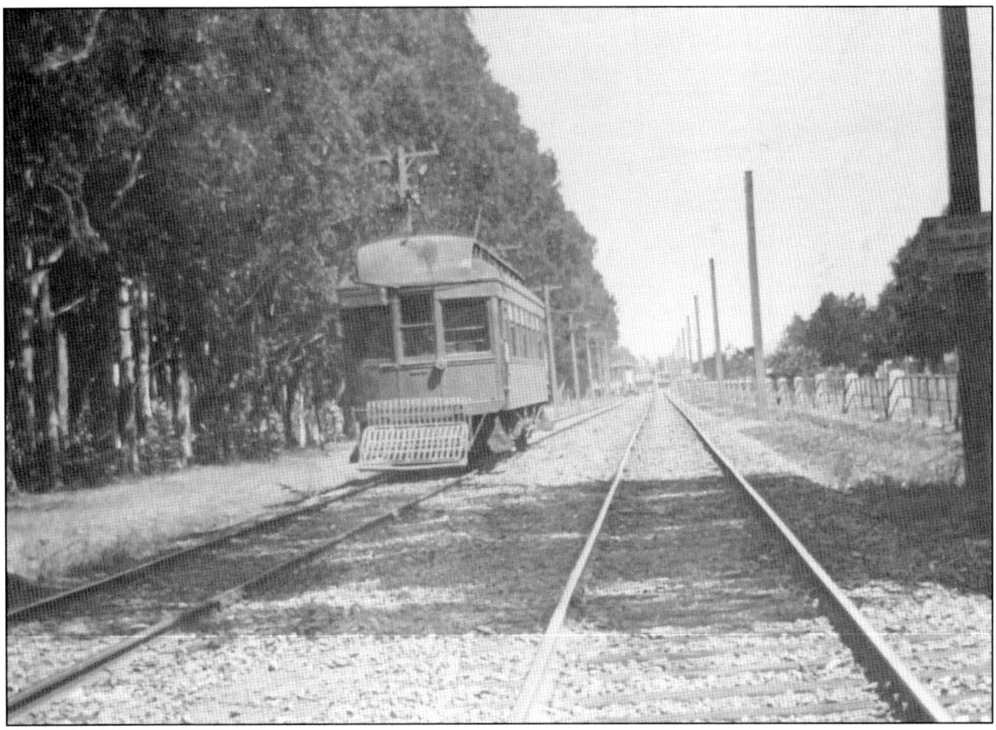

Car No. 12 with motorman Briggs at the helm is caught at speed, northbound near Oak Grove in 1922. The car now bears Market Street Railway's name, and the end is near as the Laclede 1225s are already being put through Elkton in preparation for the replacement of these large cars. (Courtesy Charles Smallwood.)

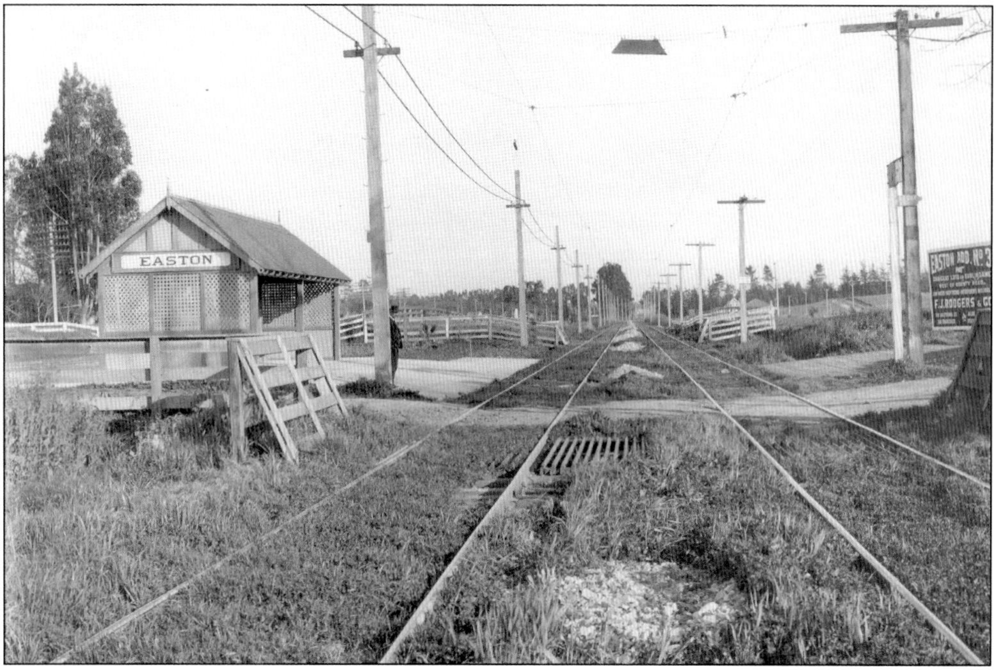

Easton Depot on the South Pacific was also used by the San Mateo line. Easton Depot, which was named for the man who originally developed the area, has long since been known as "Broadway." This photograph was taken March 13, 1908, by John Henry Mentz, URR's head staff photographer for the railway's entire existence from 1902 to 1921. (Courtesy Rudy Brandt.)

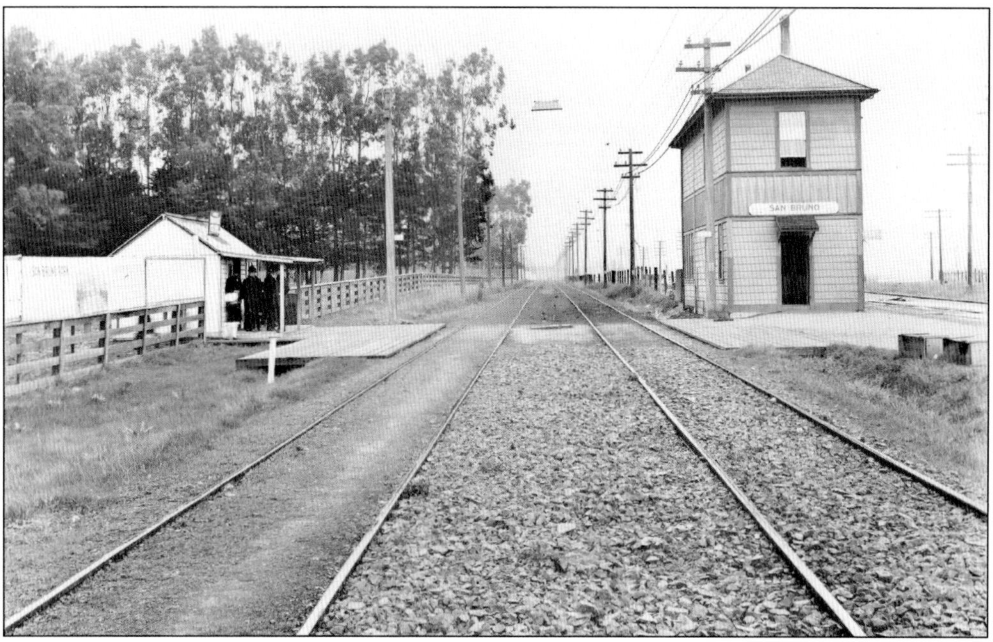

The San Mateo line paralleled the Southern Pacific for several miles between Colma and San Mateo. With the opening of the San Mateo line, Southern Pacific faced serious commuter competition. The solution was the Bayshore Cutoff completed in 1907. Here in February 1906, is the San Bruno tower, built in anticipation of the new line. (Courtesy Rudy Brandt.)

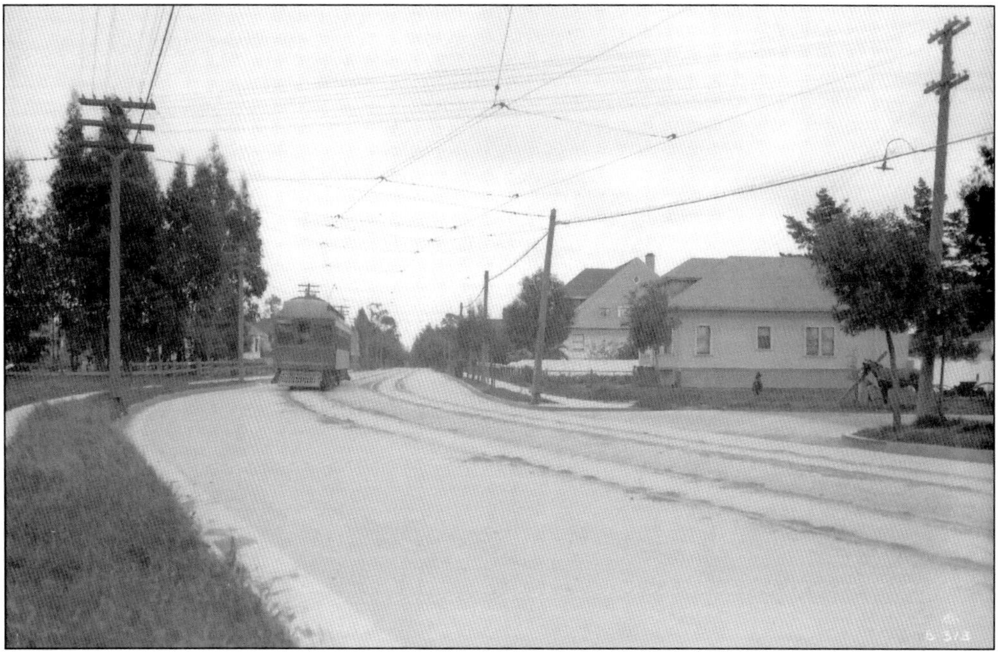

A Big Sub rounds the curve on San Mateo Drive at State Street in San Mateo. These 12 large interurbans, originally destined for the Philadelphia & Western in Pennsylvania, ran their entire service lives in sunny California. Four mates to these cars ran on the Sacramento Northern until 1940. (Courtesy Western Railroad Museum.)

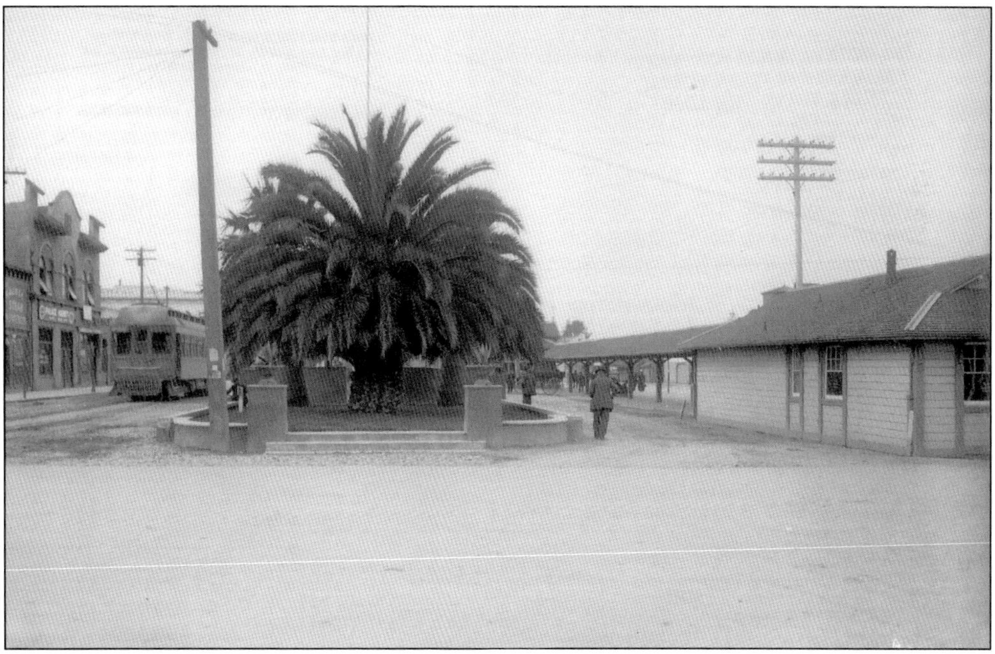

This Big Sub was photographed when the line was still young, opposite the Southern Pacific depot in San Mateo, URR's southernmost reach. Here homebound passengers could debark, shop for a few things, or take the Southern Pacific trains to other points. (Courtesy Western Railroad Museum.)

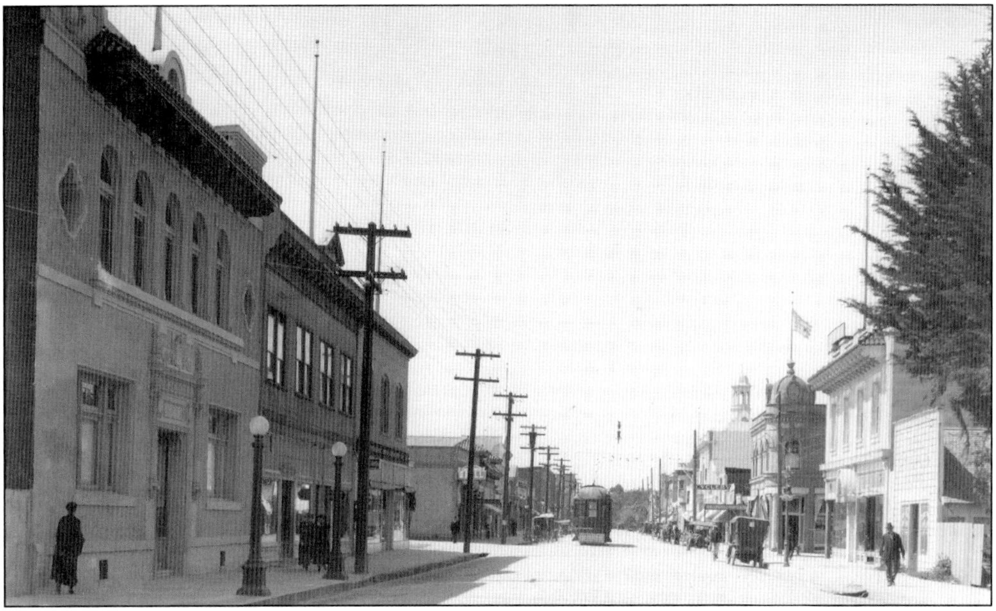

Yes the Midwest lived on the peninsula! Here on B Street at Third Avenue in San Mateo, a car that would appear more at home on rails in Pennsylvania or Indiana than California approaches the camera. Big, comfortable cars and good service, what more could a commuter want? In those days, the cities of the peninsula were much more isolated than they are today. The building at the far left is the first home of Elks Lodge 1112. (Courtesy Rudy Brandt.)

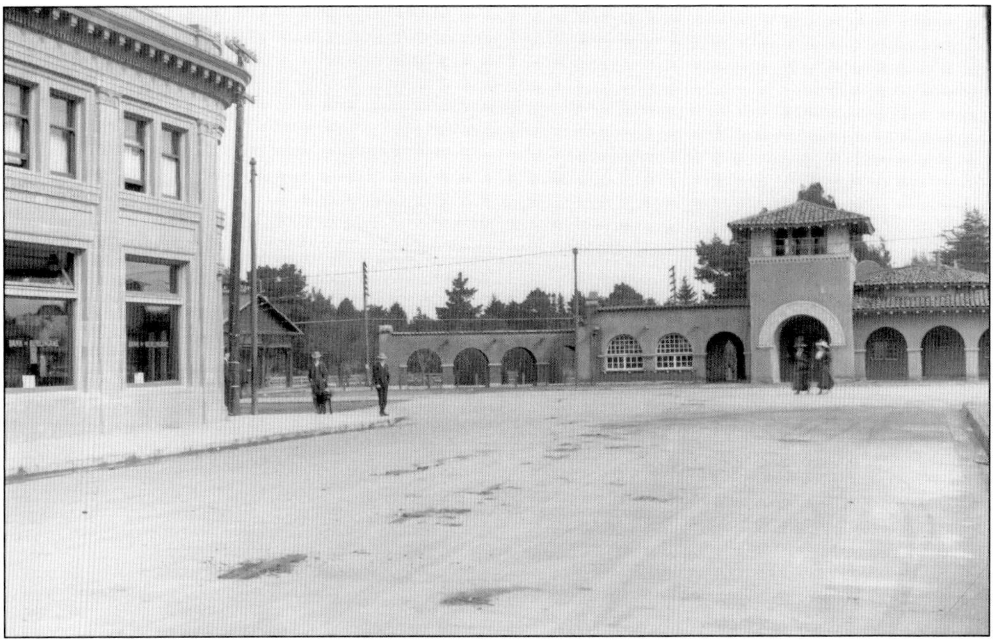

This is the Burlingame Depot as seen from town in 1911. The San Mateo tracks ran in front of the depot, while the Southern Pacific trains ran behind. Some of the tiles on the roof of the depot were from the old *Asistencia* built in San Mateo by the Mission padres. The depot had a Moorish arch over the center entrance that was later removed for safety reasons. (Courtesy Rudy Brandt.)

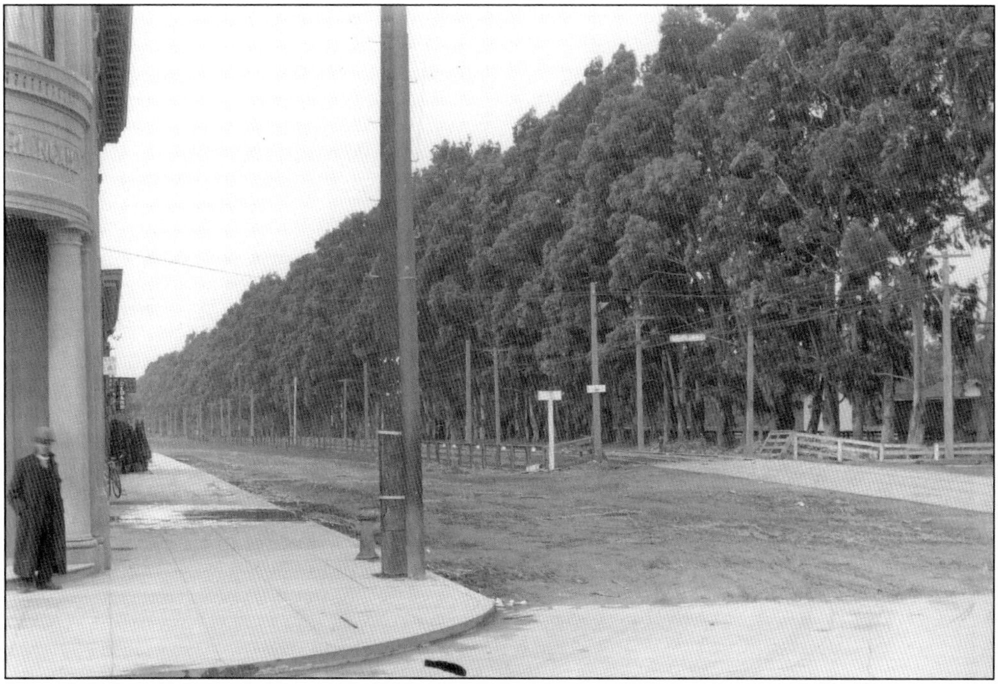

Once it neared the Southern Pacific depot in Burlingame, the San Mateo line left its private right-of-way, shown here right center in this 1911 photograph, for street running for the remainder of the line. California Drive parallels the line to the left. The Bank of Burlingame, with many changes of ownership, stands today. (Courtesy Rudy Brandt.)

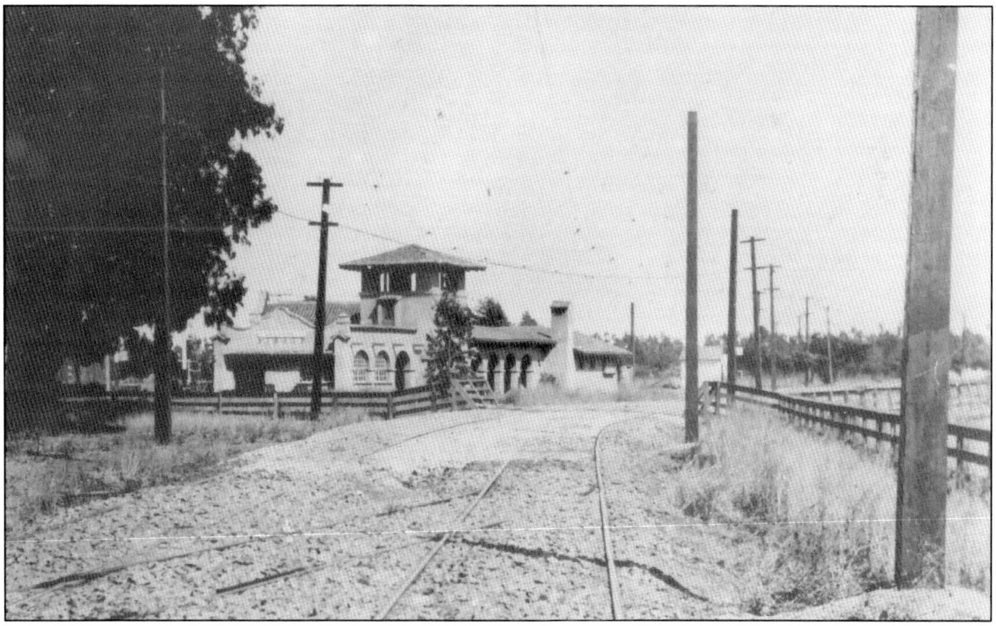

Constructed in 1894, the Burlingame Depot was the first building designed in what was to become the Mission Revival style that became popular during the first two decades of the 20th century. At the time this view was taken in about 1903, there was no business district in Burlingame near the depot. (Courtesy Richard Schlaich.)

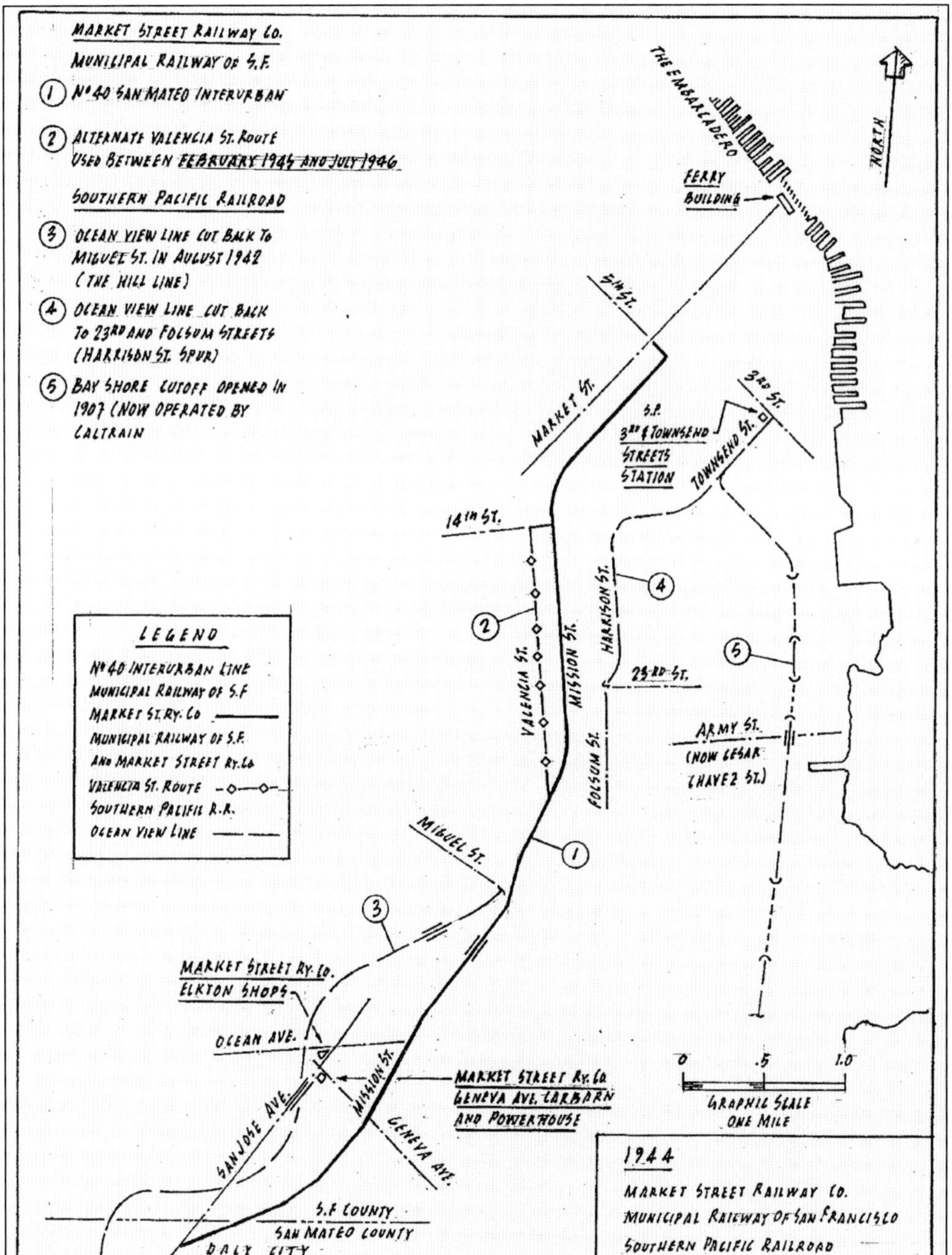

Here is the 40 line route in San Francisco in 1944 at the time of the merger with Muni Railway. (Courtesy Don Holmgren.)

Three

The Era of the 40 line

All aboard! It is time to board the 40-line car at San Francisco's Fifth and Market Streets for a 20-mile photographic journey to San Mateo. To guide the reader in this trip over the 40 line, the following is a listing of stations (excluding those in San Francisco and San Mateo), in sequence, and the page on which photographs appear at that location.

Station	Pg.	Station	Pg.	Station	Pg.	Station	Pg.
Daly City	46	Chinese Cemetery	-	Euclid Ave	65	Millbrae	76
Colma	-	Molloy's Tavern	51	San Bruno Ave	66	Millbrae Dairy	79
Estradas	-	Holy Cross	53	San Mateo Ave	68	Dufferin	80
Motorville	-	Duck Ranch	55	Angus	68	Rosedale	81
Millets	-	South City Jct.	56	Sylvan	69	Burlingame Grove	81
Italian Cemetery	50	Buri Buri	59	Huntington	70	Broadway	82
Woodlawn	50	Baden	60	Lomita Park	70	Sanchez	83
Greenlawn	-	Orange Ave	61	San Benito Ave	71	Burlingame Terrace	84
Eternal Cemetery	-	Kennel Club	62	South Lomita	72	Oak Grove	85
Mount Olivet	-	Lindenville	63	16 Mile House	73	Burlingame	89
Salem Cemetery	-	Poetsch	63	Aqua	73	Howard Ave	90
Pacific Nursery	-	Stanley	64	Millbrae Park	74	San Mateo	95
Home of Peace	-	Buena Vista	64	Millbrae Highlands	75		

The line from Daly City to Colma (Market Street) was street running, while south to Cypress Lawn Cemetery, the line was on private right-of-way in the median of El Camino Real. The line then crossed the northbound lanes of El Camino Real at grade and continued along the east side of Mission Road to Molloy's Tavern, thence on private right-of-way a short distance to Holy Cross. There were no station shelters adjacent to the tracks from Daly City to Holy Cross.

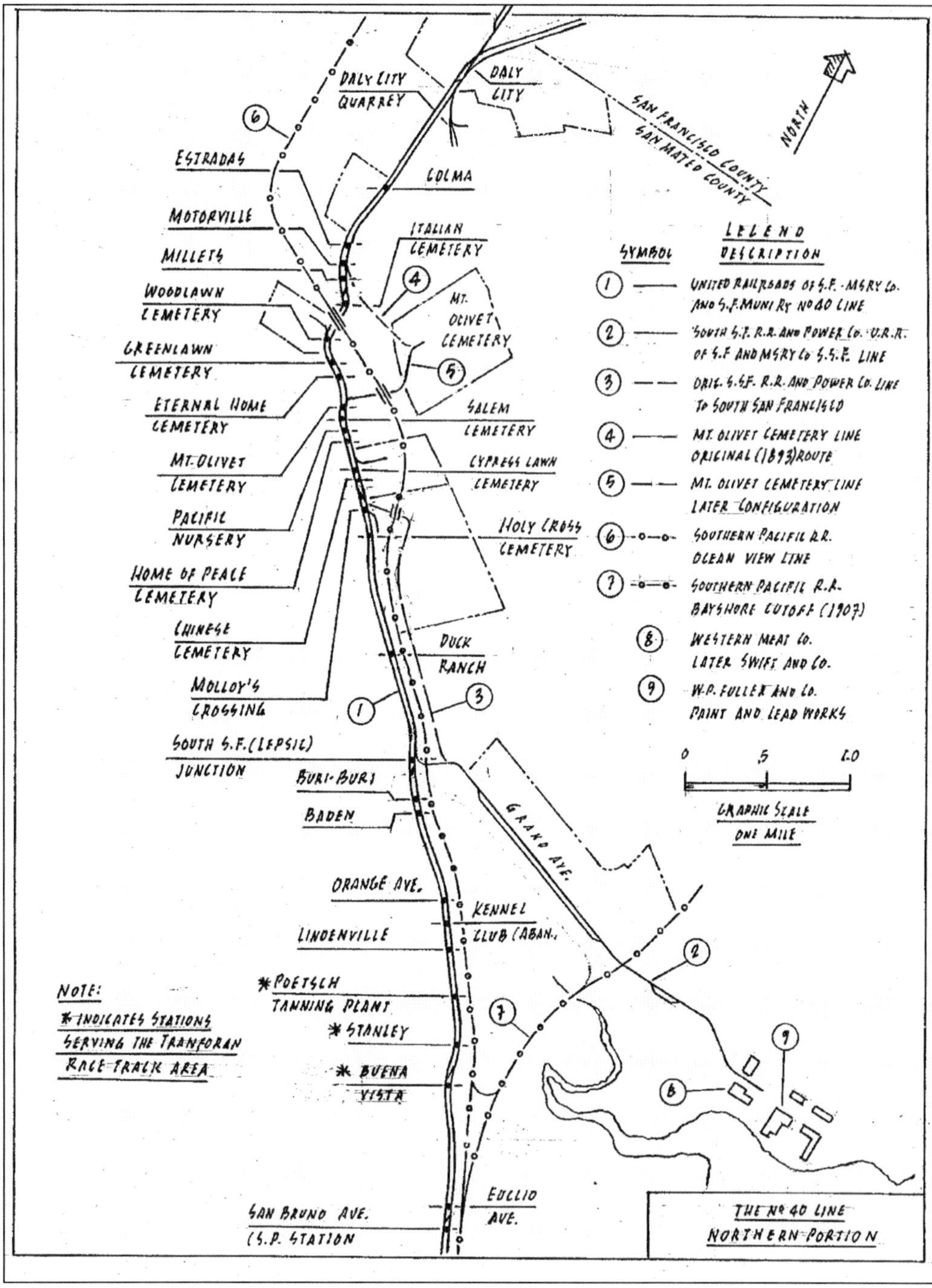

This map shows the track running from Daly City (San Mateo County) to San Bruno. (Courtesy Don Holmgren.)

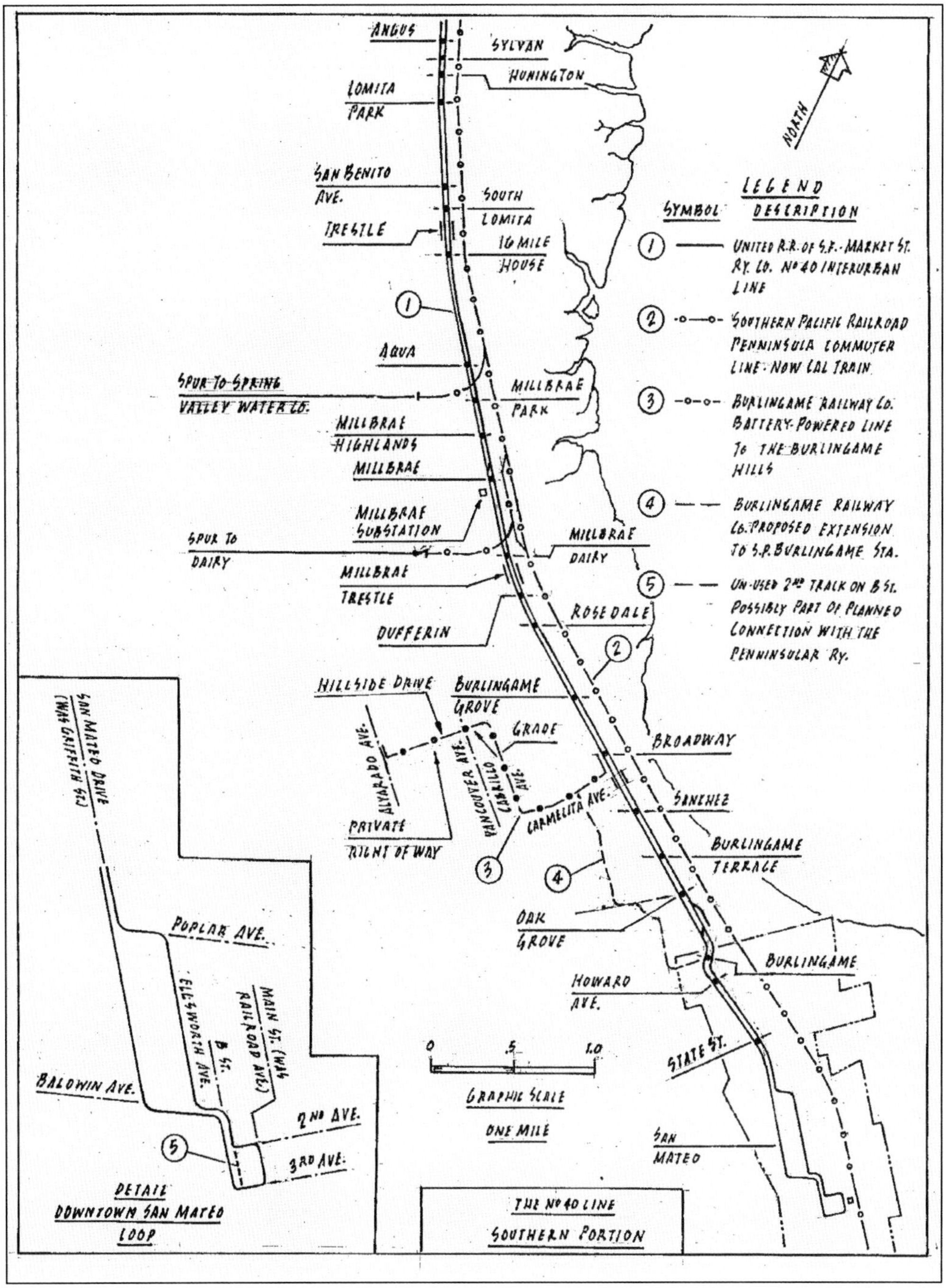

Here is a track map showing the San Bruno-to-San Mateo route and showing the Burlingame Railway. (Courtesy Don Holmgren.)

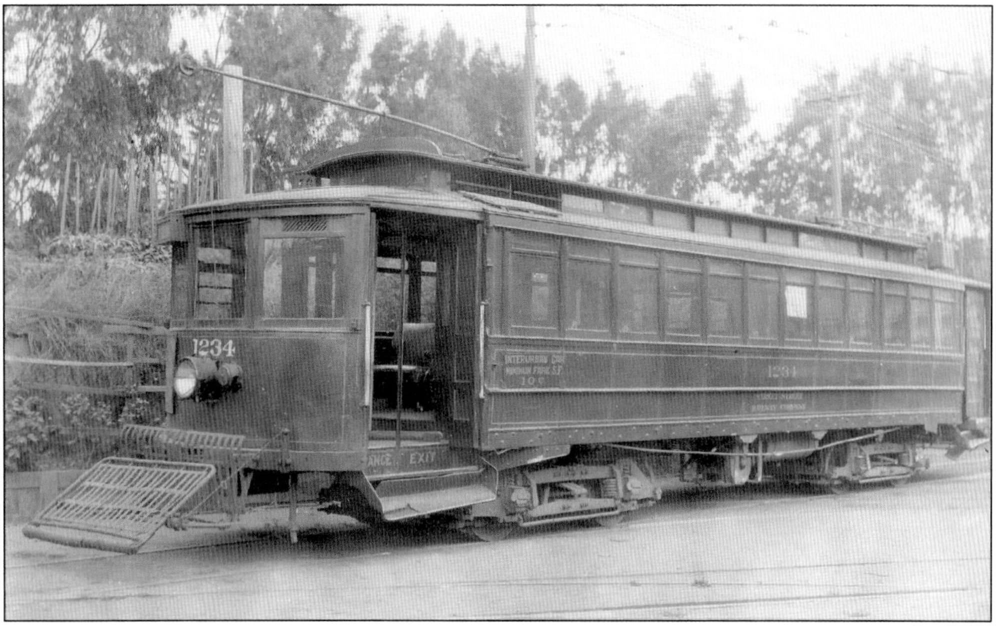

In this early 1920s view, car No. 1234 is at Elkton Shops waiting to get its steps repaired. The car is in the original MSR colors prior to the adoption of the white front paint scheme. Note that the car still has the original-style route number boxes mounted on the front right window, as well as original truss rods. The longer platforms are a result of the 1921–1922 rebuilding program to ingratiate the new "Pay As You Enter" (PAYE) fare collection program. (Courtesy Don Holmgren.)

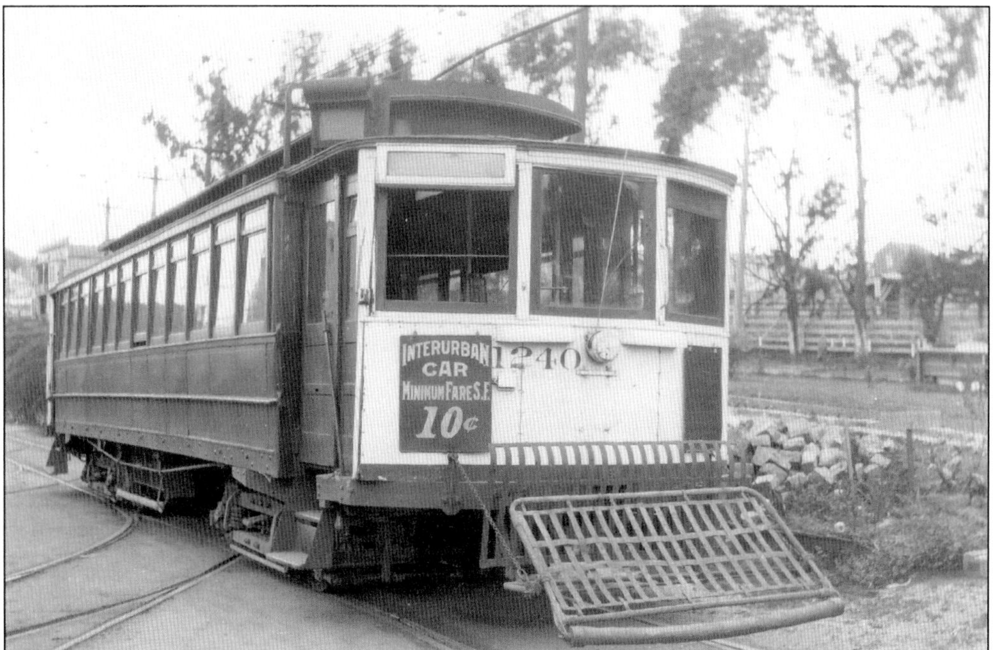

Car No. 1240, shown here at Elkton Shops, sports the white front paint scheme. The car has an exterior destination sign box, which was later built into the window.

This is a front-end view of car No. 1227 at the Geneva car house. Note the use of a light bulb carton on one of the platform lights to shield the light. (Courtesy Robert Townley.)

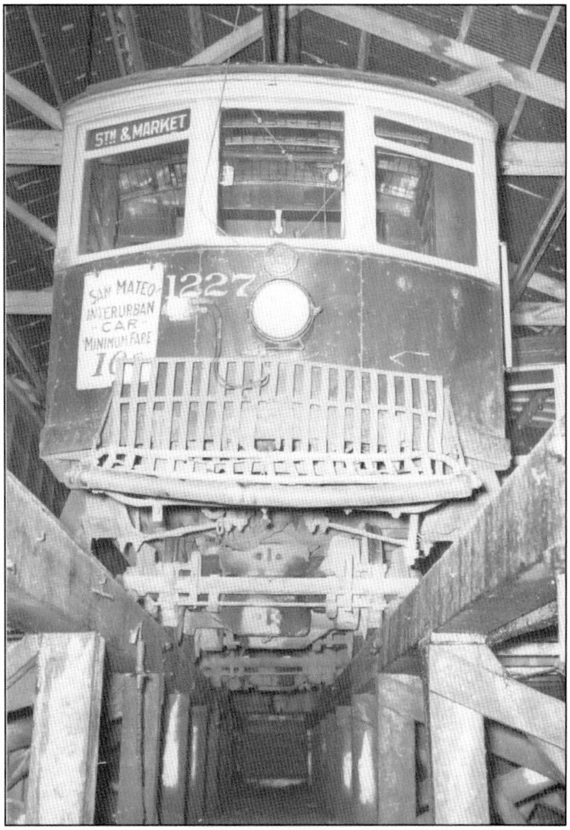

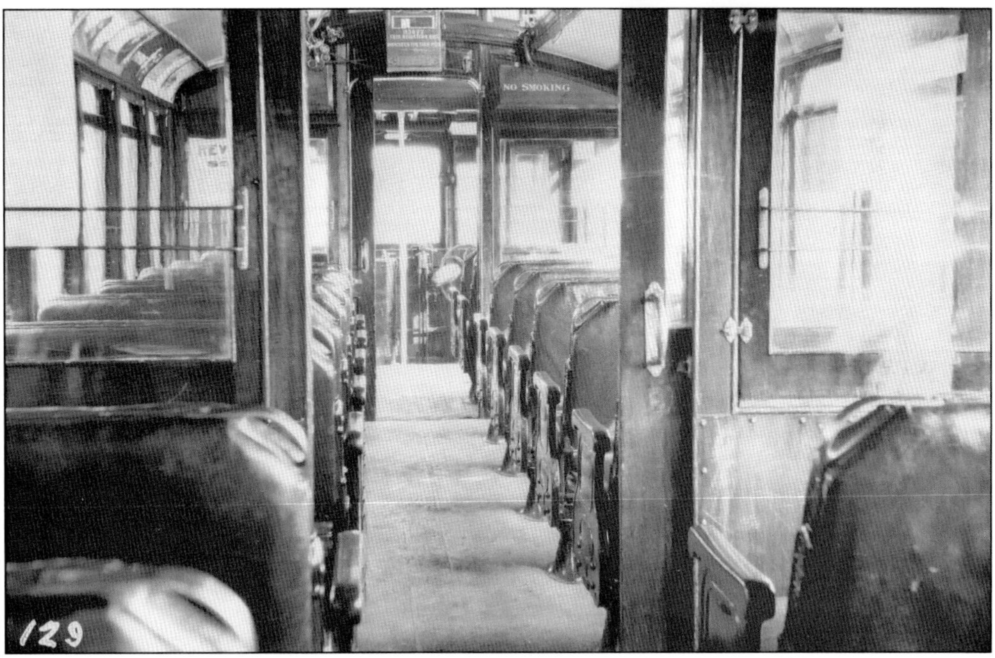

This interior view of a 1225 dates back to the late 1920s. Note that the car still has its fare register mounted on the bulkhead. (Courtesy Emiliano Echeverria.)

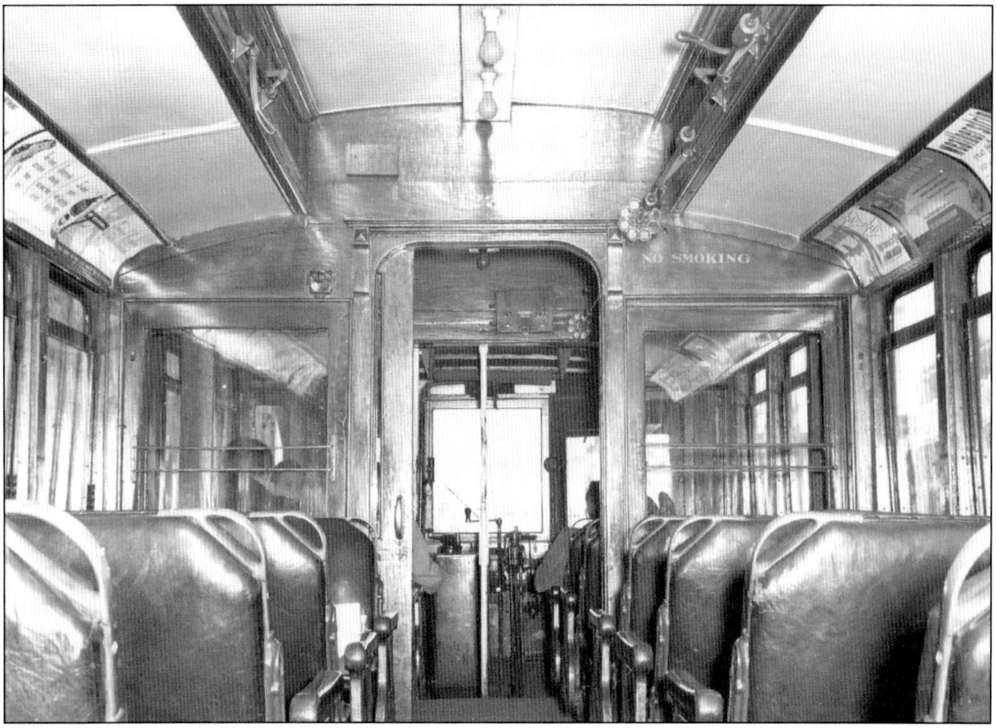

This interior view of car No. 1234 dates to January 1949, just prior to abandonment. Note that the car no longer has its fare registers but that the rods were left in place. (Courtesy Robert Townley.)

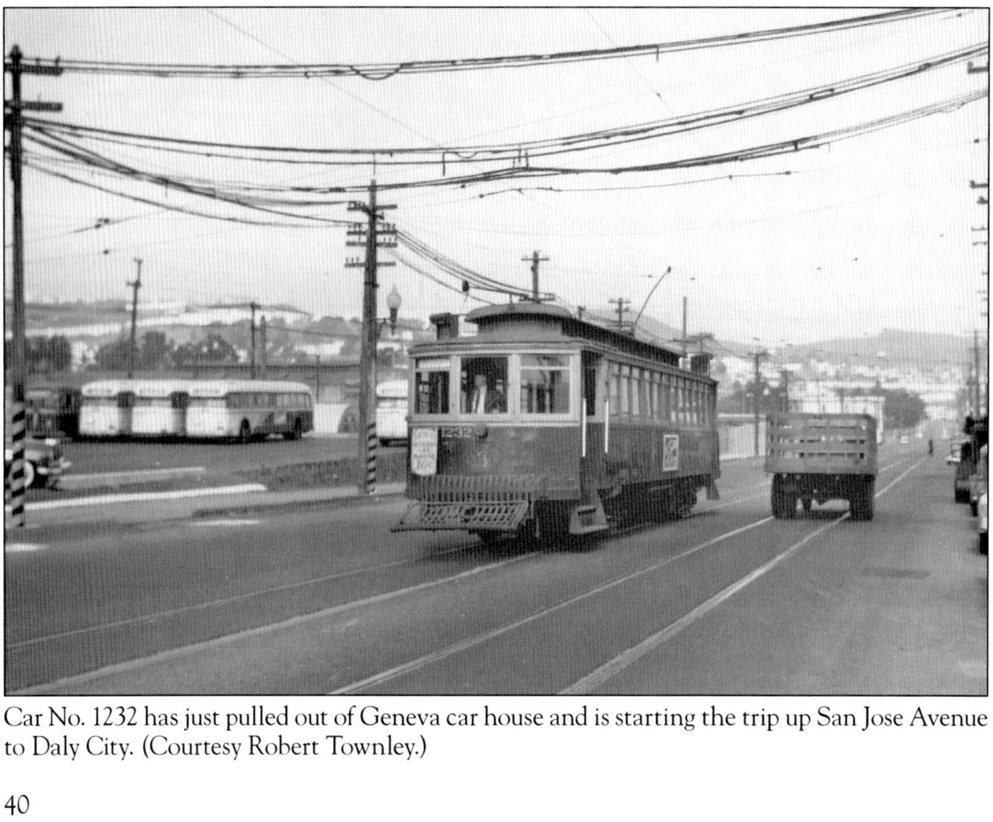

Car No. 1232 has just pulled out of Geneva car house and is starting the trip up San Jose Avenue to Daly City. (Courtesy Robert Townley.)

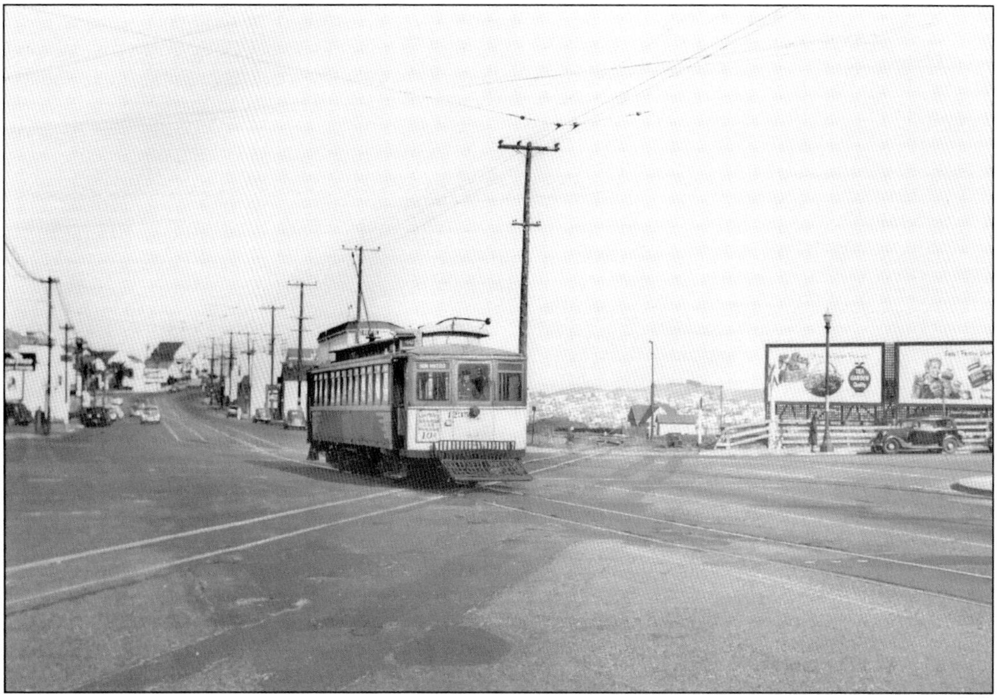

Car No. 1235 is on San Jose Avenue crossing the Southern Pacific Bernal Branch tracks. Today BART and Interstate 280 cross this intersection on aerial structures. (Courtesy Walter Vielbaum.)

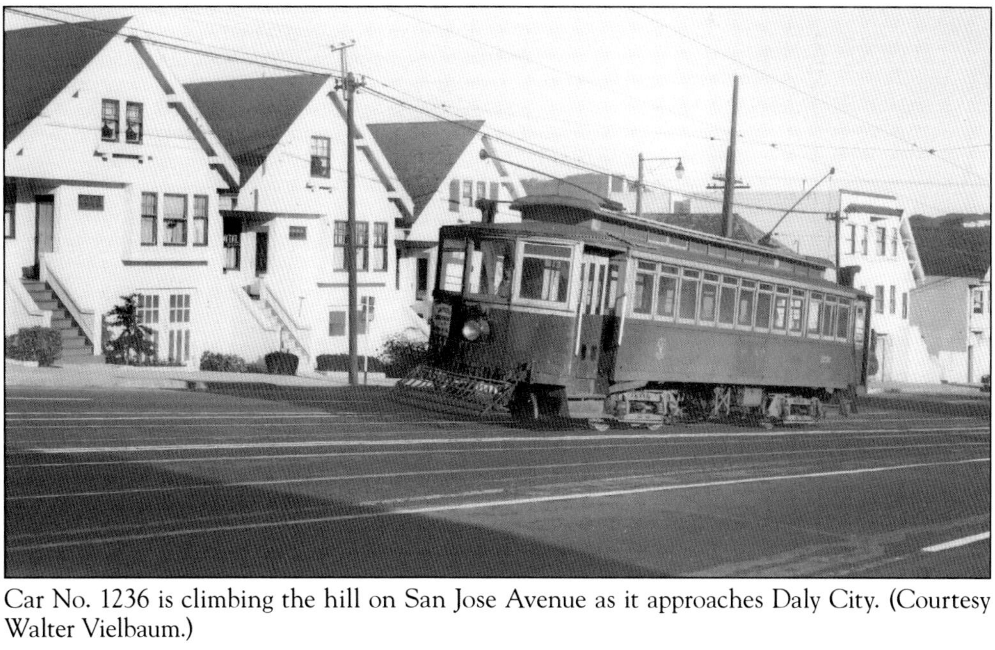

Car No. 1236 is climbing the hill on San Jose Avenue as it approaches Daly City. (Courtesy Walter Vielbaum.)

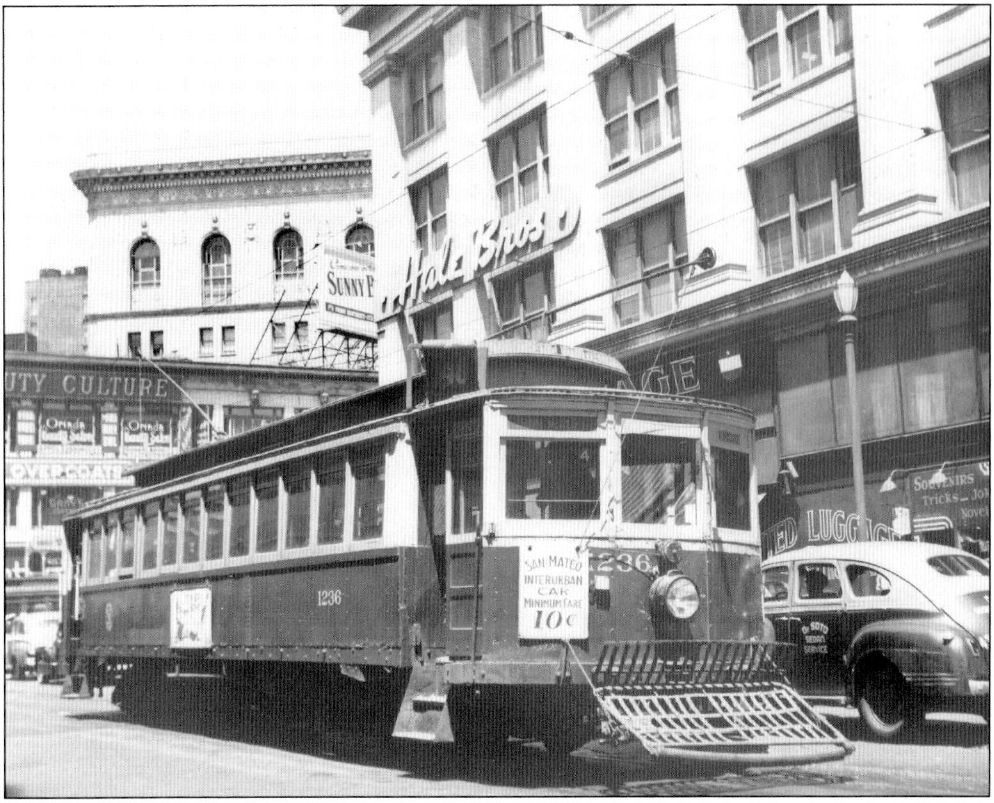

The San Francisco terminal of the 40 line was Fifth and Market Streets. Here car No. 1236 lays over prior to its departure to San Mateo. (Courtesy Al Thoman.)

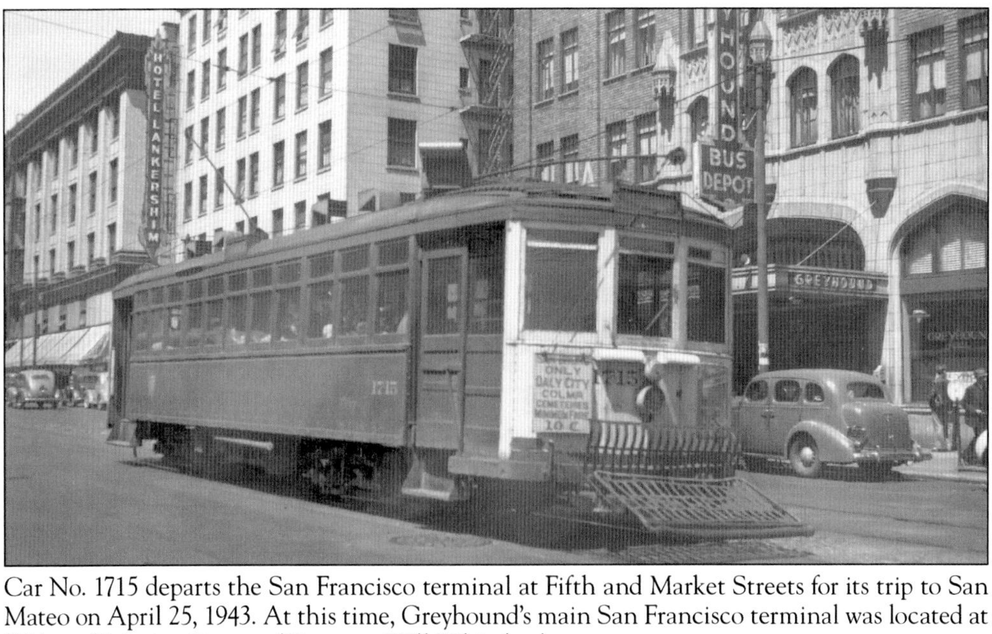

Car No. 1715 departs the San Francisco terminal at Fifth and Market Streets for its trip to San Mateo on April 25, 1943. At this time, Greyhound's main San Francisco terminal was located at Fifth and Mission Streets. (Courtesy Will Whitaker.)

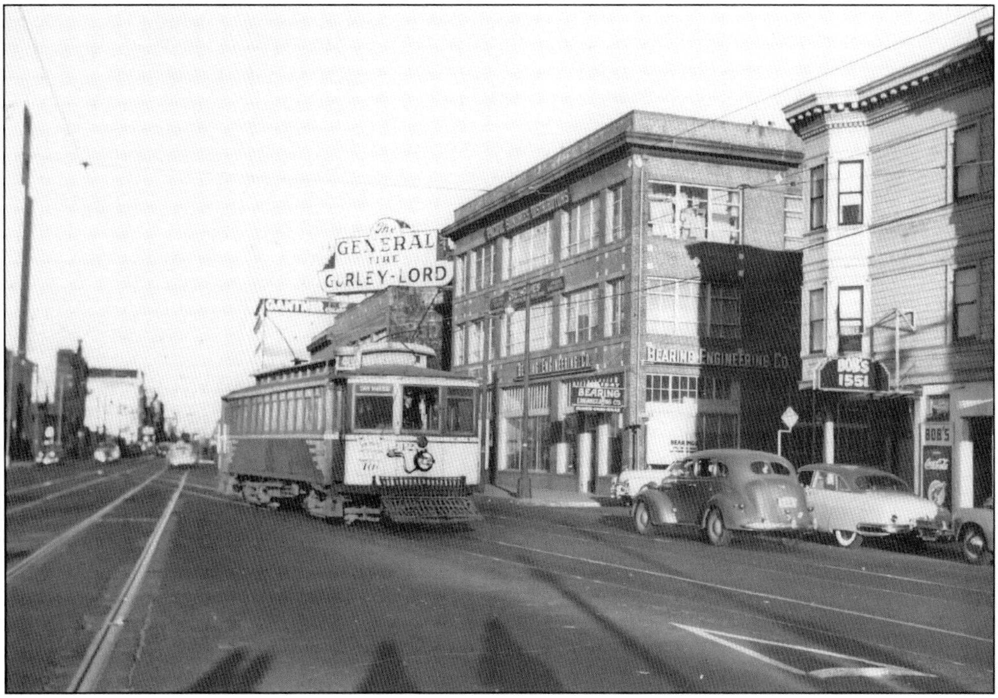

Car No. 1242 makes the turn on Mission Street at Otis in this late afternoon view. The straight tracks on the left side of the picture were at one time used to service the MSR track department's material yard at Market and Gough Streets. (Courtesy Robert Townley.)

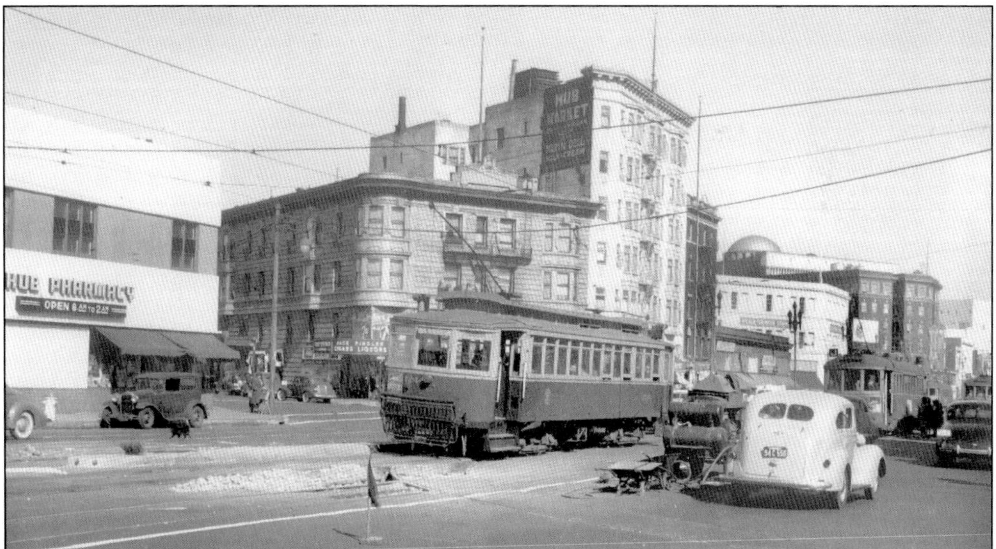

Car No. 1244 is inbound on Market Street at Gough Street in this unusual operation during 1945. At this time, the route of the 40 line was over Valencia Street, Fourteenth Street, and then back onto Mission Street. During the re-railing of the curve on Mission Street at Otis, the 40-line cars continued on Valencia Street to Market Street and then down Market Street and over Twelfth to Mission Street. The track turning off Market Street in the foreground leads to the Gough and Market Streets material yard. (Courtesy J. G. Graham.)

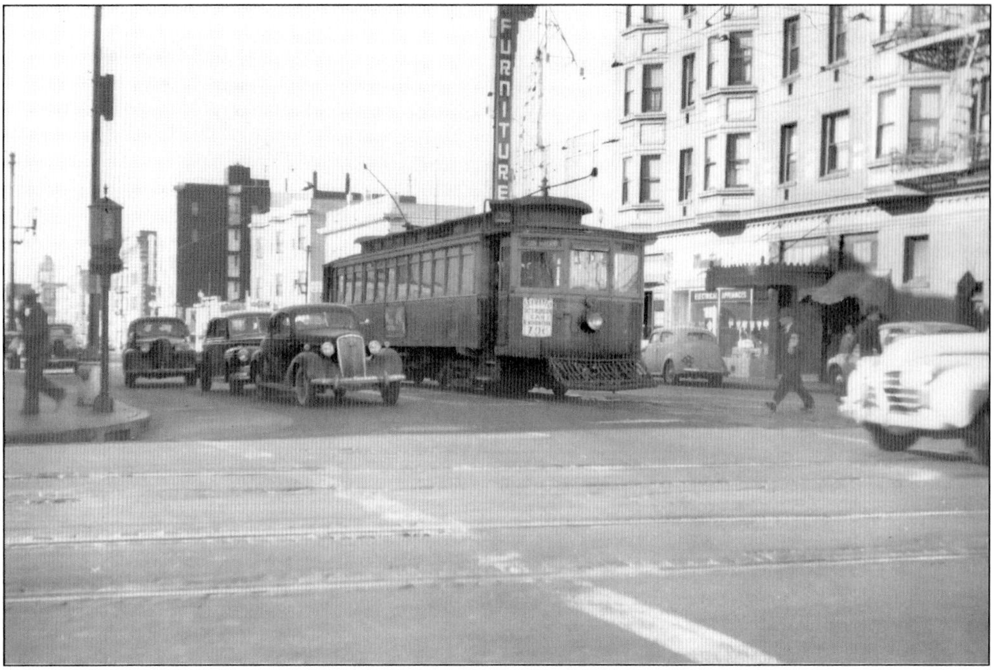

This No. 1225 is outbound on Valencia Street at Sixteenth Street. The tracks on Sixteenth Street were used by the No. 22 Sixteenth and Fillmore line. (Courtesy Jack Tillmany.)

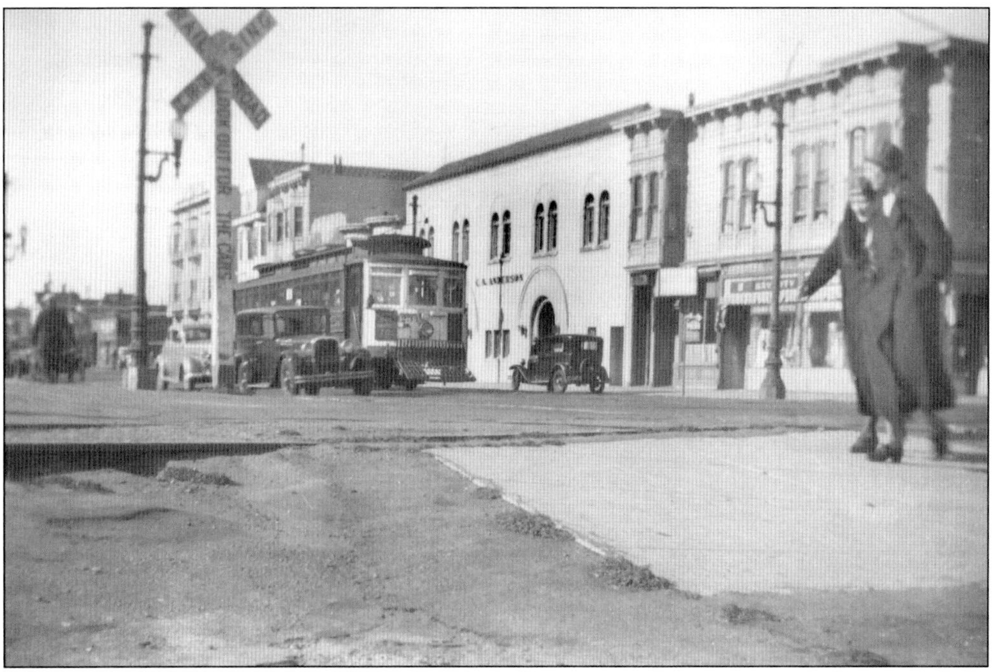

Car No. 1234 crosses the Southern Pacific Bernal Branch in this rare view from the 1930s. One can only speculate what caused this diversion of 40-line cars onto Valencia Street. (Courtesy Jack Tillmany.)

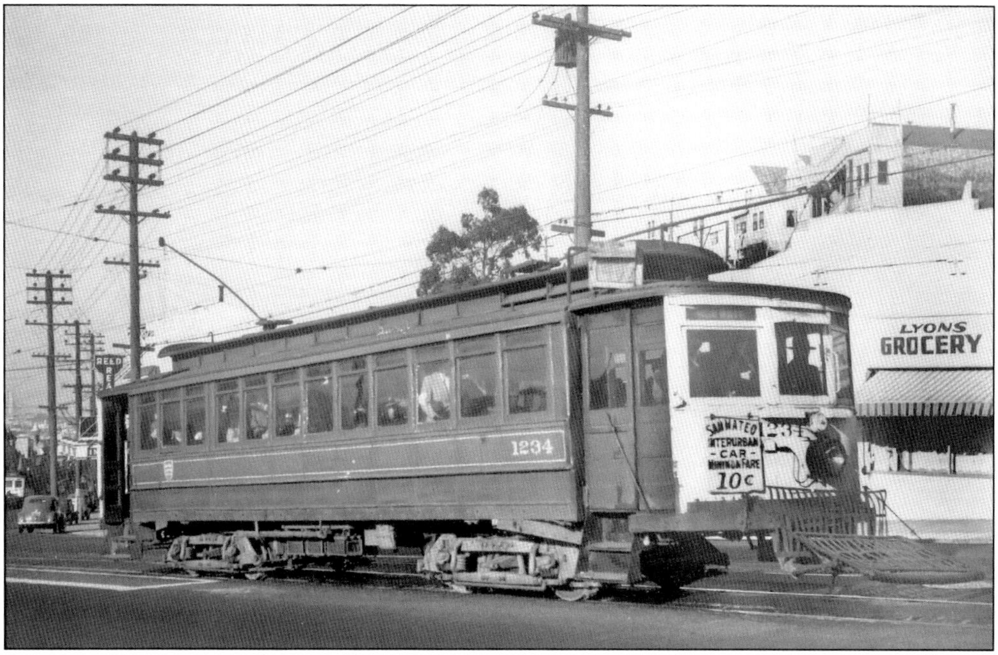

Car No. 1234 comes up the grade by Appleton Avenue on Mission Street on its way to Daly City during Market Street Railroad days. (Courtesy Will Whittaker.)

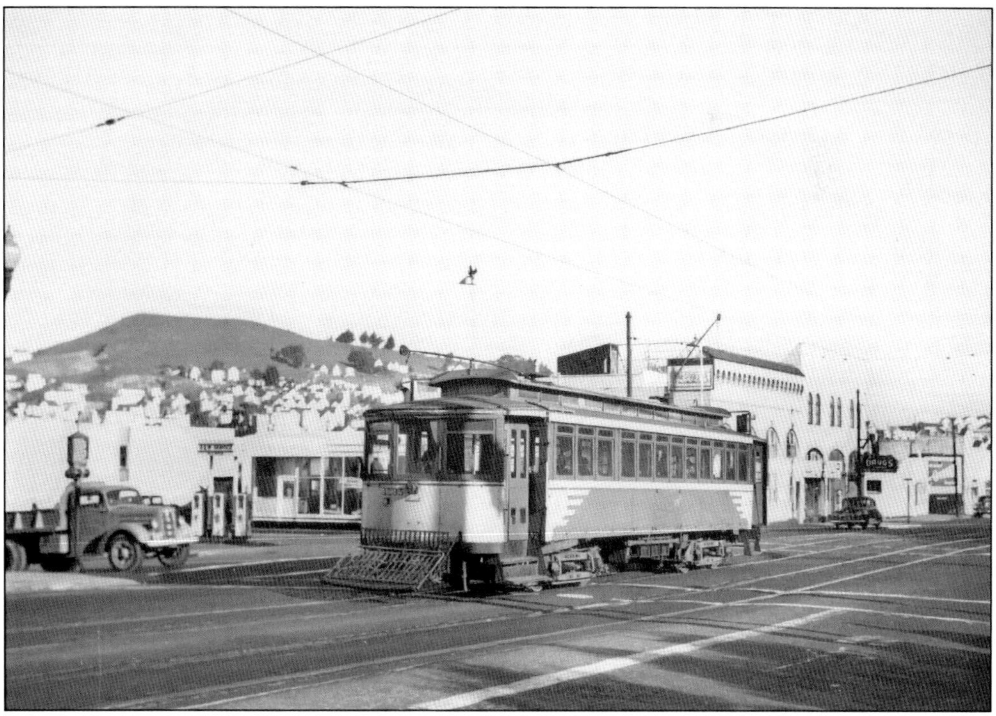

Car No. 1235 is outbound on Mission Street near Daly City.

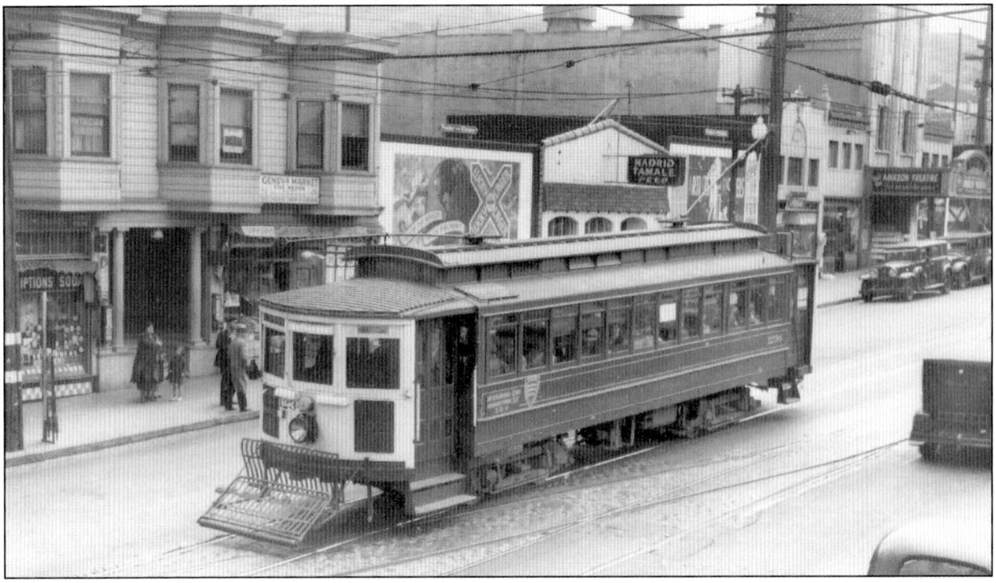

Car No. 1234 is inbound on Mission Street approaching Geneva Avenue about 1937. In the background is the Rialto Theatre. The sign on the now closed theatre marquee reads, "Visit the Amazon Theatre," which is around the corner on Geneva Avenue. The Rialto is now a billiard parlor. (Courtesy Jack Tillmany.)

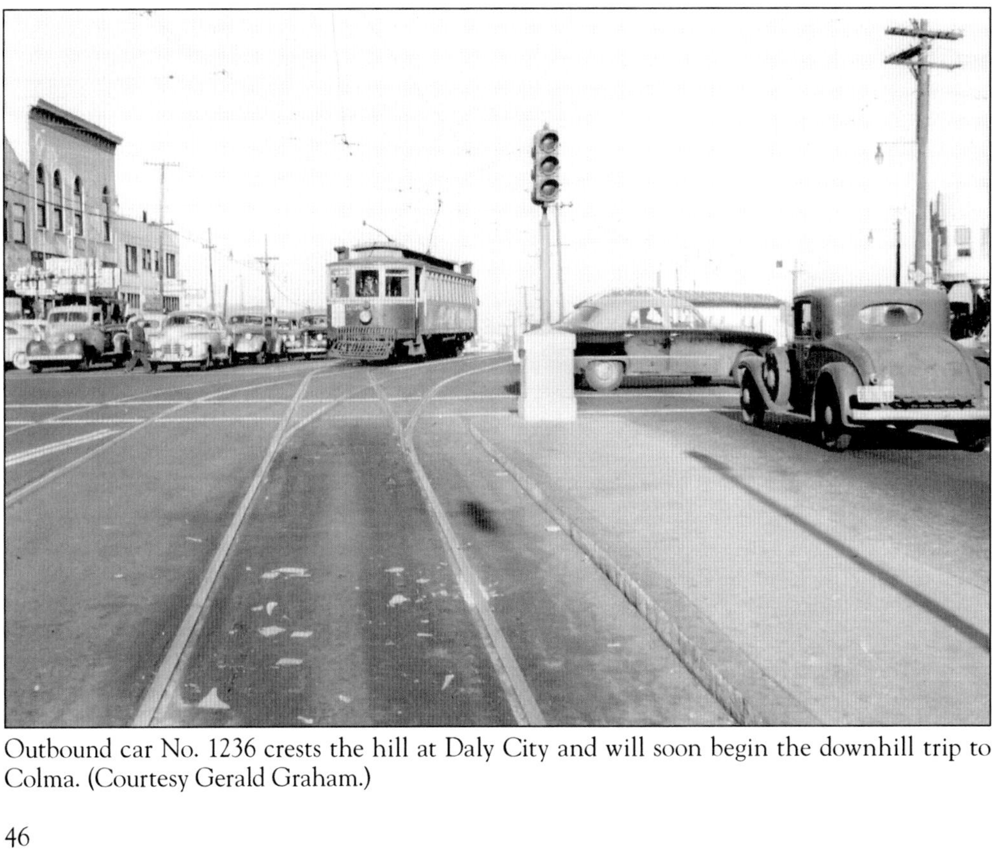
Outbound car No. 1236 crests the hill at Daly City and will soon begin the downhill trip to Colma. (Courtesy Gerald Graham.)

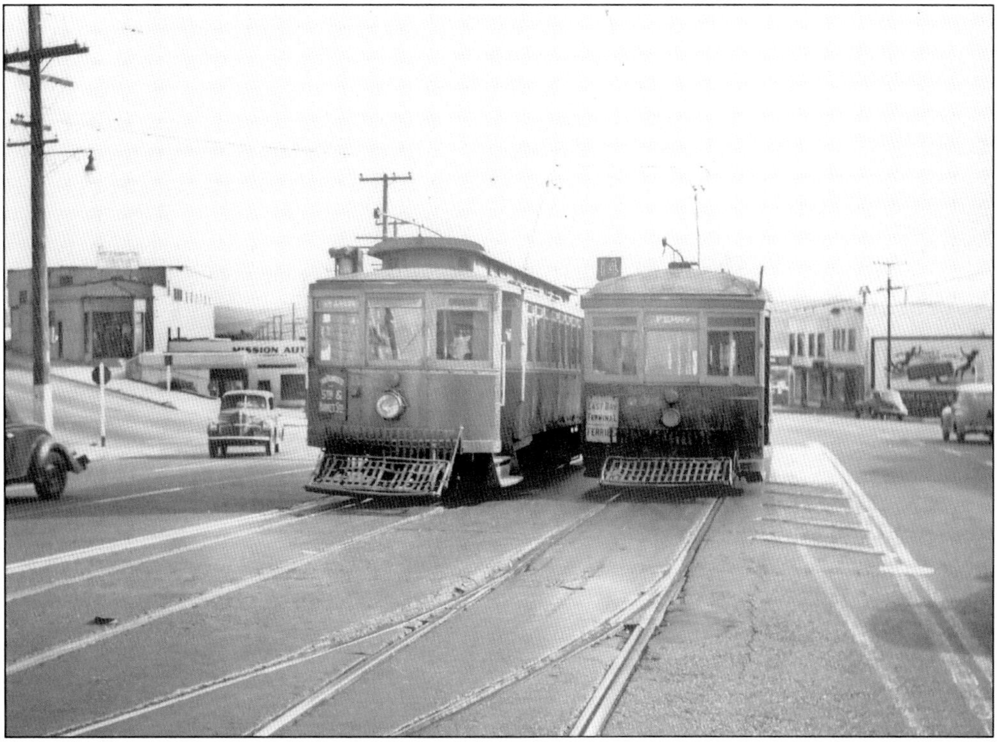

The 14-line car is waiting at the switchback at Daly City for the 40-line car to clear the loading zone at the top of the hill. The 40-line car has priority to continue down Mission Street.

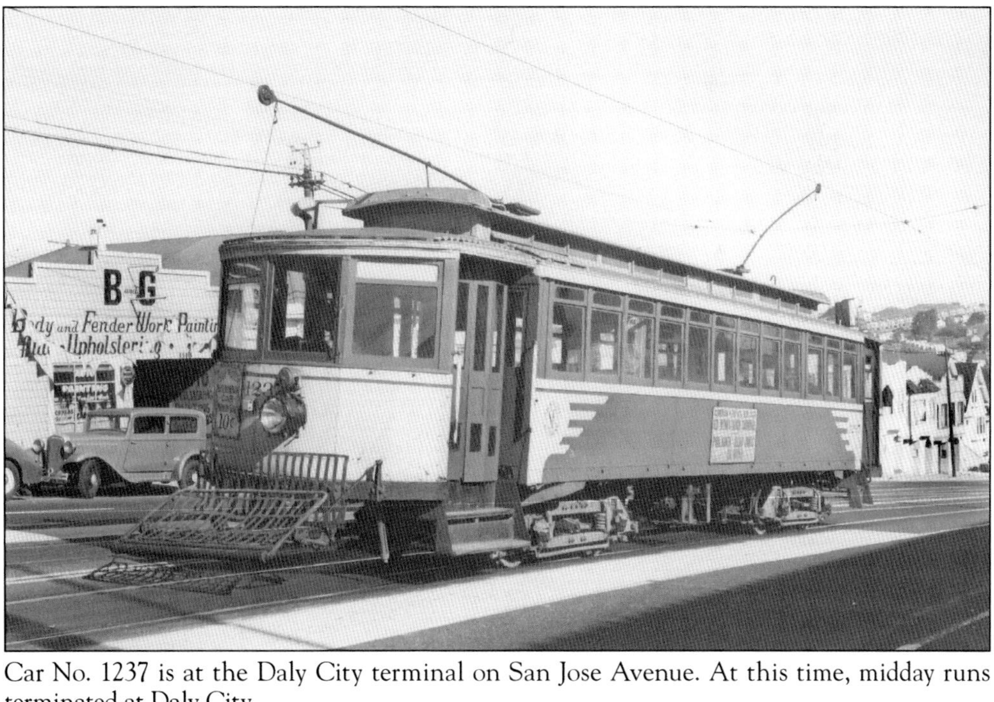

Car No. 1237 is at the Daly City terminal on San Jose Avenue. At this time, midday runs terminated at Daly City.

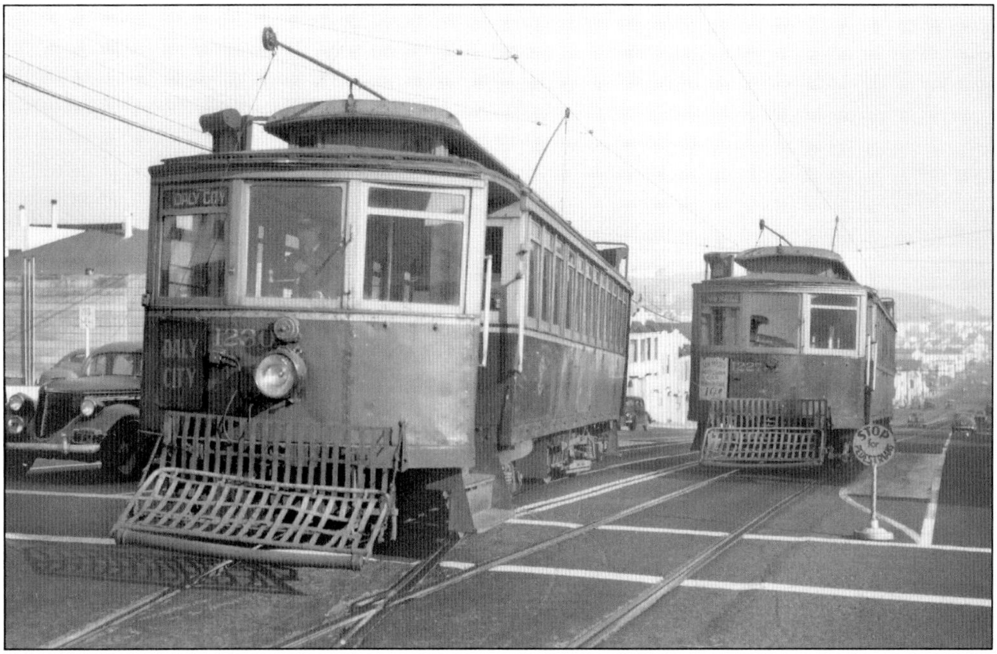

This car is leaving for San Mateo from the Daly City terminal on San Jose Avenue. Notice the Daly City dash sign that the crew forgot to change. (Courtesy Walter Vielbaum.)

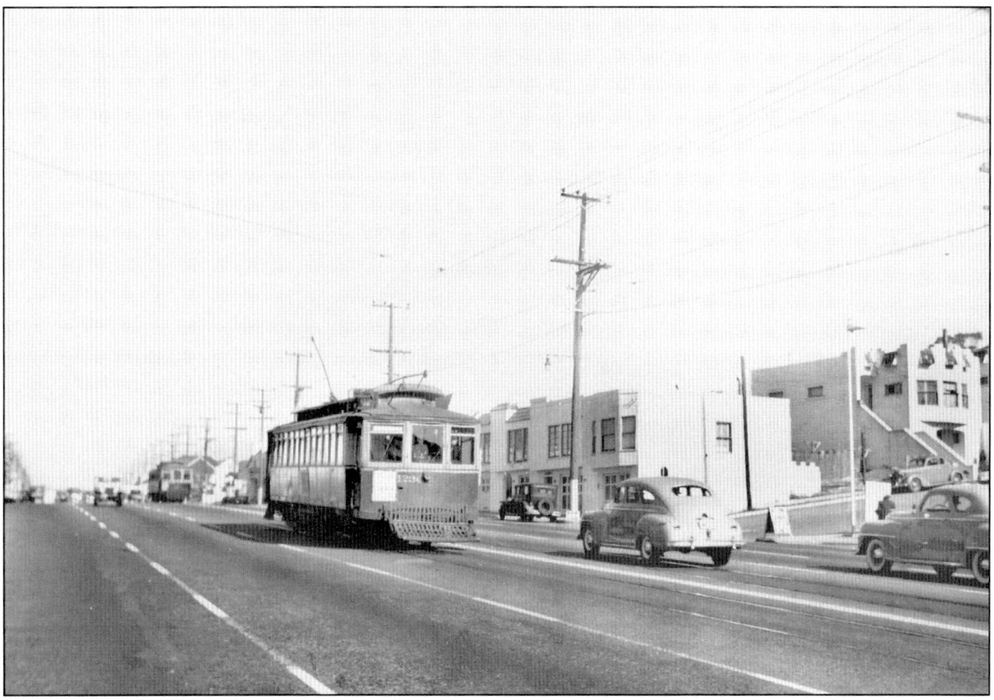

Car No. 1236 is speeding downhill from Daly City toward Colma. This stretch of line was one of the fastest downhill rides on the system. (Courtesy Robert Townley.)

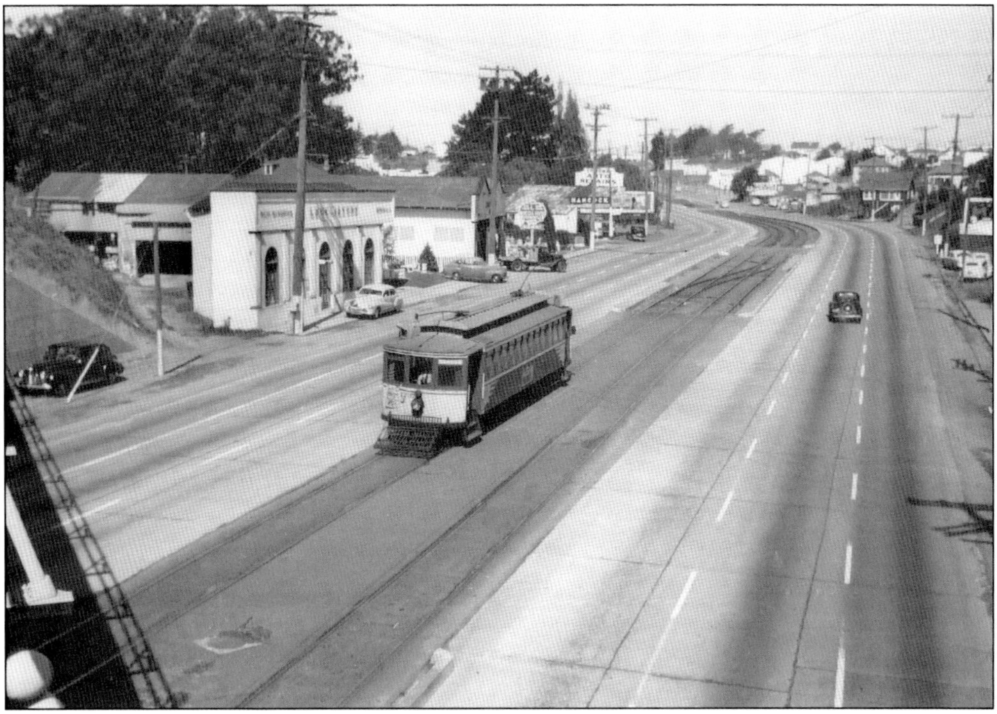

This view was taken from the Southern Pacific overpass looking toward Daly City. BART now occupies the overpass site, and the Colma BART station is on the left.

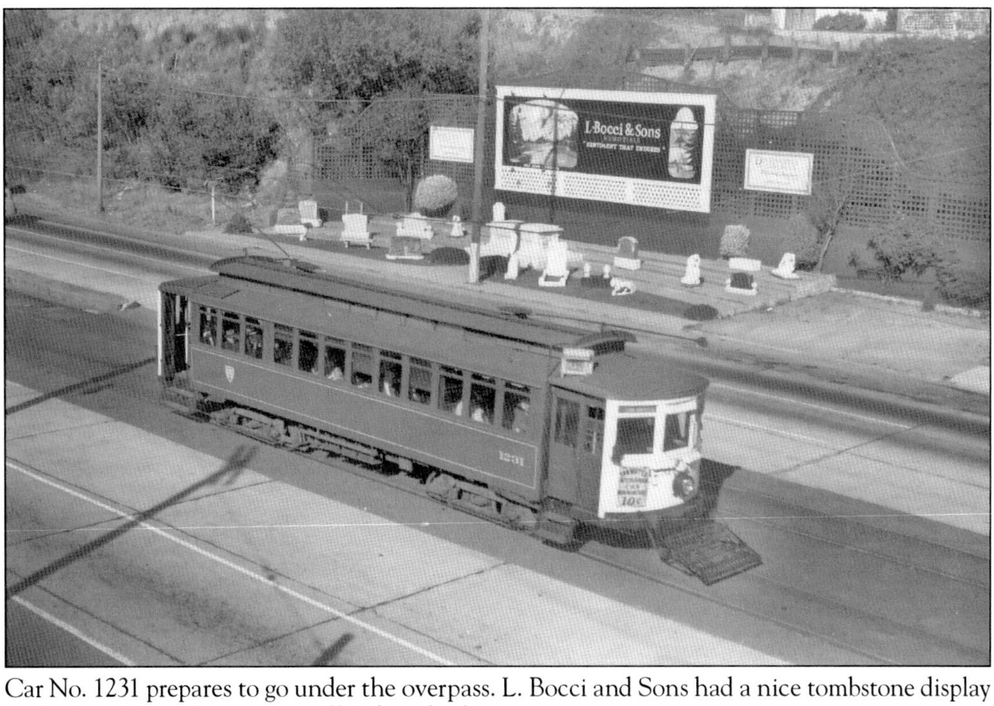

Car No. 1231 prepares to go under the overpass. L. Bocci and Sons had a nice tombstone display in the late 1930s. (Courtesy Will Whittaker.)

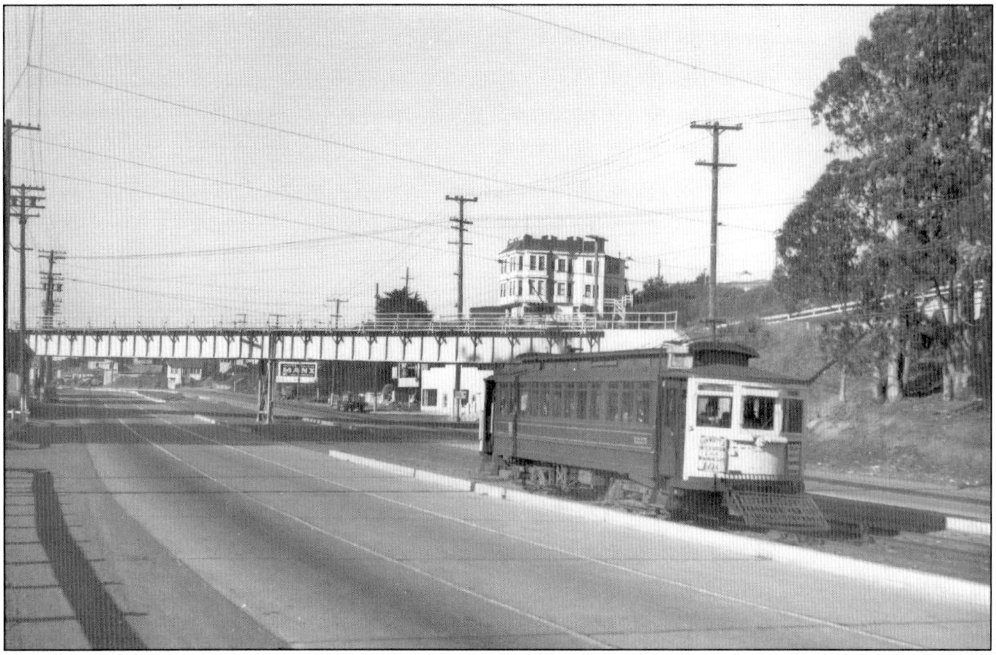

This view was taken from south of the overpass looking north. Today BART riders go over a similar overpass at the same location, but their view from the train is blocked by high walls. To the right is the Italian cemetery. (Courtesy Will Whittaker.)

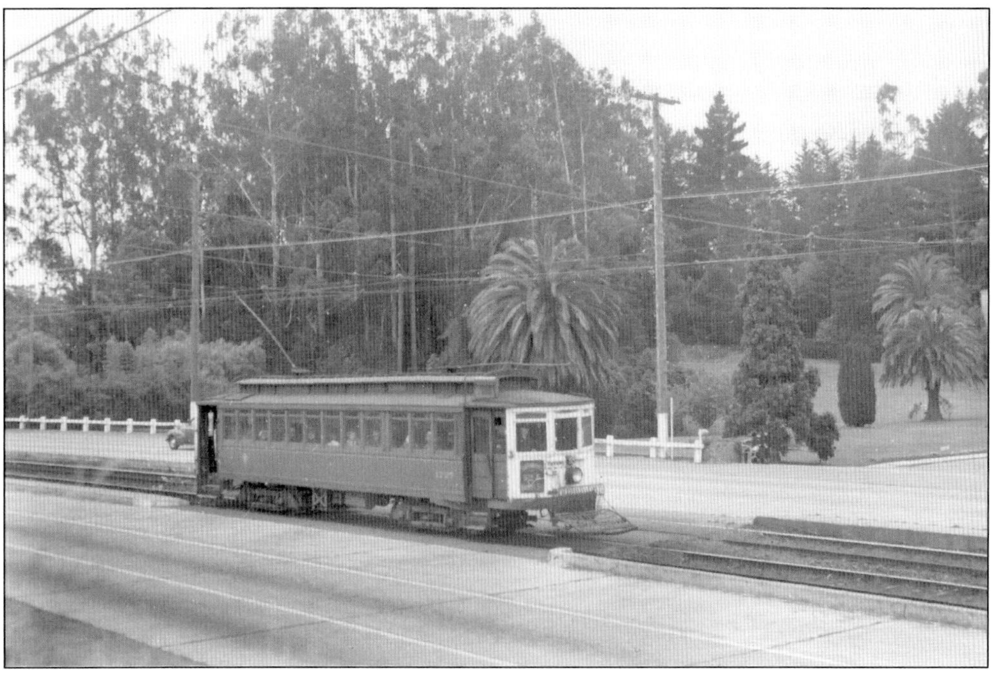

Car No. 1227 is northbound passing Woodlawn Cemetery. When El Camino Real was widened, the track was placed in the center on a reserved right-of-way. This was a great boom for the 40 line as it speeded up schedules. (Courtesy Will Whittaker.)

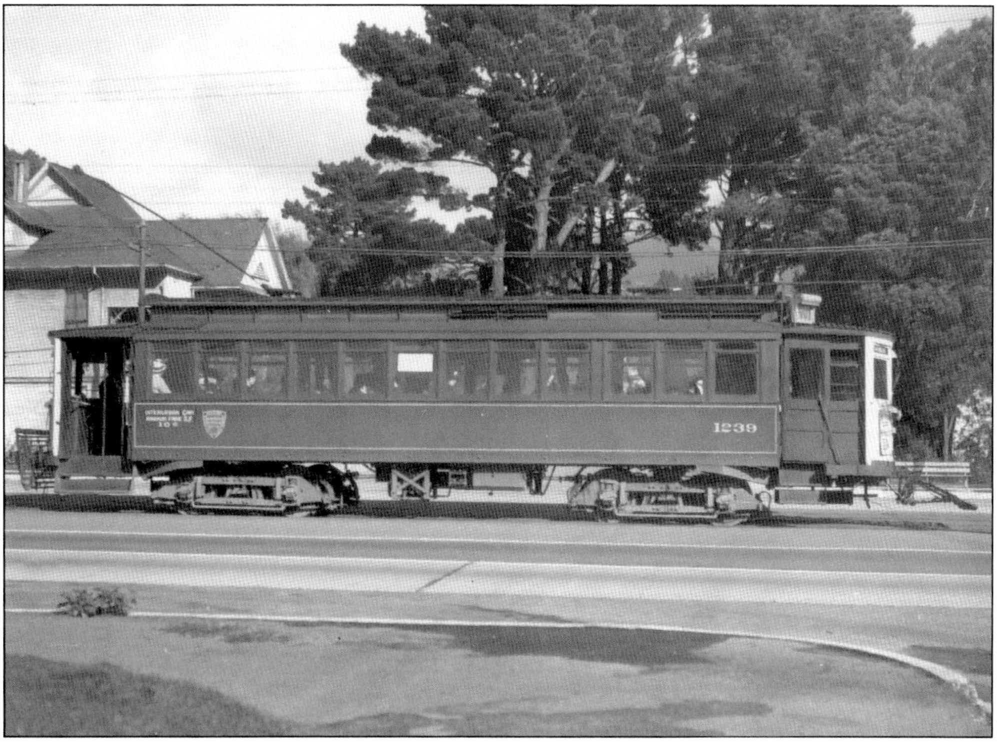

Car No. 1239 shows off its late-1930s dress, consisting of the Byllesby shield, the minimum fare 10¢ sign, the white front, and the green car body, as it goes along cemetery row in Colma. (Courtesy Will Whittaker.)

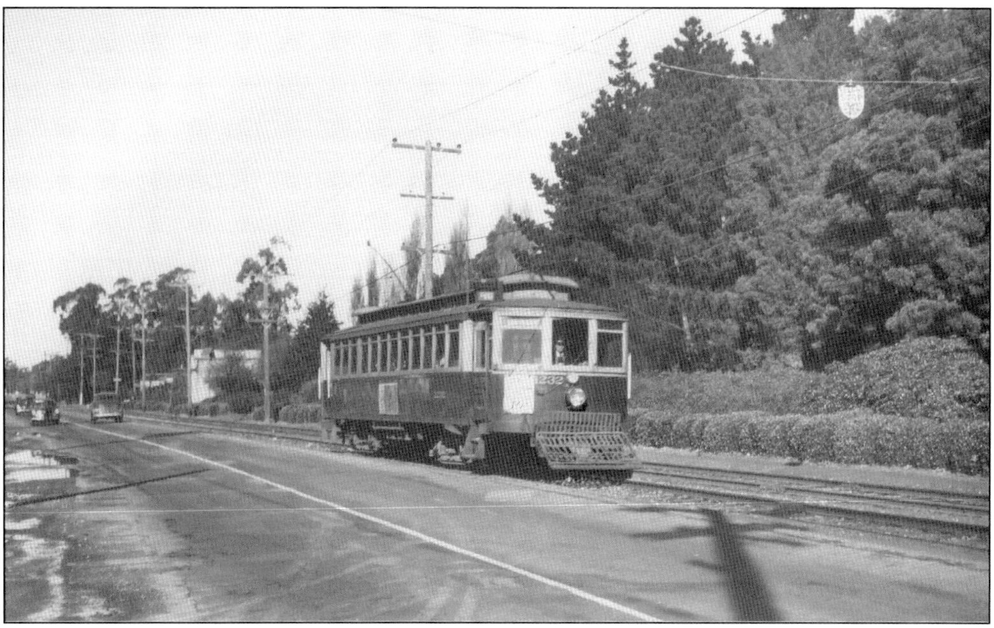

Car No. 1232 approaches the car stop for Molloy's Tavern. This short stretch of side-of-the-road operation along Mission Road, is indicative of the way the whole line through Colma used to be. (Courtesy Walter Vielbaum.)

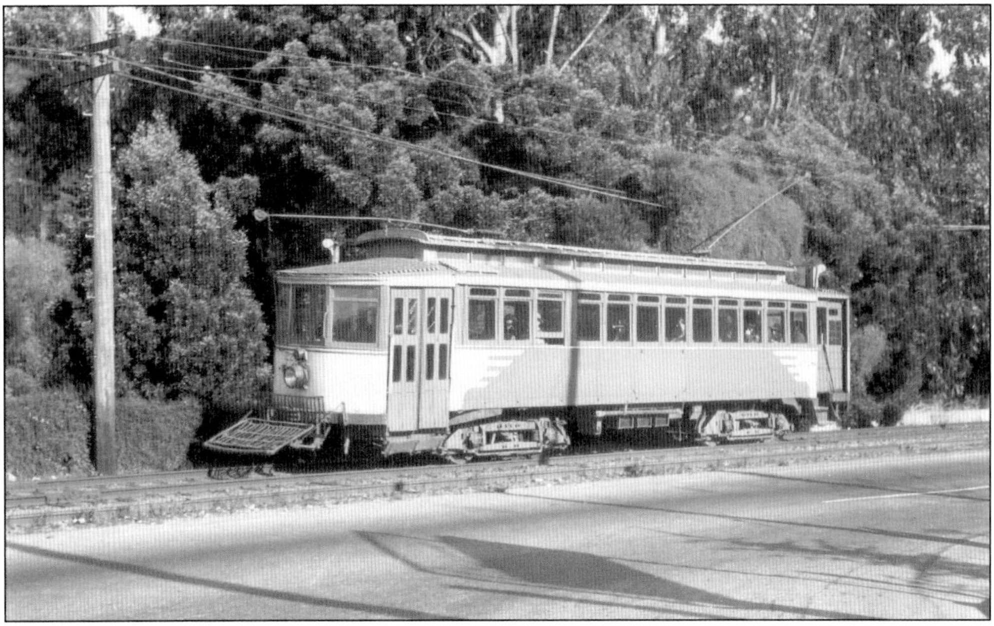

Car No. 1228 is northbound on the side-of-the-road section near Cypress Lawn Cemetery. Note the folding steps and doors left over from the ill-fated one-man conversion. (Courtesy Walter Vielbaum.)

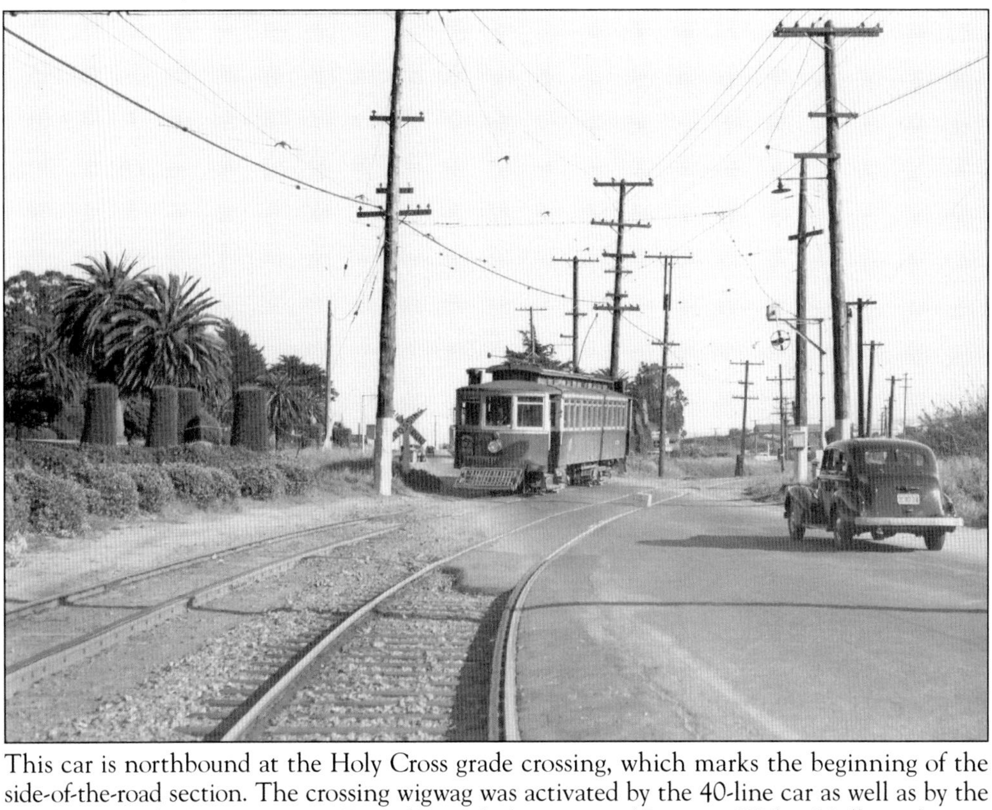

This car is northbound at the Holy Cross grade crossing, which marks the beginning of the side-of-the-road section. The crossing wigwag was activated by the 40-line car as well as by the Southern Pacific Ocean View or Bernal Branch–line trains. (Courtesy Walter Vielbaum.)

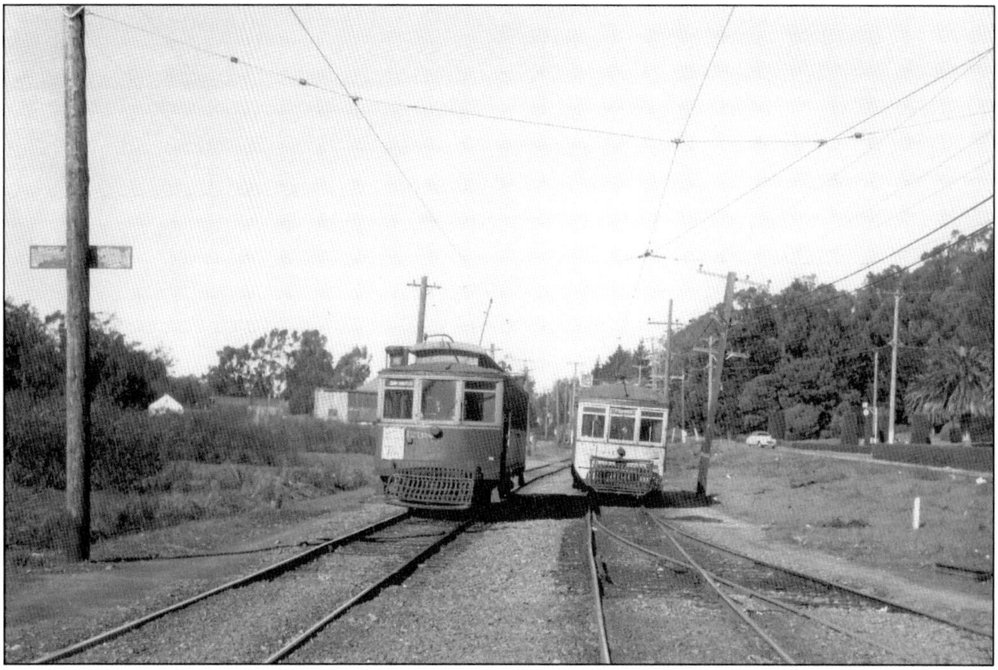

Car No. 1238 is southbound approaching the Holy Cross station while car No. 941 on the 14 line has just departed to return to San Francisco.

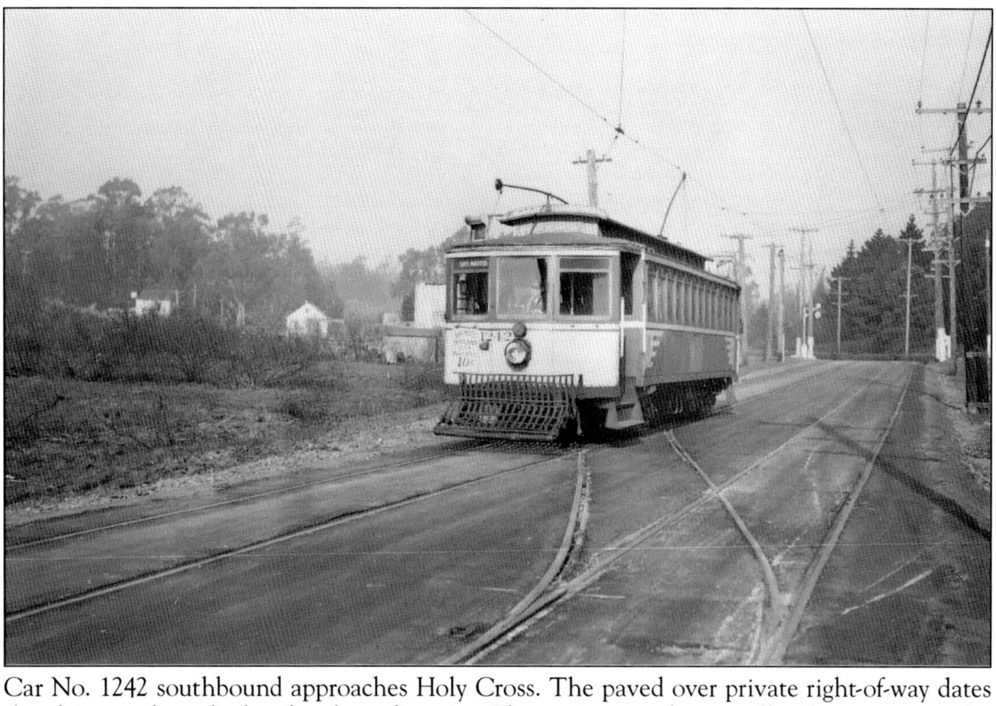

Car No. 1242 southbound approaches Holy Cross. The paved over private right-of-way dates the photograph to the last few days of service. The paving was done to allow buses to serve the Holy Cross station.

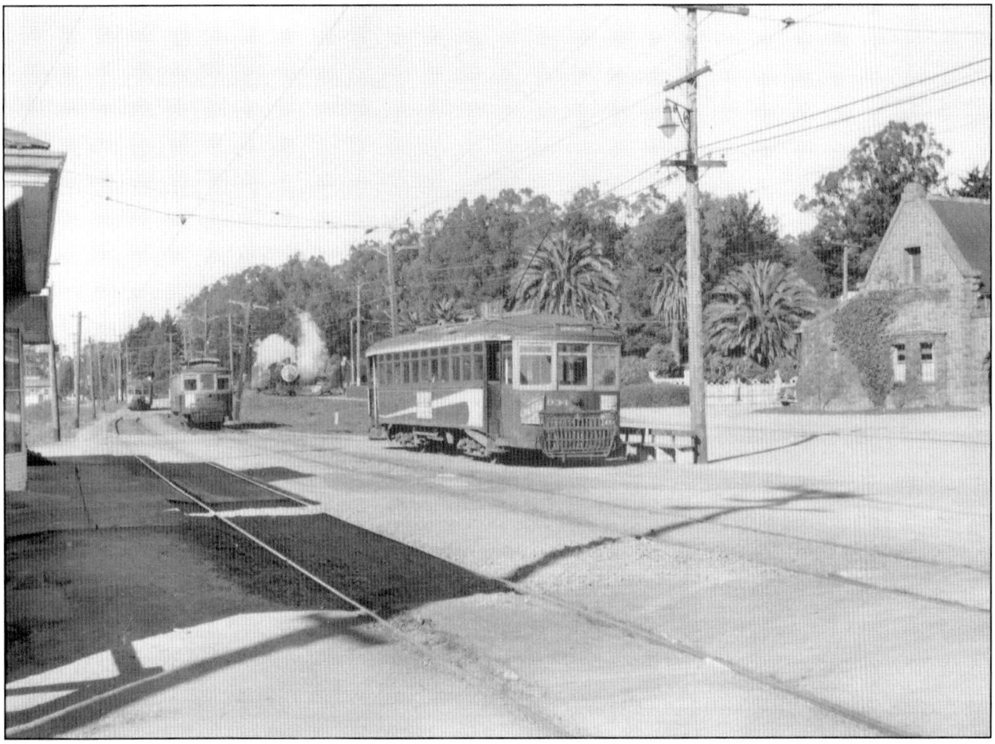

In this view at Holy Cross, car No. 934 on the 14 line is laying over on the spur track as a No. 1225 leaves the station northbound. Another 14-line car waits to enter the station while a Southern Pacific freight train, headed by a steam engine, approaches. (Courtesy Gerald Graham.)

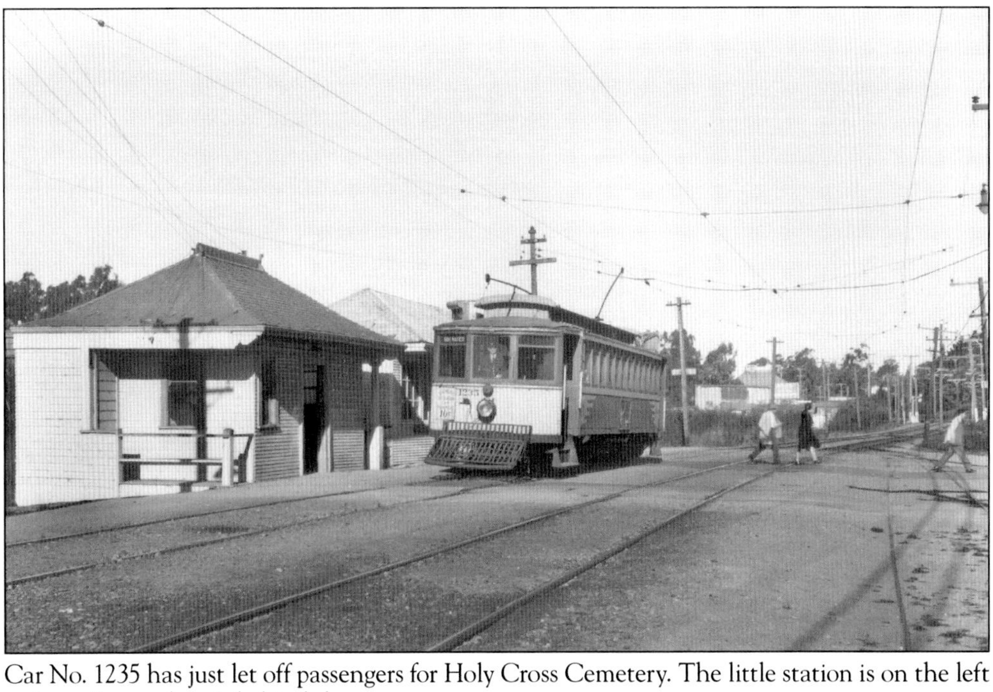

Car No. 1235 has just let off passengers for Holy Cross Cemetery. The little station is on the left and the flower shop is behind the car.

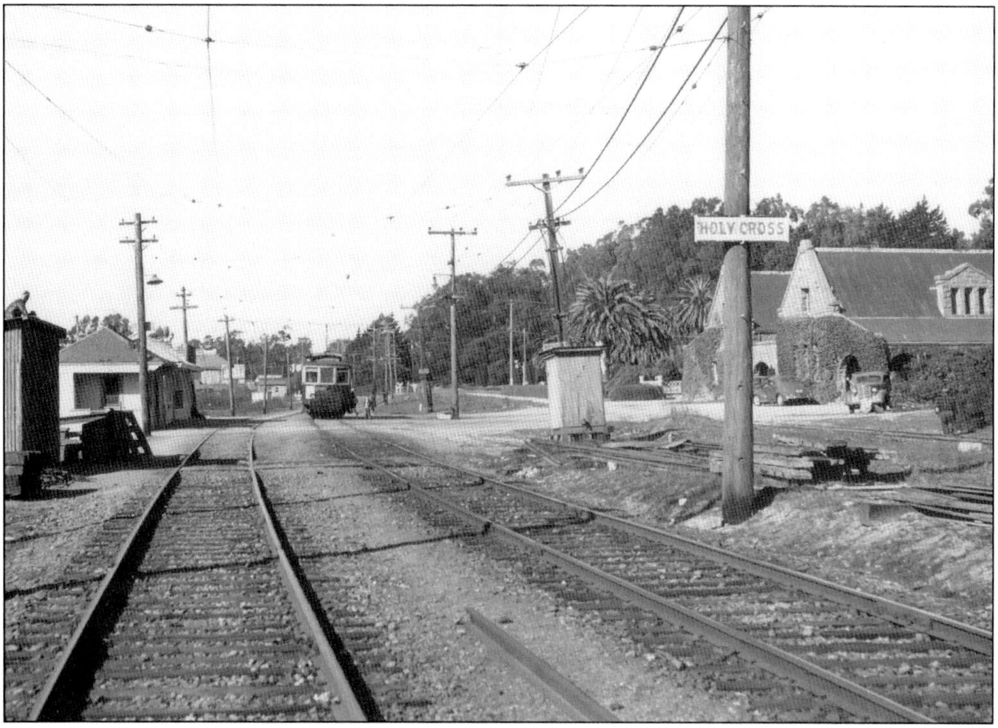

This is an overview of the Holy Cross station area looking north. The little corrugated iron shed on the left housed the track maintainers's speeder.

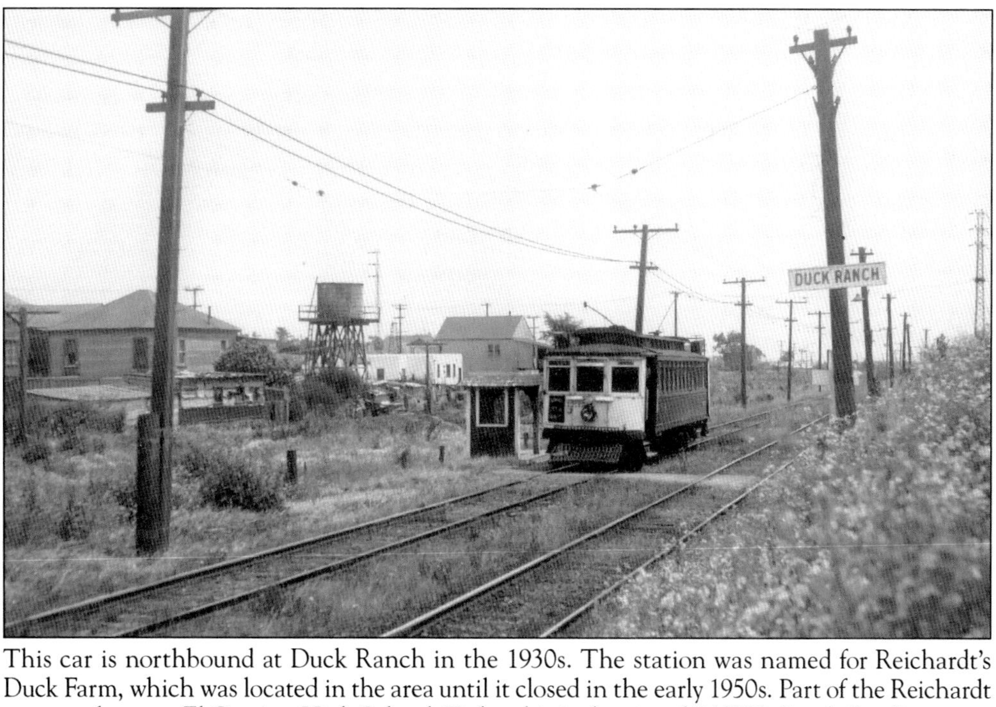

This car is northbound at Duck Ranch in the 1930s. The station was named for Reichardt's Duck Farm, which was located in the area until it closed in the early 1950s. Part of the Reichardt property became El Camino High School. Today this is the site of BART's South San Francisco Station. (Courtesy Will Whittaker.)

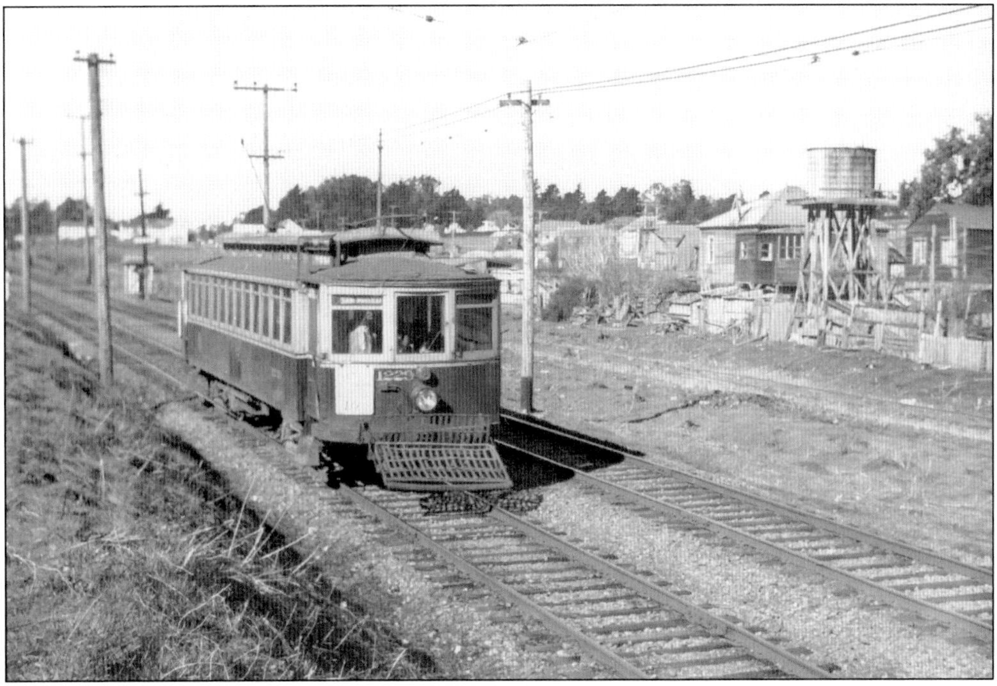

Car No. 1229 is southbound at Duck Ranch in the late 1940s. The track on the far right is the Southern Pacific Bernal Branch, which, before 1906, was the main line to San Francisco.

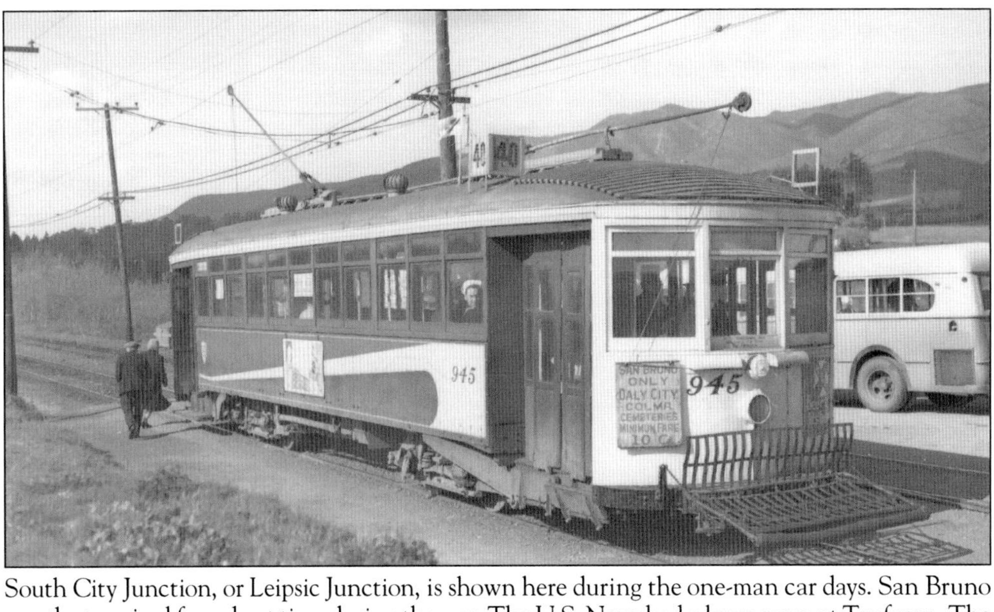

South City Junction, or Leipsic Junction, is shown here during the one-man car days. San Bruno was the terminal for a short time during the war. The U.S. Navy had a large camp at Tanforan. The Ford Transit bus is ready to depart for South San Francisco. (Courtesy Emiliano Echeverria.)

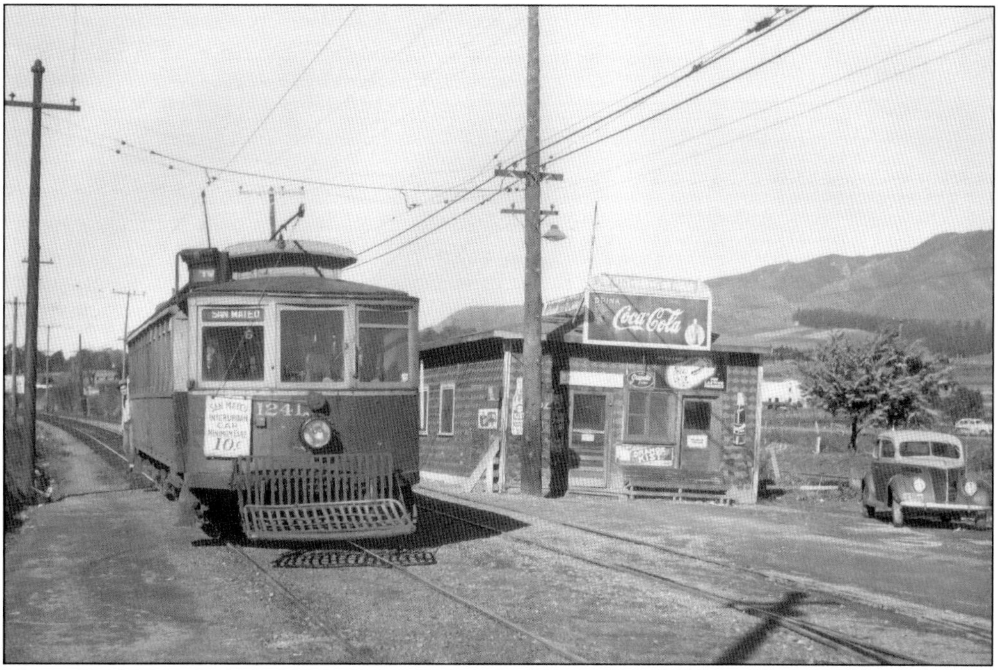

This car is heading south at South City Junction. At one time the South City car line took off here for South San Francisco. The 1937 Ford on the right belonged to the photographer. (Courtesy Walter Vielbaum.)

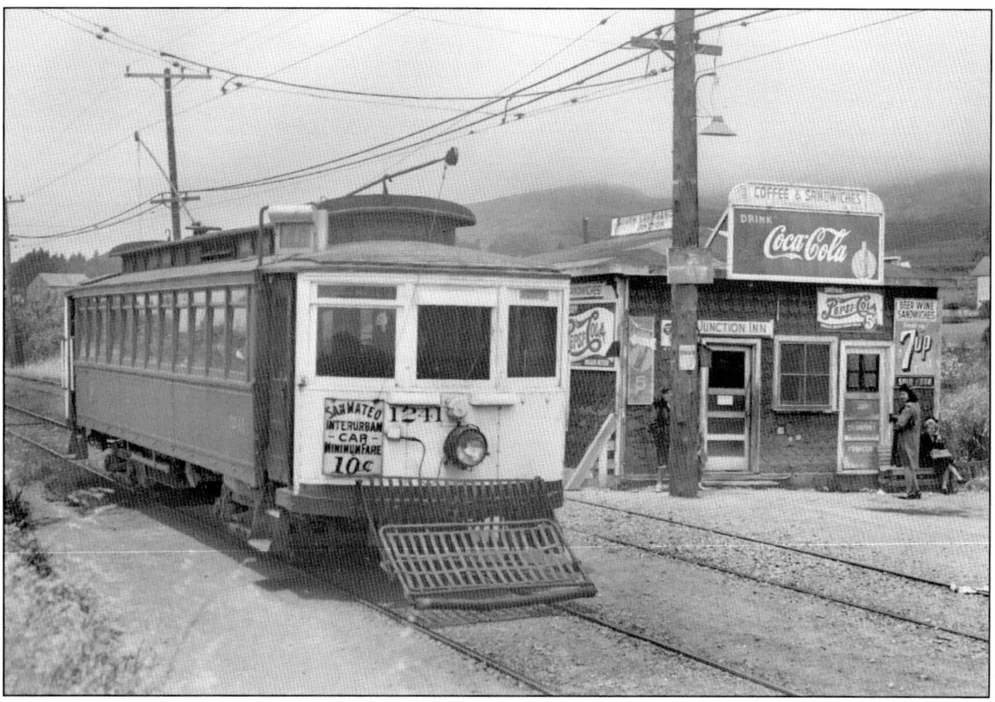

It's an overcast day in the late 1930s at South City Junction. The ladies on the right are dressed to go to the city and are waiting for the northbound 40-line car. (Courtesy Will Whittaker.)

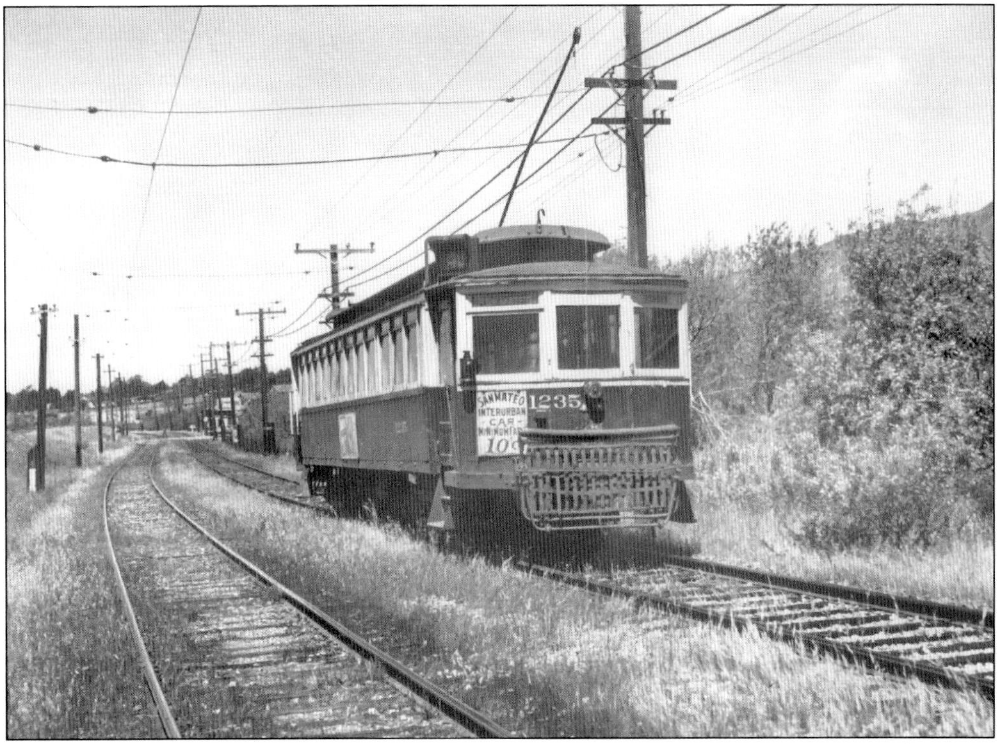

Car No. 1235 is northbound entering South City Junction. Today this whole area is built up. (Courtesy Richard Brown.)

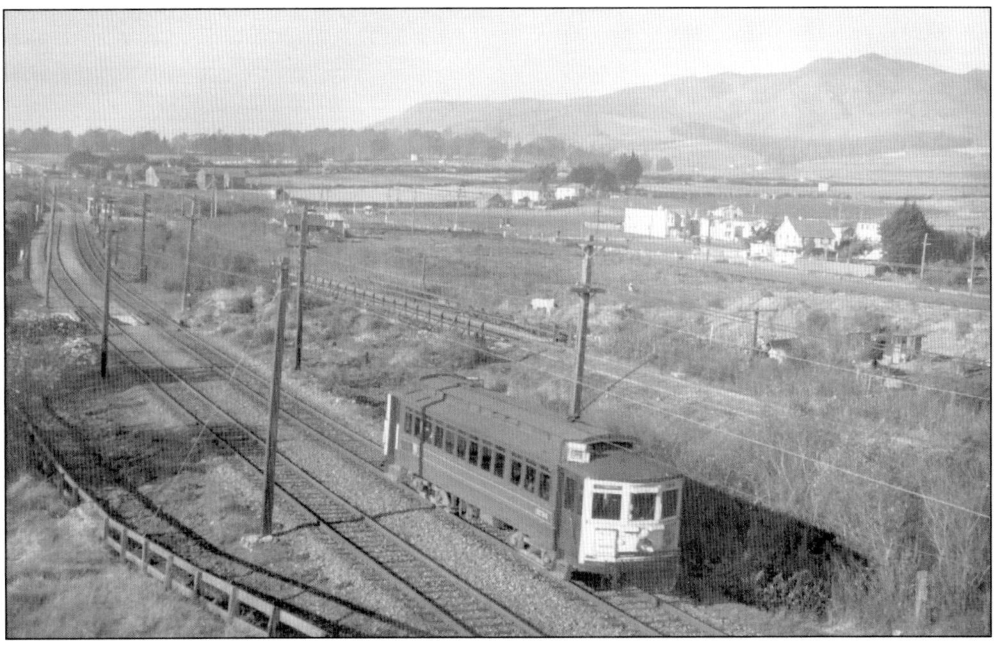

This overview looks north toward South City Junction with the old Southern Pacific main line on the right. (Courtesy Will Whittaker.)

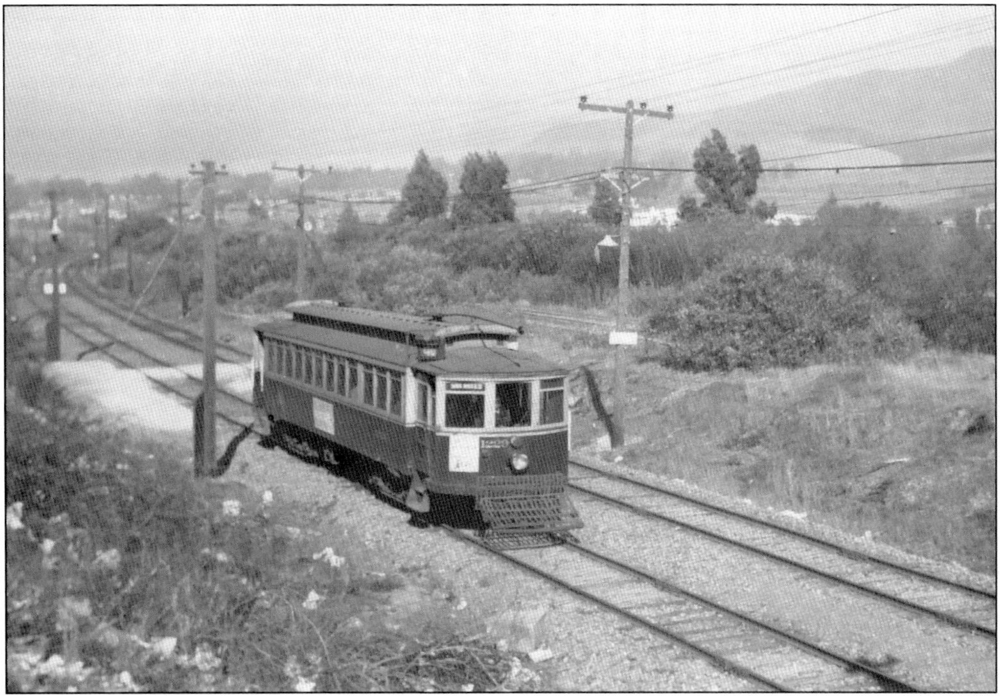

Car No. 1229 is southbound just leaving Buri Buri station. The next stop is Baden. (Courtesy Walter Vielbaum.)

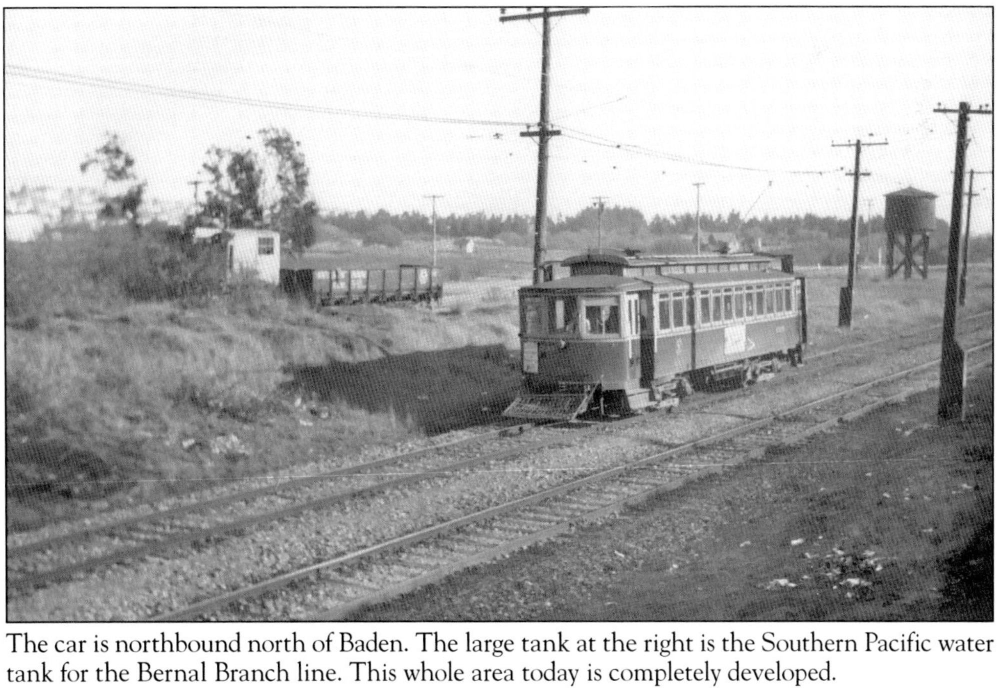

The car is northbound north of Baden. The large tank at the right is the Southern Pacific water tank for the Bernal Branch line. This whole area today is completely developed.

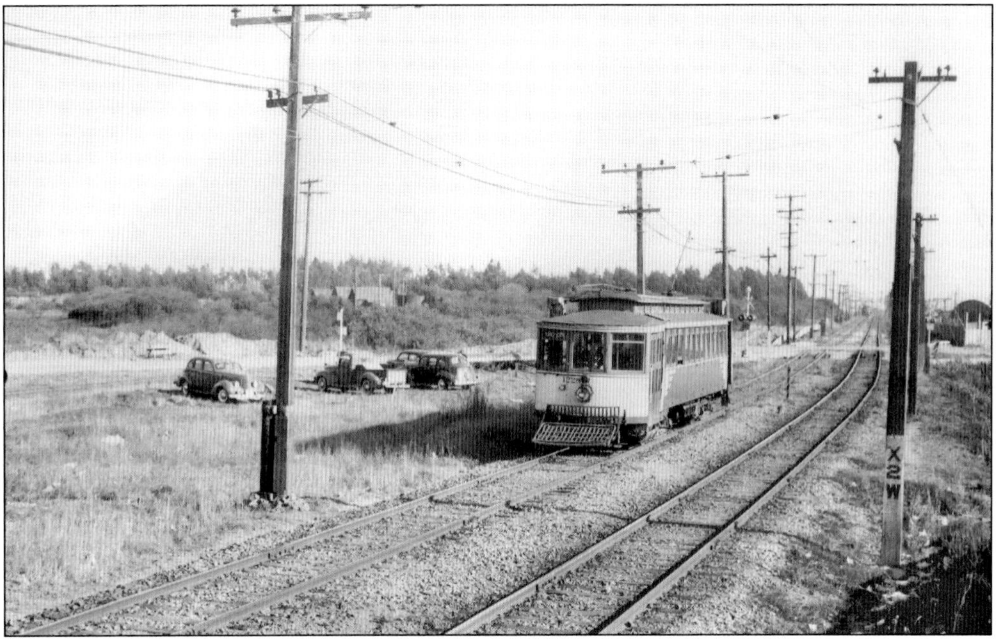

Car No. 1228 is northbound at Baden. The "X2W" on the line pole is the sign to blow two blasts on the whistle for the crossing, which is now Chestnut Street.

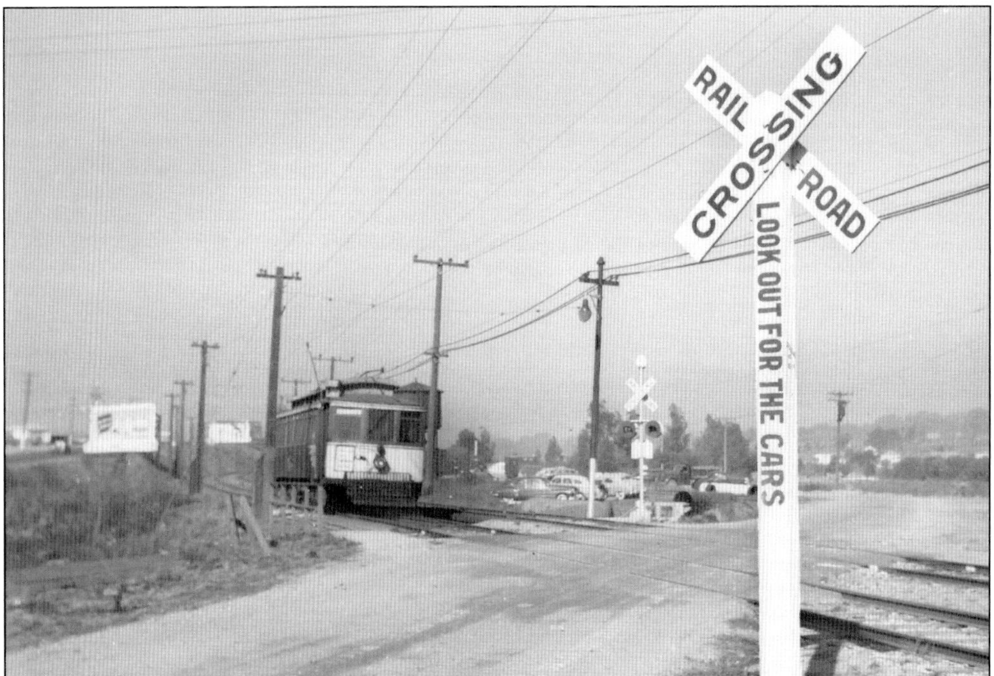

This is the way Baden crossing used to look. Muni Railway installed the red flashing lights, which gave a touch of class to the line. Behind the car is the Southern Pacific water tank.

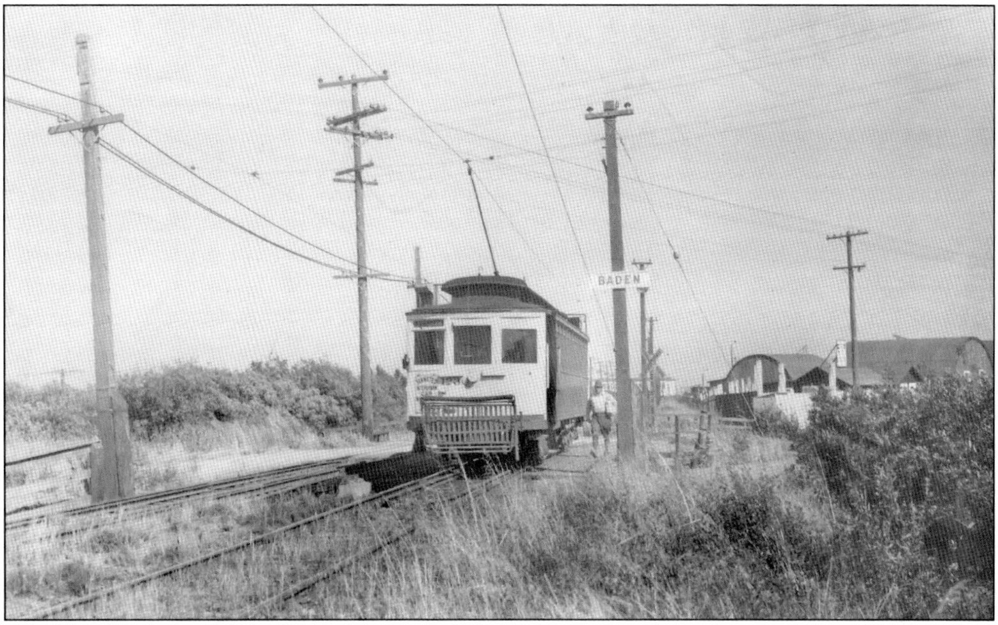

Southbound car No. 1230 stops at Baden crossing in the late 1930s. At that time, the area was largely undeveloped. (Courtesy Emiliano Echeverria.)

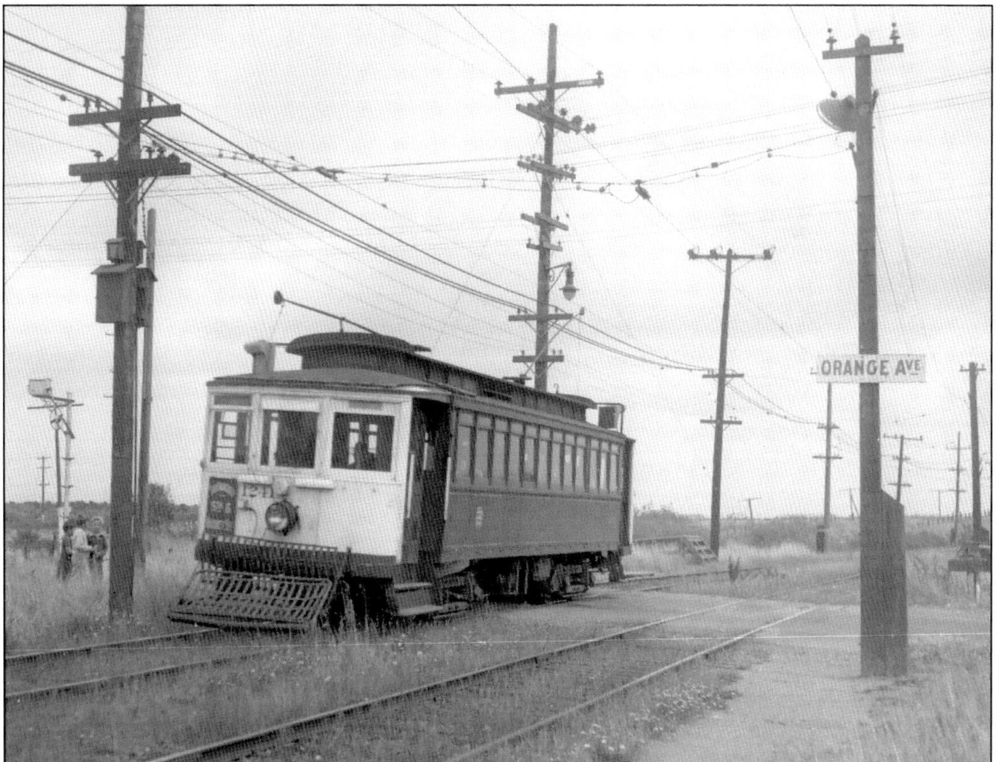

Orange Avenue was rural in the late 1930s. The wigwag signal on the left is on the pre-1906 Southern Pacific mainline line.

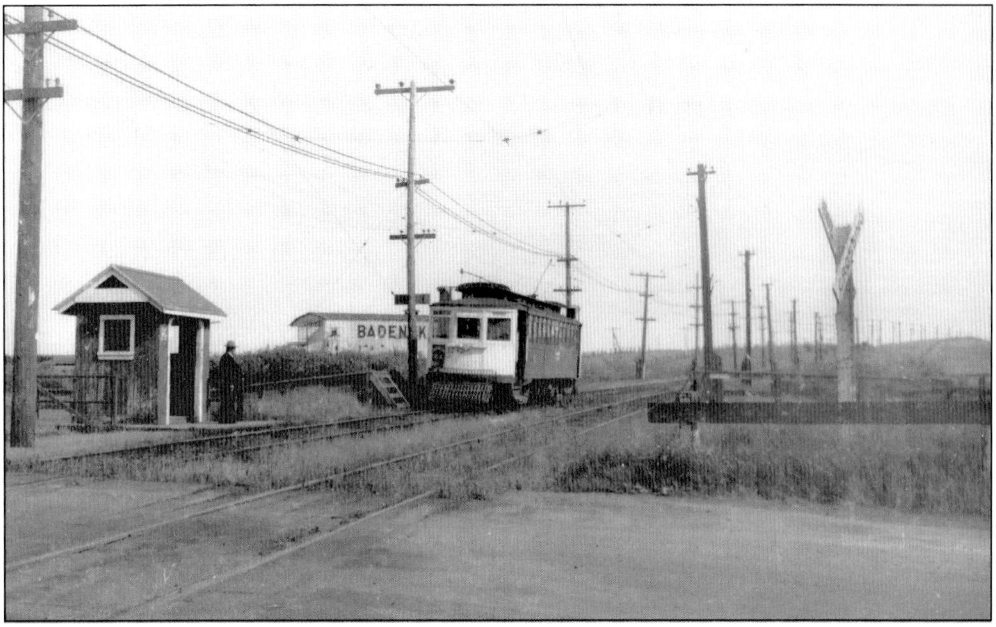

In the early 1930s, dog racing was legal in California. The grandstand for the Baden Kennel Club is behind the car approaching Orange Avenue northbound.

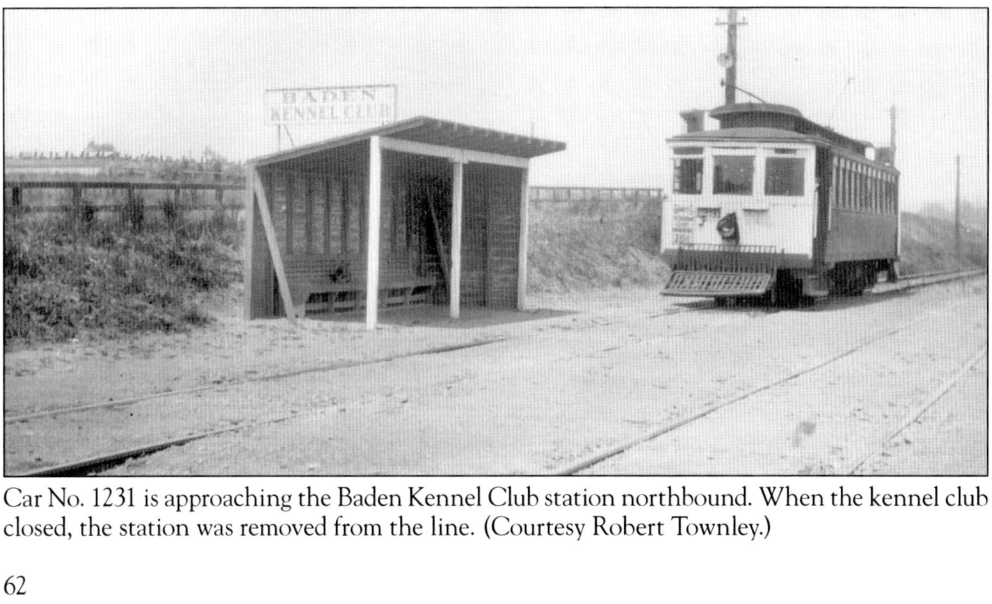

Car No. 1231 is approaching the Baden Kennel Club station northbound. When the kennel club closed, the station was removed from the line. (Courtesy Robert Townley.)

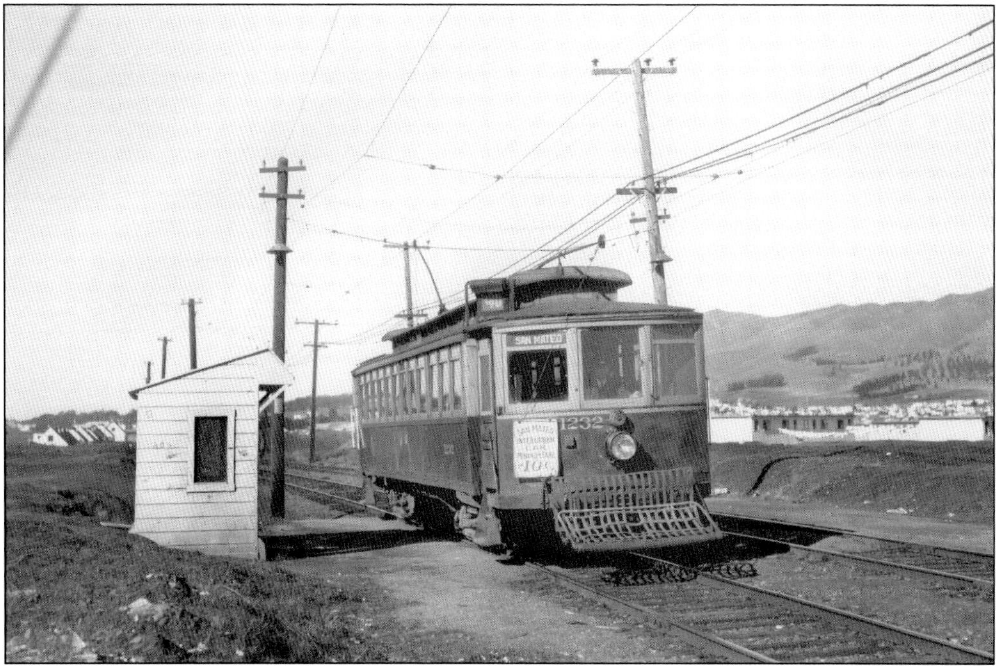

Car No. 1232 is southbound at Lindenville. This stop was added during World War II to serve the wartime housing at the right for the Tanforan Navy Base. (Courtesy Walter Vielbaum.)

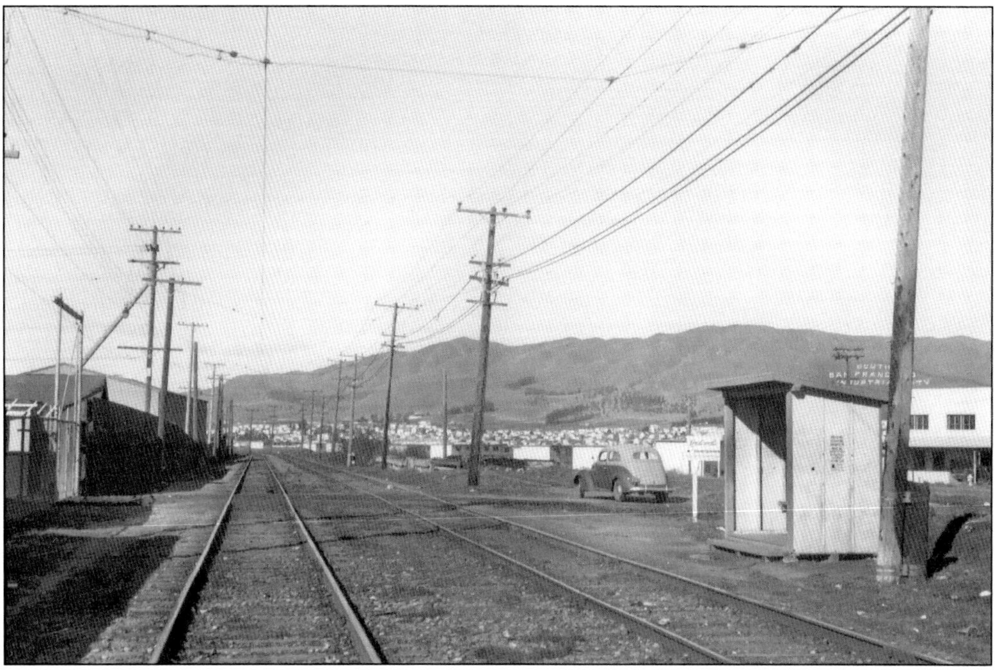

Poetsch was the first stop southbound behind the Tanforan Racetrack. Today this is BART's San Bruno Station. The same 1937 Ford appears again on the right. (Courtesy Walter Vielbaum.)

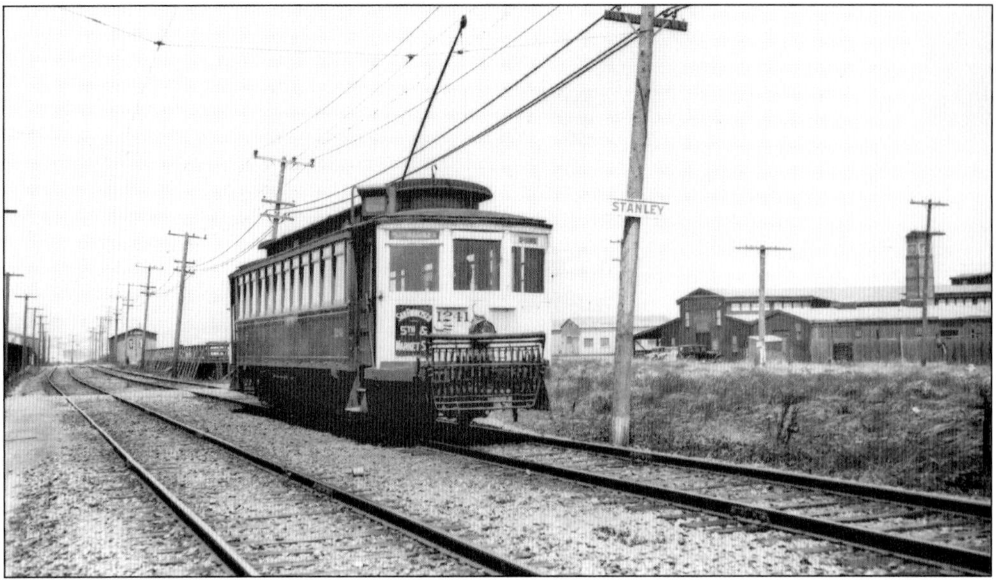

Car No. 1241 is northbound at Stanley, the second station behind the Tanforan Racetrack. Just ahead of No. 1241, on the Southern Pacific line, is the hay barn and loading dock for the horses. (Courtesy Will Whittaker.)

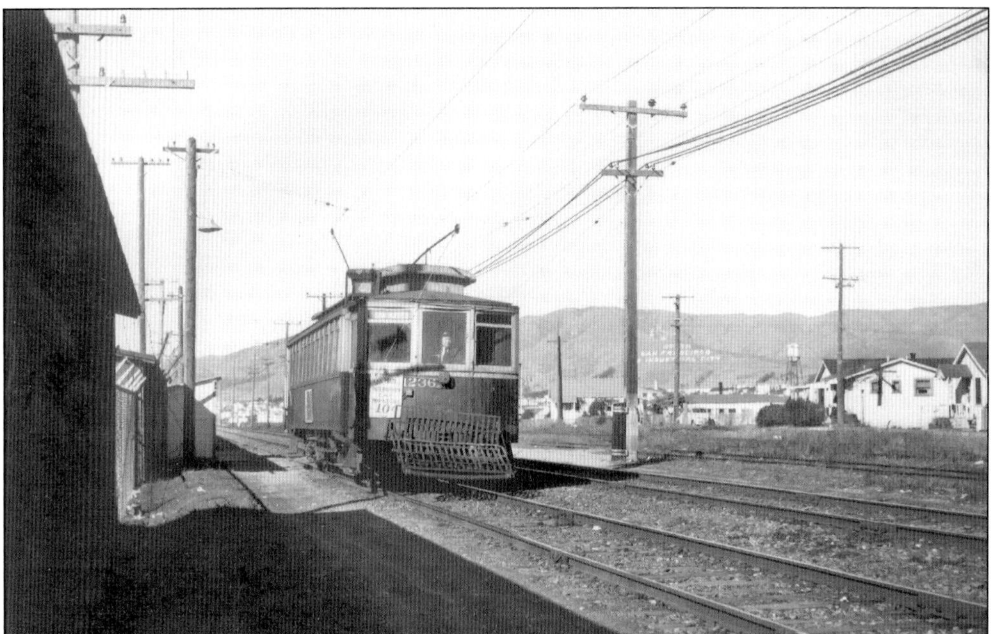

Car No. 1236 is speeding southbound by Buena Vista, the last station behind the Tanforan Racetrack. These stops were used during racing season by the Tanforan specials. (Courtesy Walter Vielbaum.)

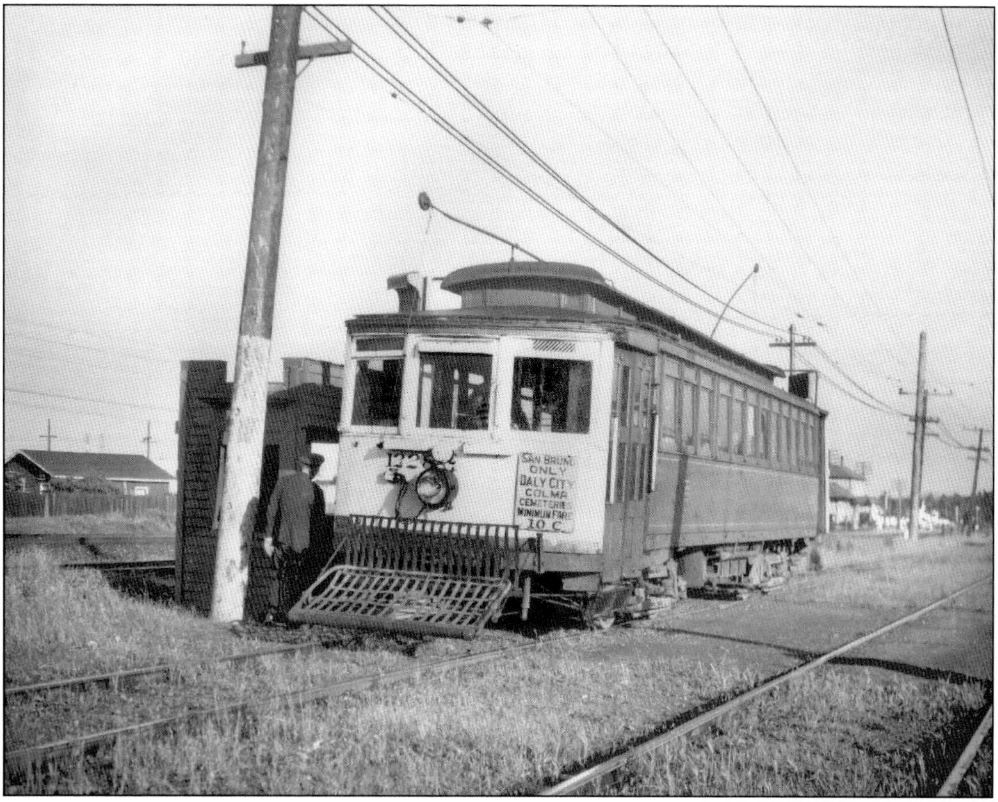

Car No. 1228 is northbound at Euclid during the San Bruno-only service during World War II. (Courtesy Emiliano Echeverria.)

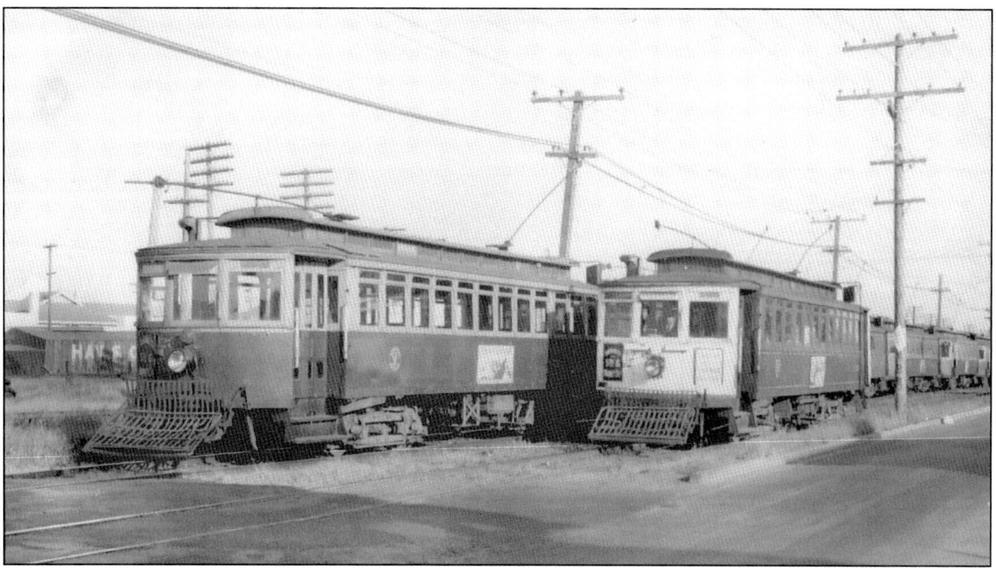

This lineup, adjacent to Euclid, is reserved for the Tanforan Racetrack service. Note that car No. 1237 is running northbound on the southbound track to pass the extra cars. (Courtesy Emiliano Echeverria.)

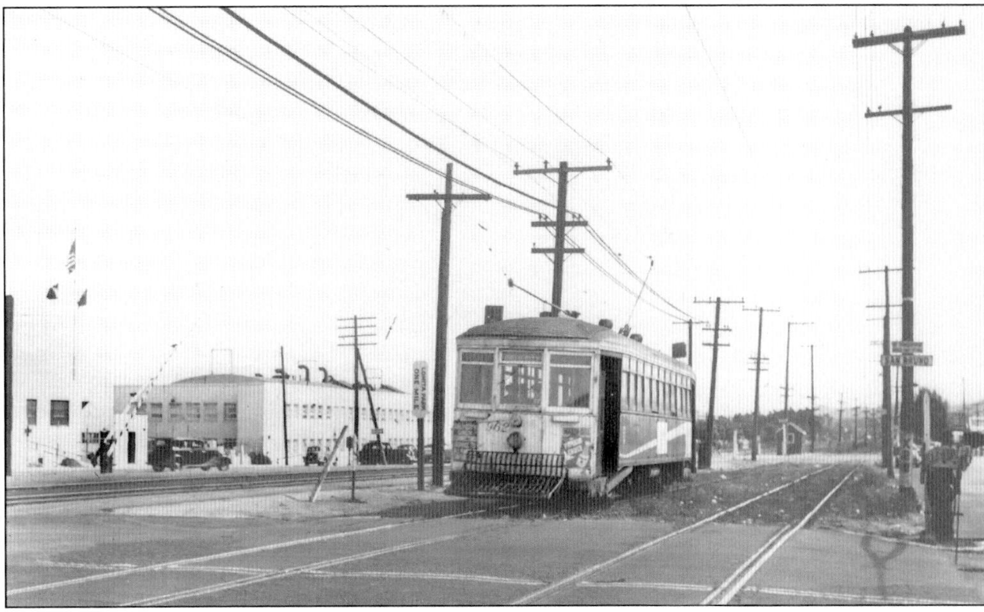

Car No. 962, a one-man car, is northbound at San Bruno Avenue crossing. The Southern Pacific crossing gates were manually operated, and the tower man has put down the gates for San Bruno Avenue for the No. 962. The other crossing behind the car is San Mateo Avenue, San Bruno. (Courtesy Emiliano Echeverria.)

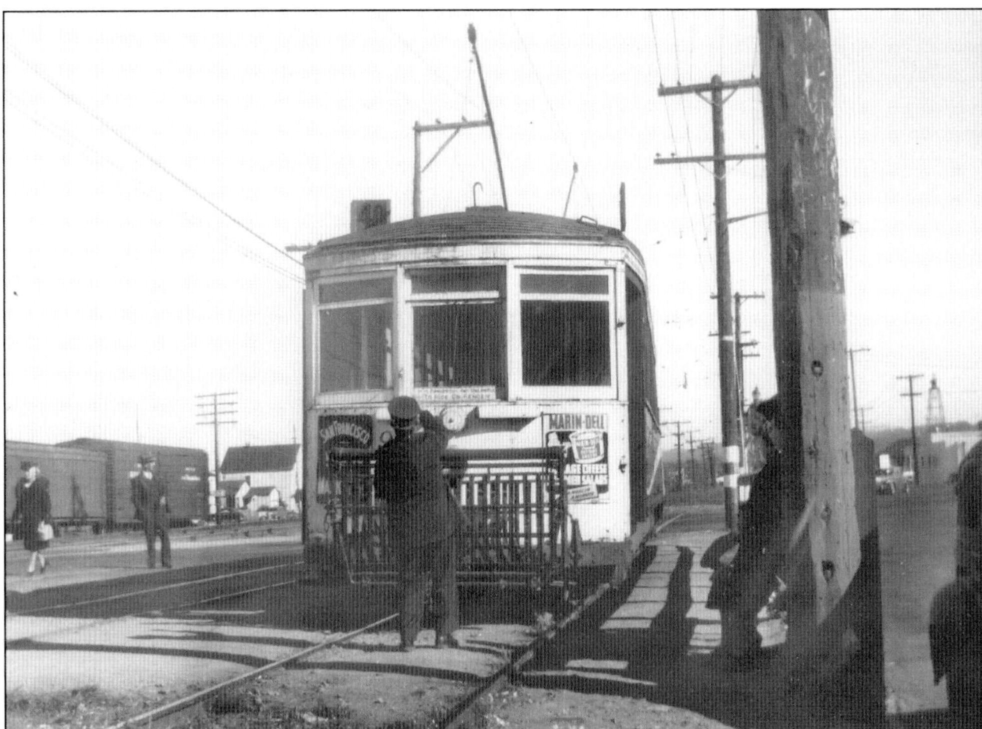

This wartime one-man car is changing ends at San Bruno's San Mateo Avenue crossing for the return trip to San Francisco..

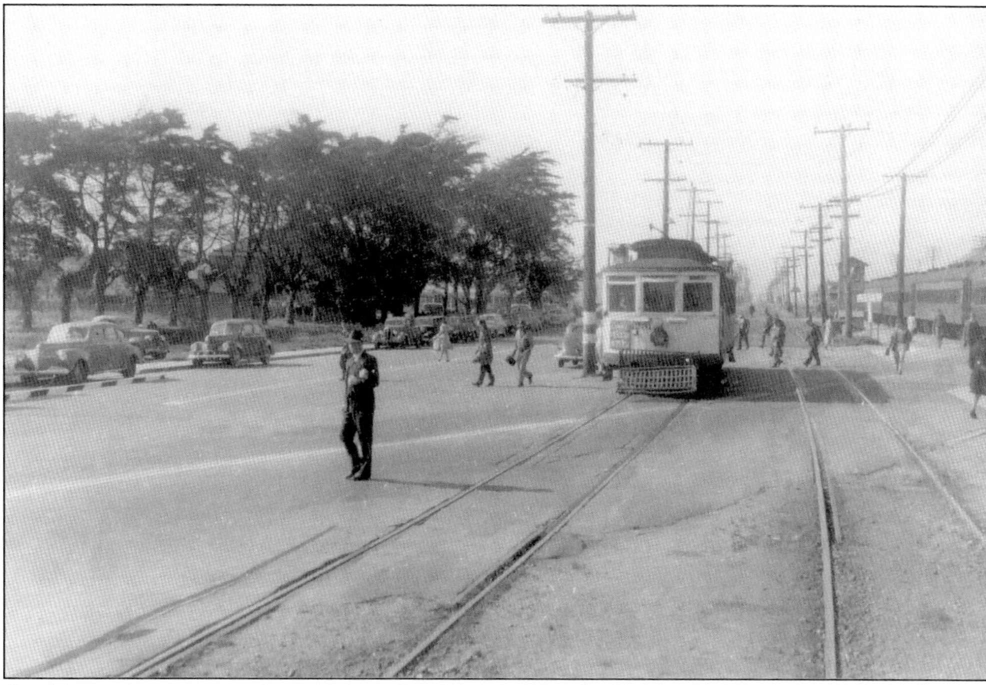

San Mateo Avenue was a busy place in San Bruno when the commuter trains stopped at the depot. Both San Mateo Avenue and San Bruno Avenue were blocked. The station was on the north side of San Bruno Avenue. The little square tower between the car and train was the crossing gate man's home. (Courtesy Emiliano Echeverria.)

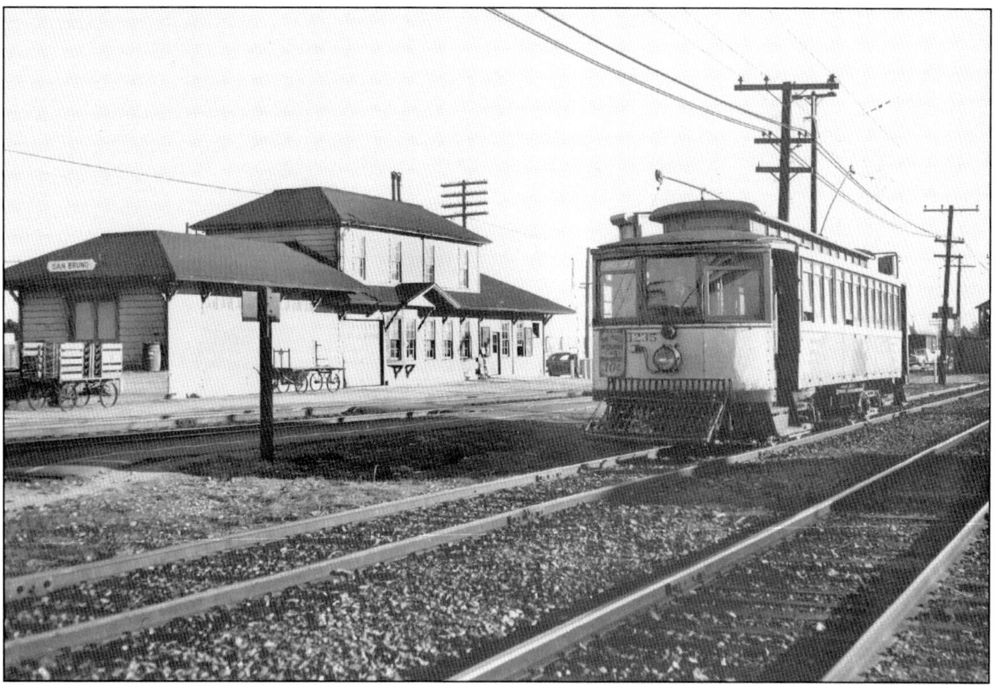

The Southern Pacific San Bruno depot was on the north side of San Bruno Avenue. Car No. 1235 is heading for San Francisco.

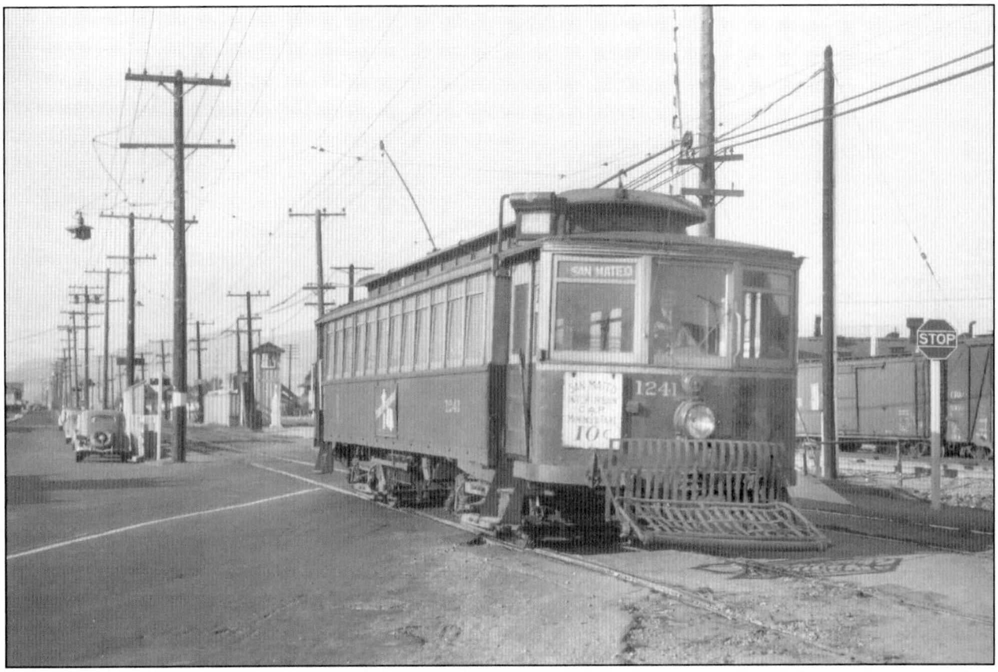

Car No. 1241, sporting the blue and yellow Muni colors, is crossing San Mateo Avenue, San Bruno. During the 1940s, San Francisco and its peninsula was a major generator of freight traffic. Therefore the sight of 1241s passing a Southern Pacific freight train was not unusual.

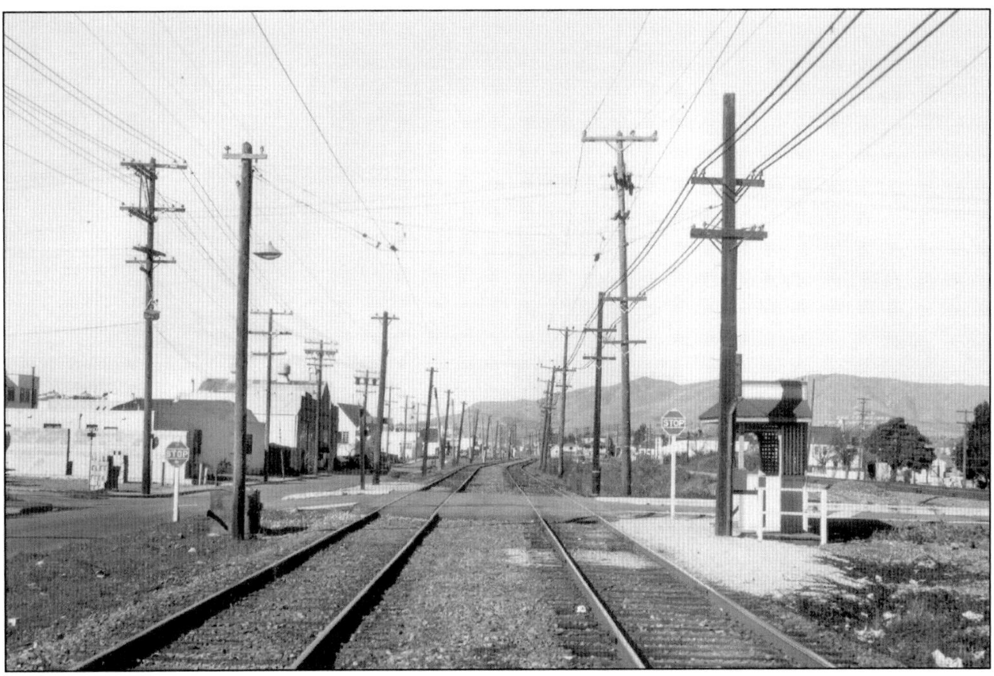

The first stop south of San Bruno's main stop at San Mateo Avenue was Angus. This northerly view provides a classic snapshot of the right-of-way and its surrounding territory in the late 1940s. Note that all northbound cars were required to stop.

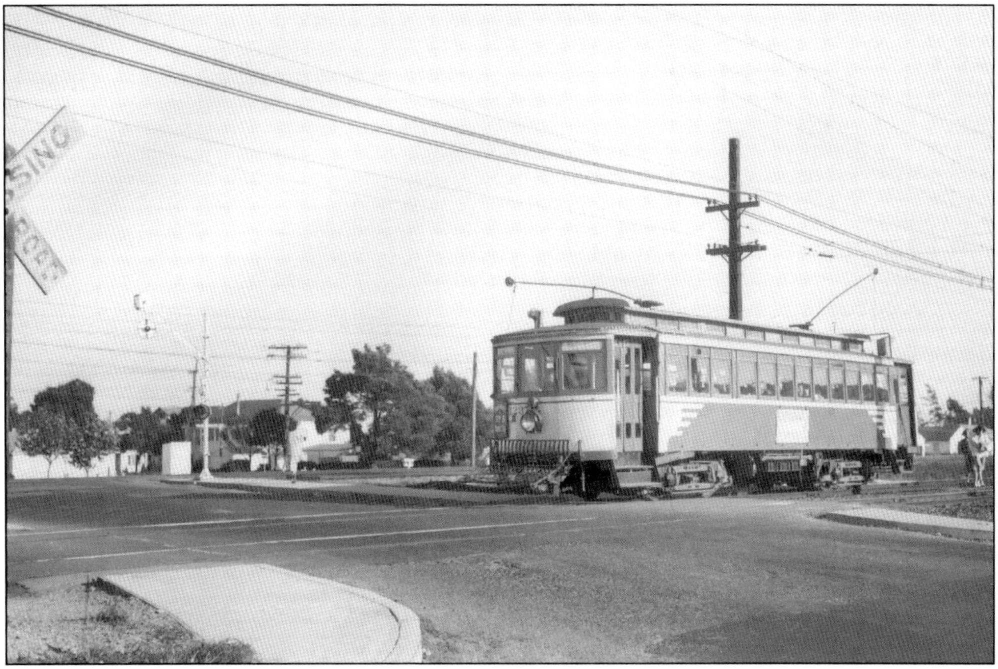

Displaying Muni's cream and green wings paint scheme, Car No. 1237 has just left Angus on its journey to San Francisco's retail center at Fifth and Market Streets. Protecting No. 1237 as it crosses the roadway is a wigwag signal, a type developed by Los Angeles' Pacific Electric.

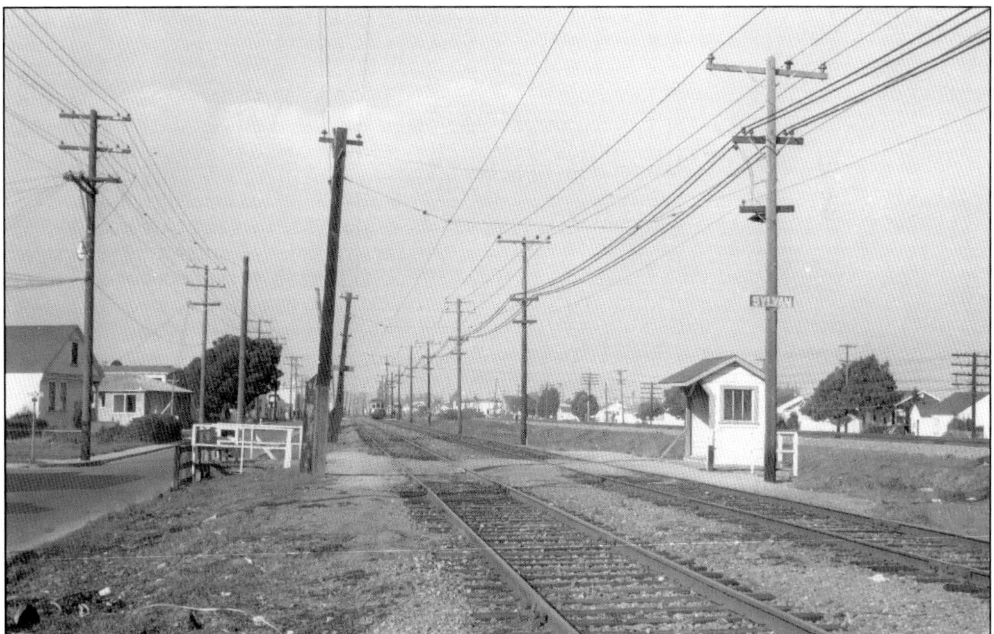

The blue and yellow 40-line car has left Sylvan and is on its way northbound to the Angus station. The small waiting room has been painted in Muni colors of cream with brown trim. (Courtesy Walter Vielbaum.)

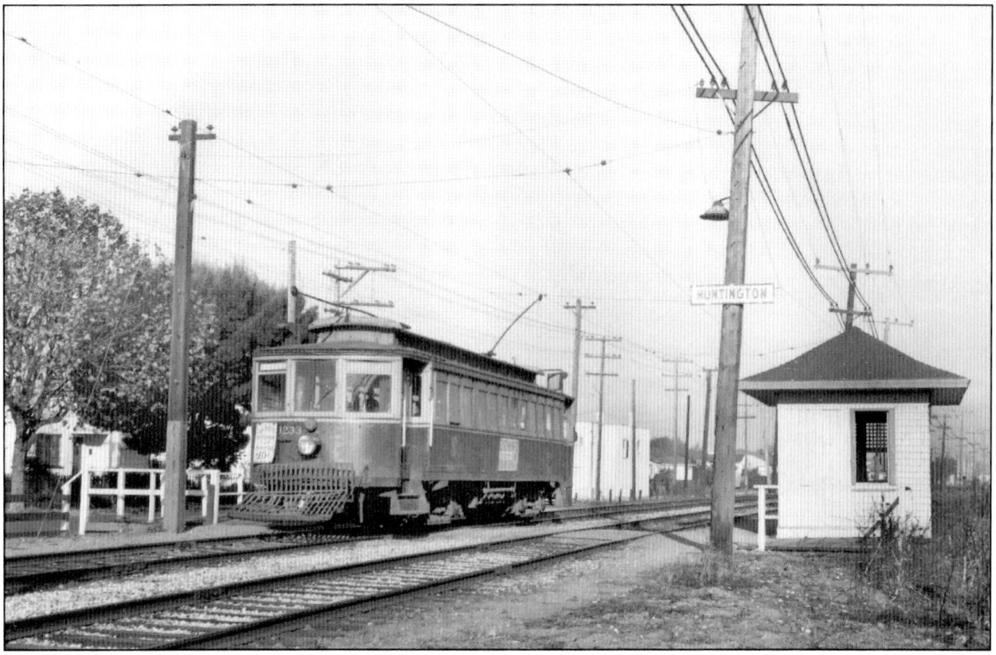

The white roller sign in the lightly loaded No. 1233's window could imply that it will end its southbound trip before reaching San Mateo, perhaps to pick up homeward bound Burlingame High School students. Car No. 1233 is passing through San Bruno's Huntington stop.

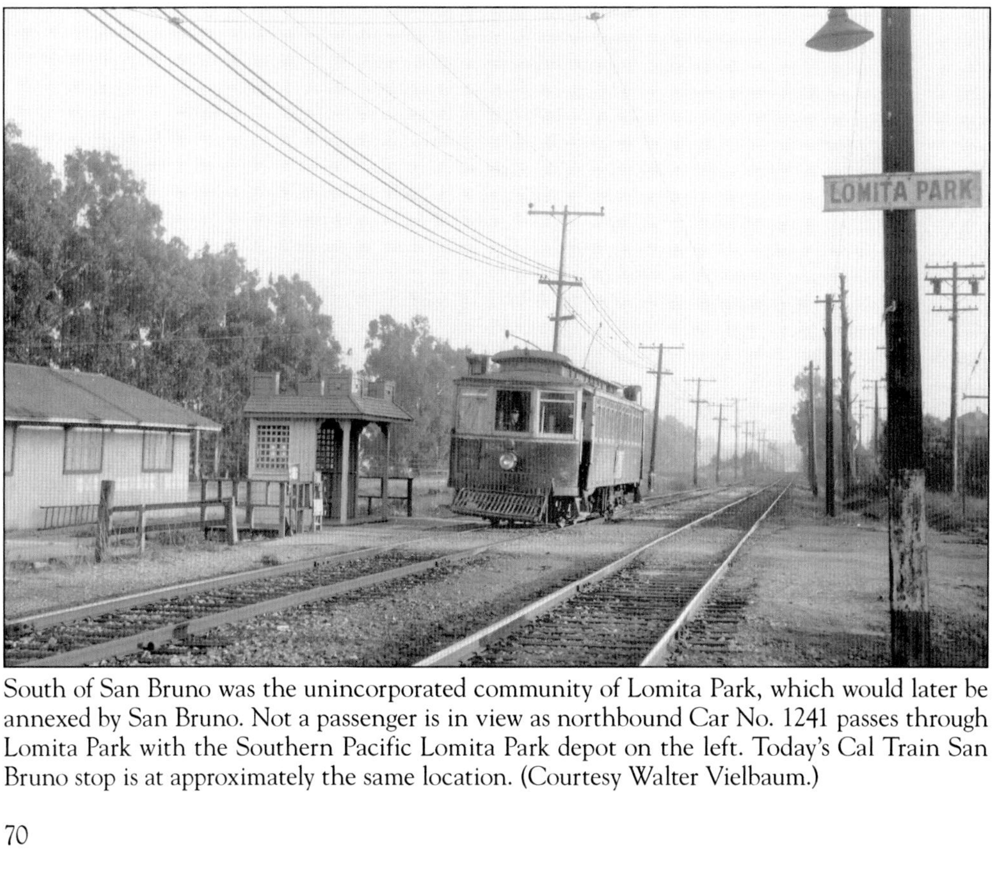

South of San Bruno was the unincorporated community of Lomita Park, which would later be annexed by San Bruno. Not a passenger is in view as northbound Car No. 1241 passes through Lomita Park with the Southern Pacific Lomita Park depot on the left. Today's Cal Train San Bruno stop is at approximately the same location. (Courtesy Walter Vielbaum.)

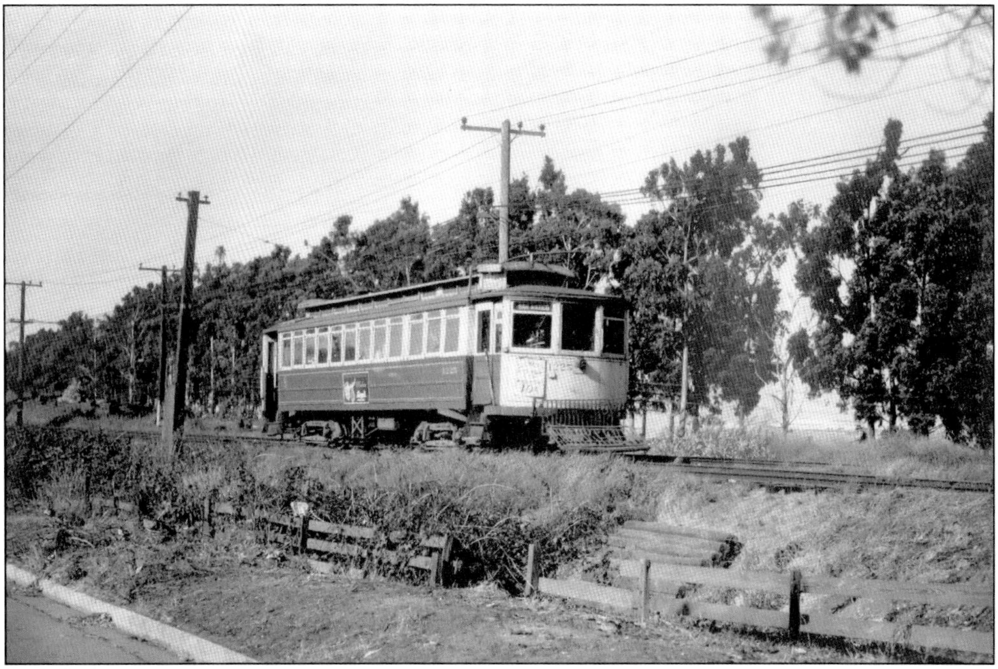

Eucalyptus trees were a characteristic trademark of much of the 40 line's private right-of-way from San Bruno south. Heading to downtown San Mateo is a speeding No. 1225 that has just left Lomita Park in its wake.

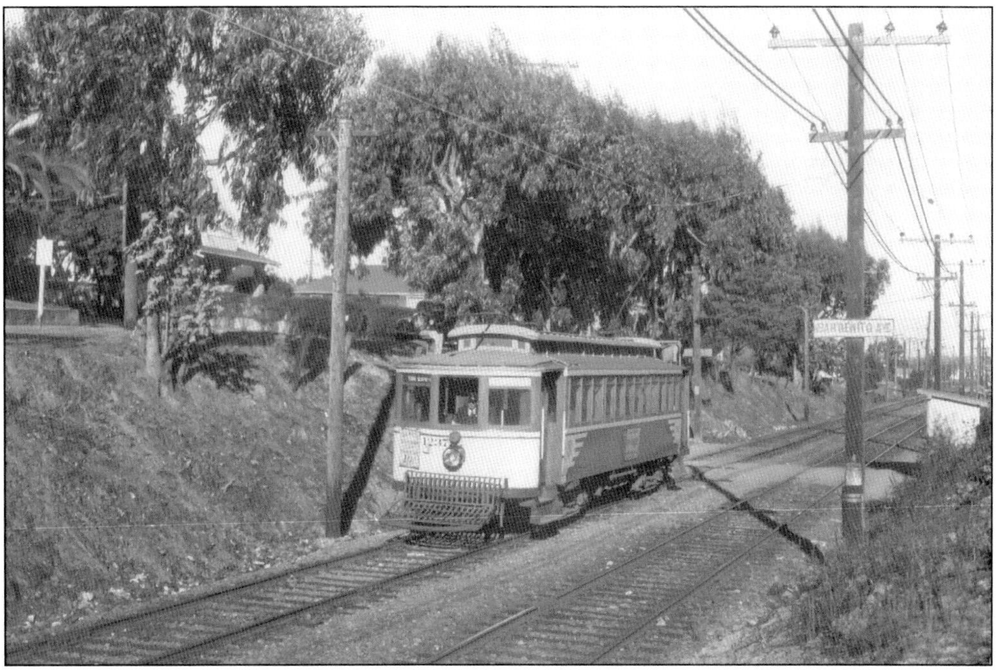

Running in a cut is southbound Car No. 1237, which has just left Lomita Park's San Benito Avenue stop. Within 20 minutes, its last southbound passenger will have disembarked in San Mateo.

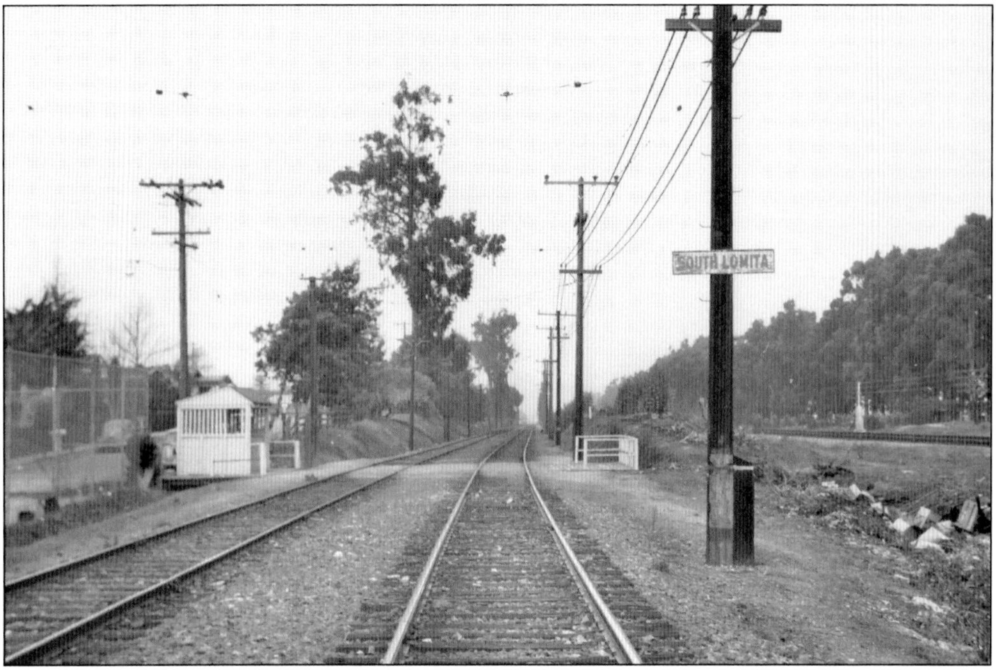

Looking north at South Lomita, the right-of-way appears in fine condition. Of interest is the fact that shelter is provided on the San Mateo-bound track instead of the more traditional location of the northbound San Francisco track. To the right are the tracks belonging to 40-line rival Southern Pacific Railroad. (Courtesy Robert Townley.)

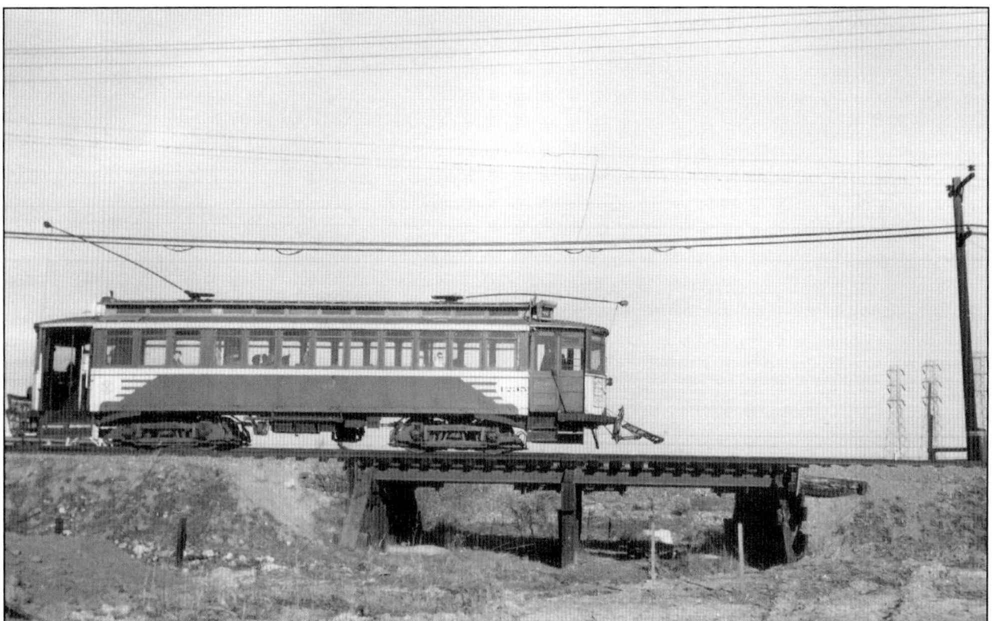

Car No. 1235 crosses one of the line's wooden trestles just north of the famous roadhouse, the 16 Mile House. This broadside view illustrates the green and cream wings paint scheme that was applied by the Muni on five cars of the 40-line fleet. (Courtesy Robert Townley.)

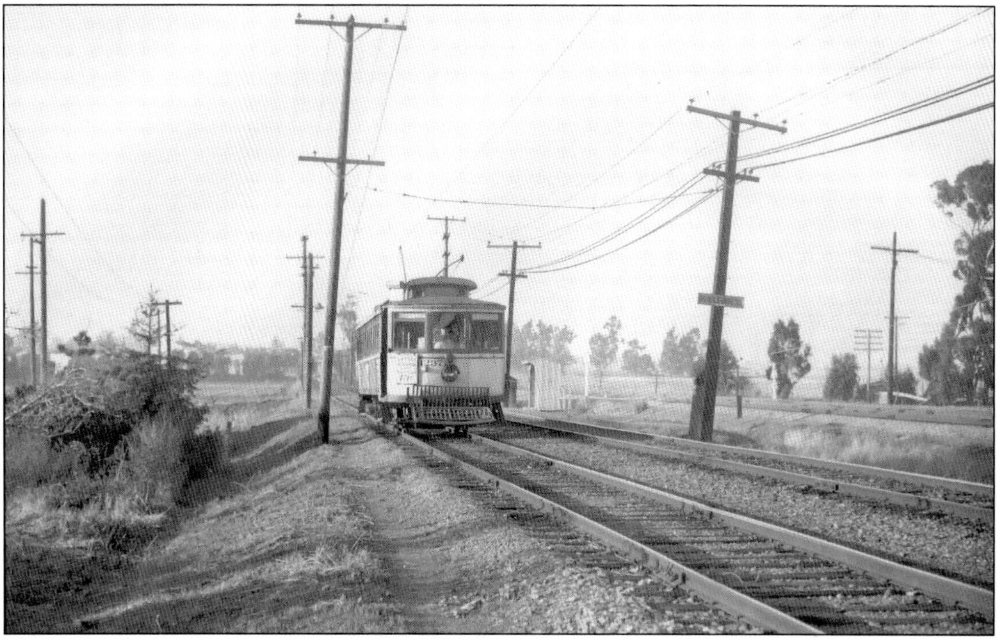

Southbound car No. 1237 is speeding past the 16 Mile House stop, the start of Millbrae in the then largely undeveloped territory of north Millbrae, in the late 1940s. Because of the 40 line's long private right-of-way, the line's average speed was relatively high, which helped make the 40 line a moneymaker even in its last months of operation. (Courtesy Walter Vielbaum.)

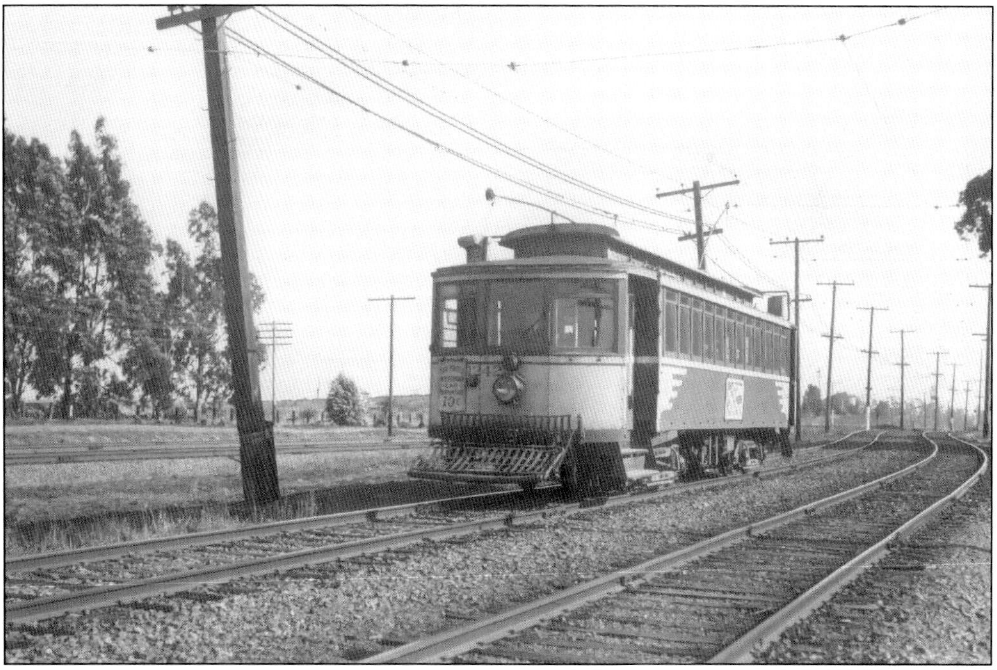

Muni-era northbound Daly City car No. 1242 passes Aqua (Spanish for "water"), the site of the City of San Francisco Water Department maintenance base for the city's Crystal Springs water facilities. The curve in the tracks is necessitated because the 40-line right-of-way north of Aqua is farther west from the Southern Pacific's San Francisco–San Jose mainline. (Courtesy Walter Vielbaum.)

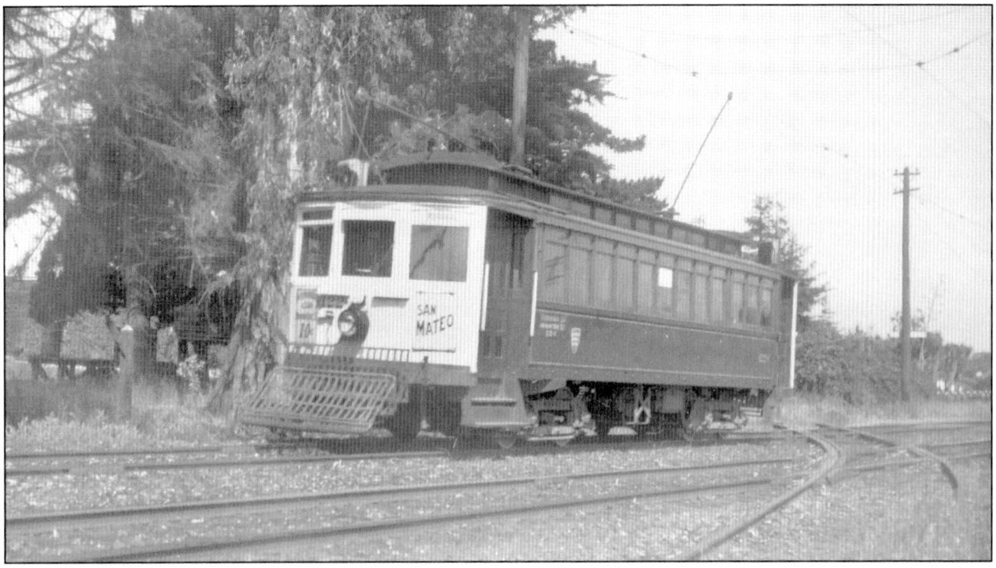

Photographed on the same day as No. 1237 at Millbrae Park on May 20, 1938, car No. 1226 has received a new paint job that has eliminated the red window trim but still features the MSR patented white front and dash lights. The dash sign that reads "Interurban Car Minimum Fare 10¢" is now white, whereas car No. 1237 bore a red dash sign. Crossing the 40-line tracks is the Southern Pacific Aqua freight spur into the City of San Francisco Water Department yard. (Courtesy Will Whittaker.)

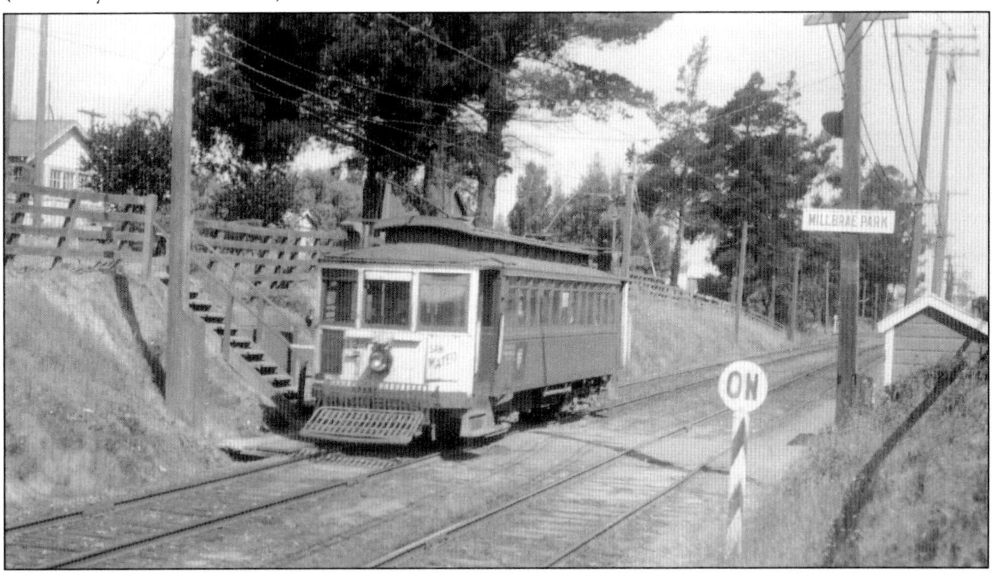

Car No. 1237, shown here at Millbrae Park, May 20, 1938, personifies the transition between Market Street railway eras. The red window trim is still on the patented white front, which will be removed at the next painting; however, the company shield on the car's side has been cut down, eliminating the reference to Byllesby as the company owner. Under the Public Utilities Holding Act of 1935, Byllesby was forced to sell the MSR. Samuel Kahn, the company's president, was now the principal owner. The "ON" sign to the right of the car in the photograph was to instruct the motorman to turn on the field taps, which were to be used only on specific locations. (Courtesy Will Whitaker.)

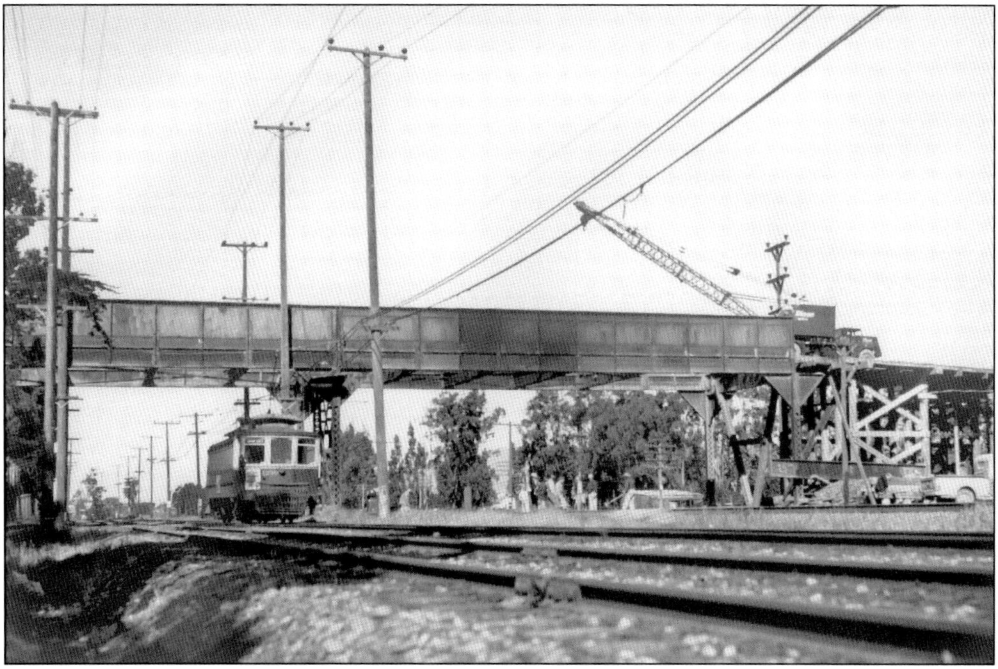

Muni blue and yellow Car No. 1230 is northbound to a Daly City hilltop terminal, where San Francisco passengers will have to transfer to a slow, 14-line Mission streetcar or a No. 26 bus on San Jose Avenue. Car No. 1230 is passing under the construction overpass at Millbrae Highlands that soon will be carrying dump trucks hauling dirt to expand the runways of the San Francisco International Airport, then known as Mills Field. (Courtesy Robert Townley.)

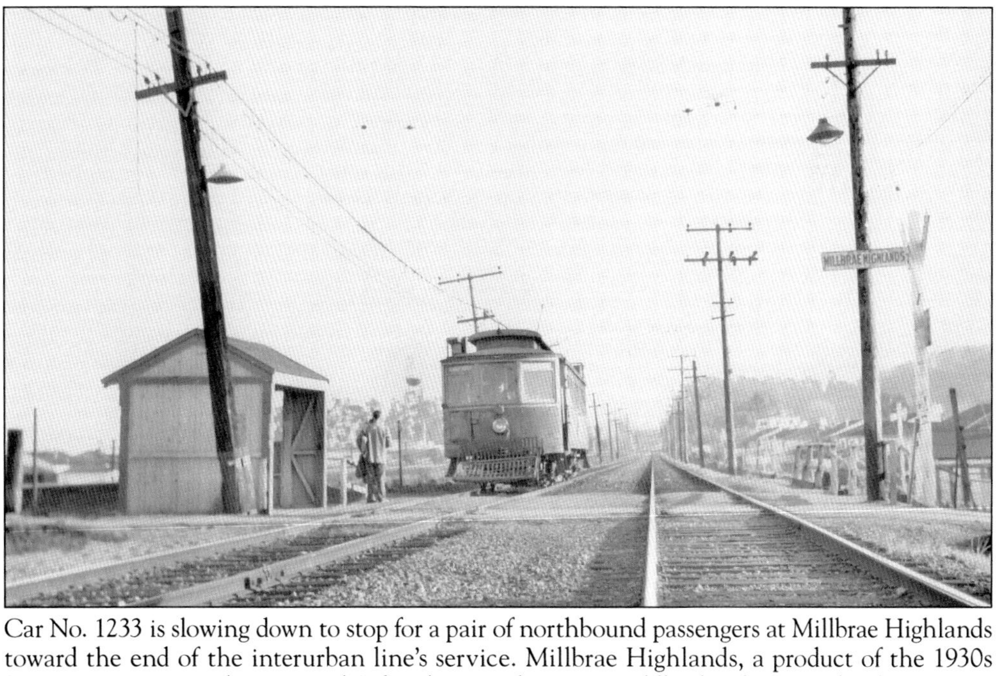

Car No. 1233 is slowing down to stop for a pair of northbound passengers at Millbrae Highlands toward the end of the interurban line's service. Millbrae Highlands, a product of the 1930s Depression era, was the peninsula's first large-scale upper middle class housing development. It reached westward to Skyline Boulevard.

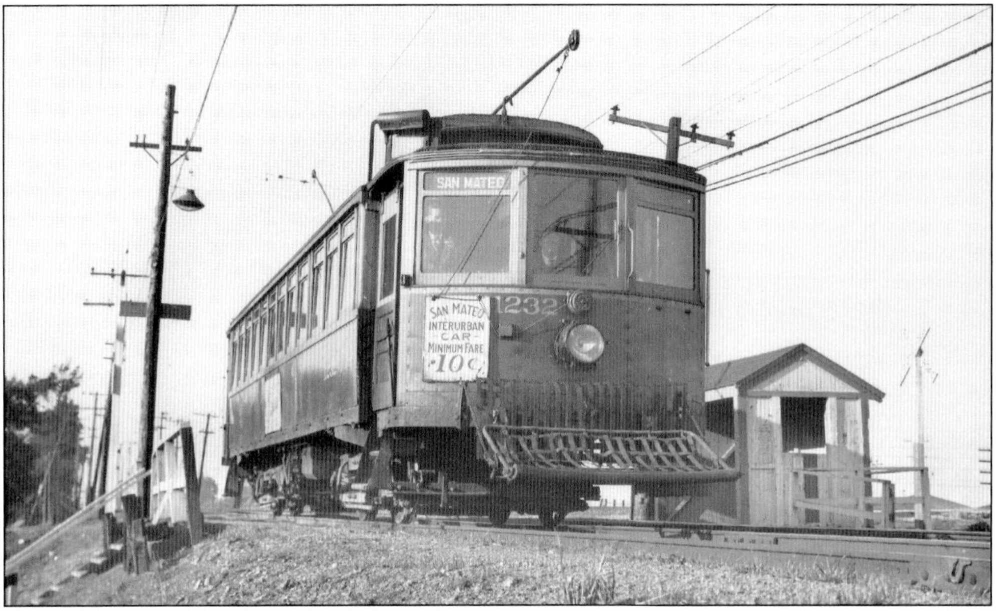

The handsome, classic lines of this 1903 Laclede No. 1232 are unmistakable even in Muni's blue and yellow colors and despite the fact that it reflects its 1923 Market Street Railway rebuilding, when all of the 1225-class cars were lengthened from 45 feet 9 inches to 48 feet one inch, their end platforms were enclosed to allow "Pay As You Enter" fare collection, and the end smoking sections were fitted with windows. In this post-war view, car No. 1232 has just left Millbrae Highlands. (Courtesy of Robert Townley.)

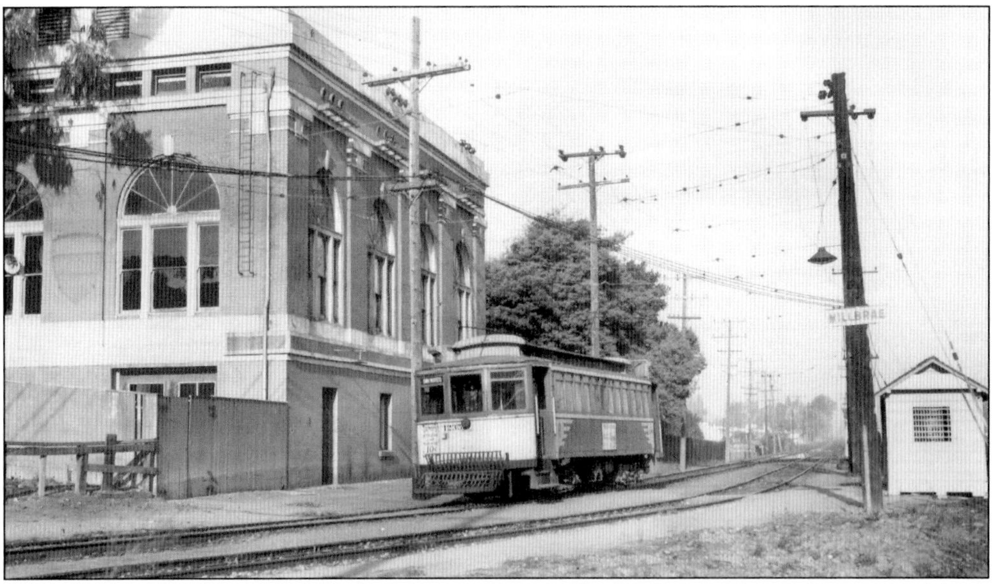

The San Mateo bound Muni No. 1225 passes the Millbrae substation at Millbrae Road (now Millbrae Avenue). The substation that powered the 40 line from Holy Cross south was built in 1903 by United Railroads. The substantially fireproof brick substation measured 40 feet by 75 feet and was painted green with white window trim by the Market Street Railway in the 1920s as part of the company's system-wide upgrading under the leadership of the railway's president, Samuel Kahn. (Courtesy Walter Vielbaum.)

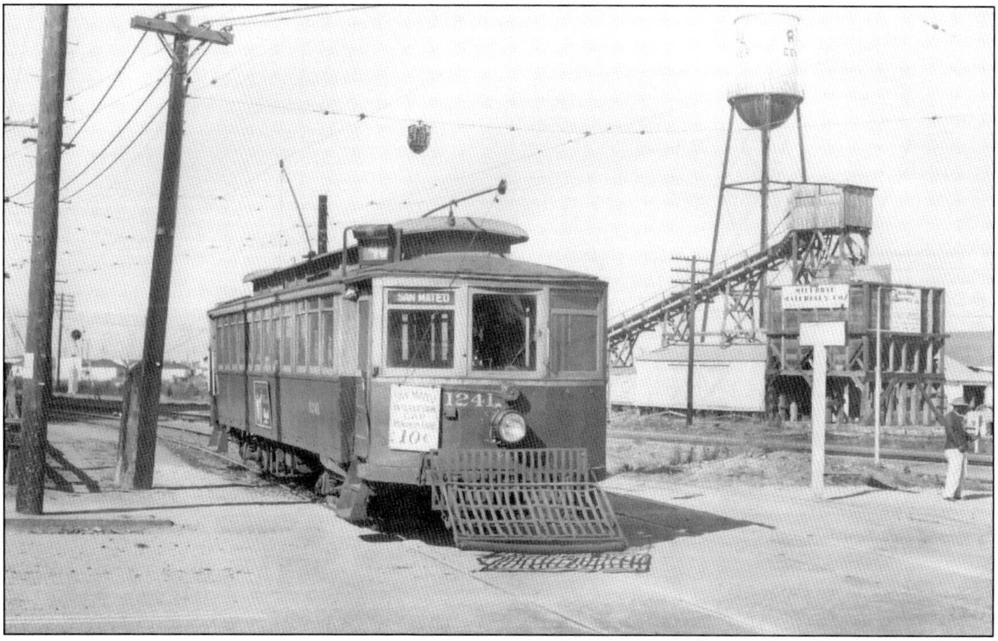

The Millbrae Materials Company, seen here in the background, is part of the peninsula's long vanished industrial heritage. Today the site is occupied by the Bay Area Rapid Transit (BART) and Caltrain (heir to the Southern Pacific's commute service) station. (Courtesy Walter Vielbaum.)

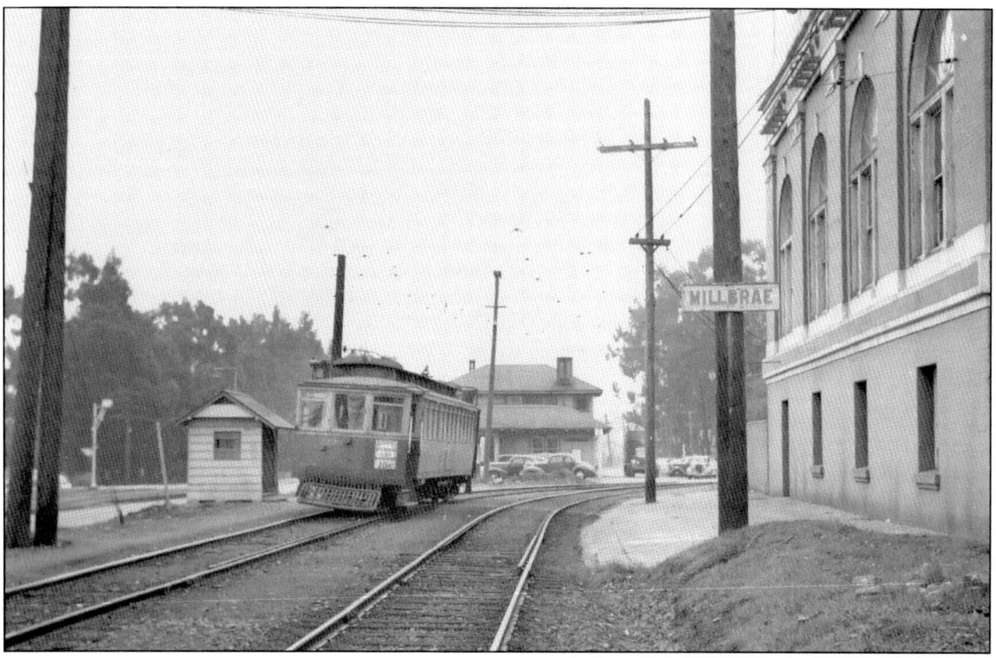

Fifteen minutes into its 75-minute San Mateo–San Francisco journey, car No. 1230 has arrived at its Millbrae stop, adjacent to the line's substation. In approximately another hour, No. 1230 will arrive at its San Francisco terminal of Fifth and Market Streets. During the United Railroads period, the substation door led to a passenger waiting room located in the substation's basement, the floor of which was level with the track. (Courtesy Robert Townley.)

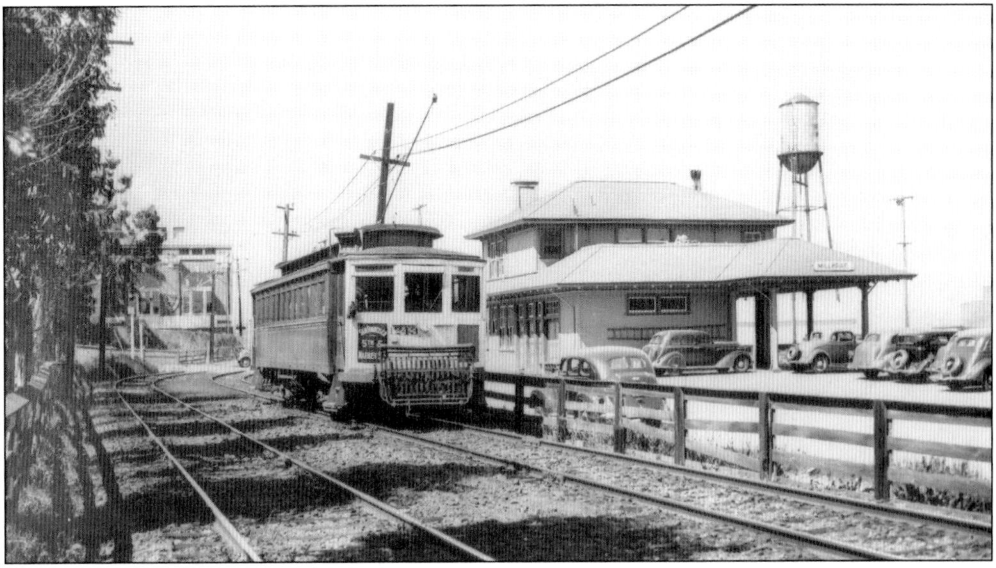

Market Street Railway northbound car No. 1243 passes Millbrae's Southern Pacific depot; this 1907 structure replaced two prior stations that burned down. Perhaps the most famous passenger ever to disembark at the station was Ulysses S. Grant, who served as president of the United States from 1869 to 1877. On September 30, 1879, the Civil War hero arrived at the Millbrae station in time for dinner at the estate of Darius Ogden Mills. The classic 1930s autos of commuters who elected to ride the train instead of the 40 line to San Francisco, as well as the solid white front on No. 1243, plus the Byllesby shield still on the Millbrae substation, date the photograph to c. 1938. (Courtesy Tom Gray.)

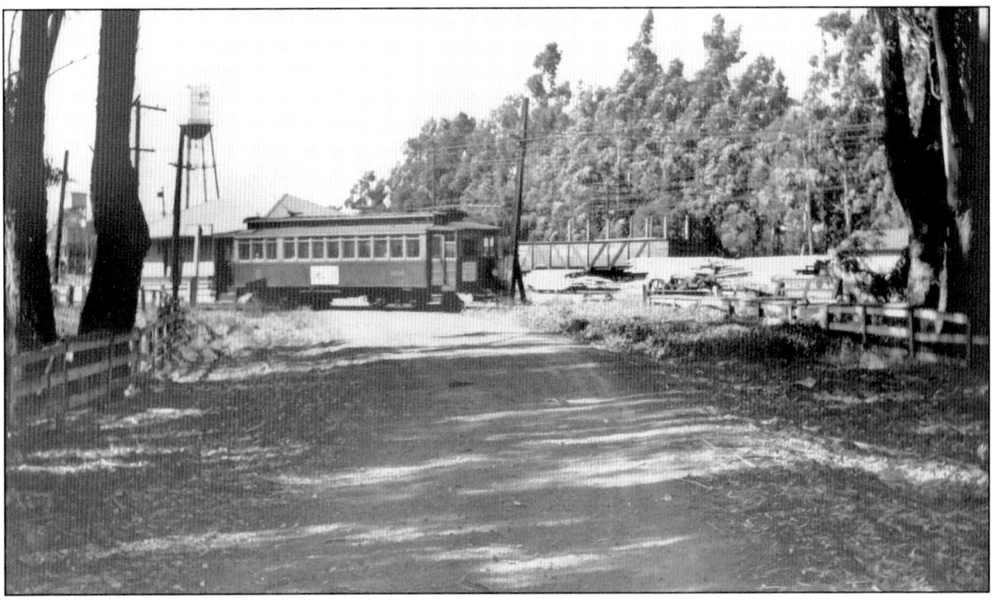

During this hot July day in 1947, the photographer chose to stand in the shade on the old road to the Mills mansion west of El Camino Real. The freight house is behind the car. Ridership from Millbrae was considerably lower when school was not in session. Millbrae's high school students rode the streetcar to attend Burlingame High School until the 40 line stopped. (Courtesy Jim Carpenter.)

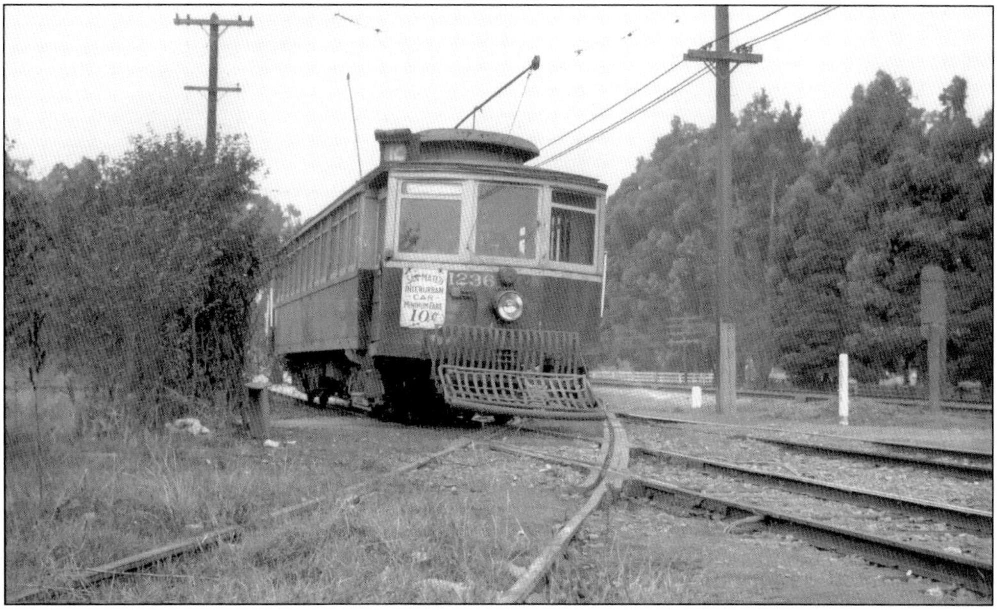

Southbound car No. 1236 crosses the Southern Pacific spur into the Millbrae Dairy. The dash sign is the correct 40-line southbound sign; however, the route box reads "12" for San Francisco's Mission Street, Ingleside, and Sloat Boulevard streetcar line. The 12 line often required extra cars on weekends since it went directly to Fleishhacker Zoo. Perhaps car No. 1230 had seen such service recently as, in addition to the 40 line, the 1225-class was used on the 12 and 14 Mission lines. (Courtesy Robert Townley.)

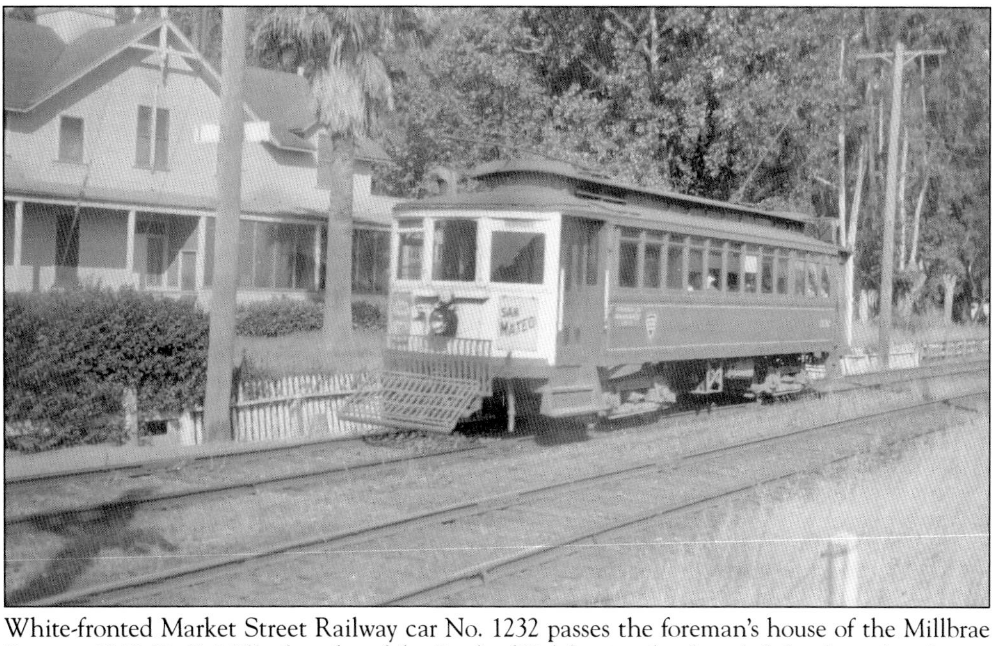

White-fronted Market Street Railway car No. 1232 passes the foreman's house of the Millbrae Diary, c. 1943. D. O. Mills, founder of the Bank of California, also founded the dairy that during the United Railroads's 40-line era was the primary source of employment in Millbrae. Mills, a Scotsman, used the word "brae" (Scottish for hills), together with "mill" (his name) for the community Millbrae. (Courtesy Will Whittaker.)

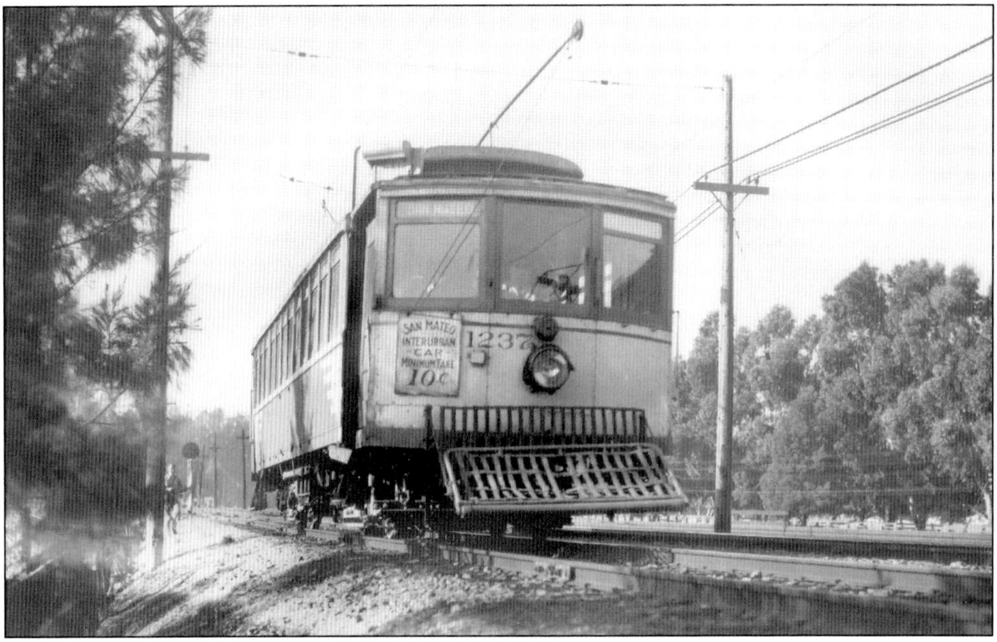

By the looks of the somewhat shabby Muni green and cream wings paint scheme, the bent eclipse fender (referred to by many San Franciscans as a cowcatcher), and the removed side advertising holder, the end is very near for car No. 1237 and the 40 line. No. 1237 is shown here south of the Millbrae Dairy. That's coauthor Robert Townley behind the car by the field tap sign. (Courtesy Walter Vielbaum.)

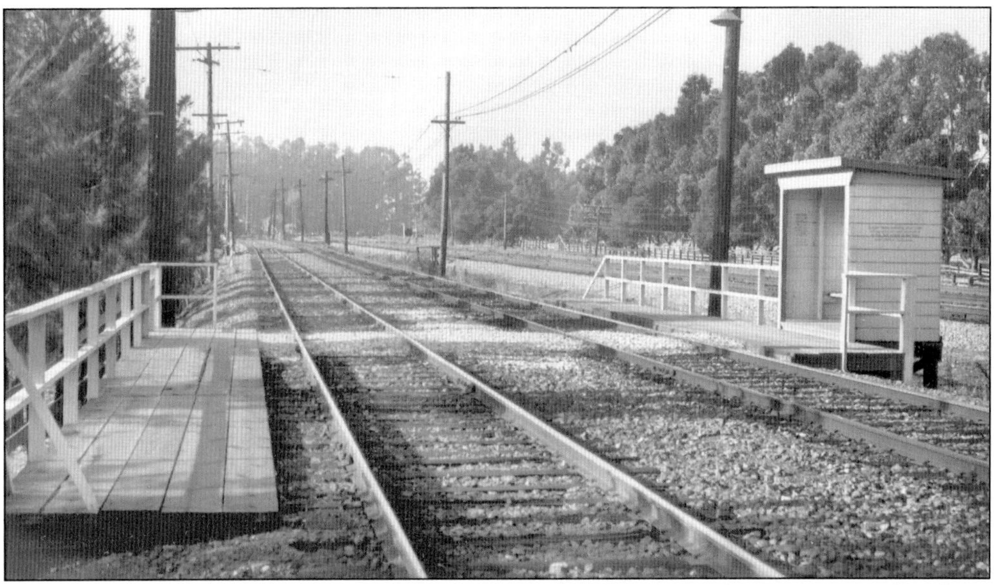

During the latter years of Market Street Railway ownership, the 40 line's private right-of-way abounded in weeds. Not so under the ownership of San Francisco's Municipal Railway, as this north looking photograph at the Dufferin stop illustrates. To the right are the Southern Pacific tracks, and everywhere it seems there are stands of elm and eucalyptus trees, which probably were originally planted to mark property boundaries. Dufferin was one of the last stations to be added to the line. (Courtesy Walter Vielbaum.)

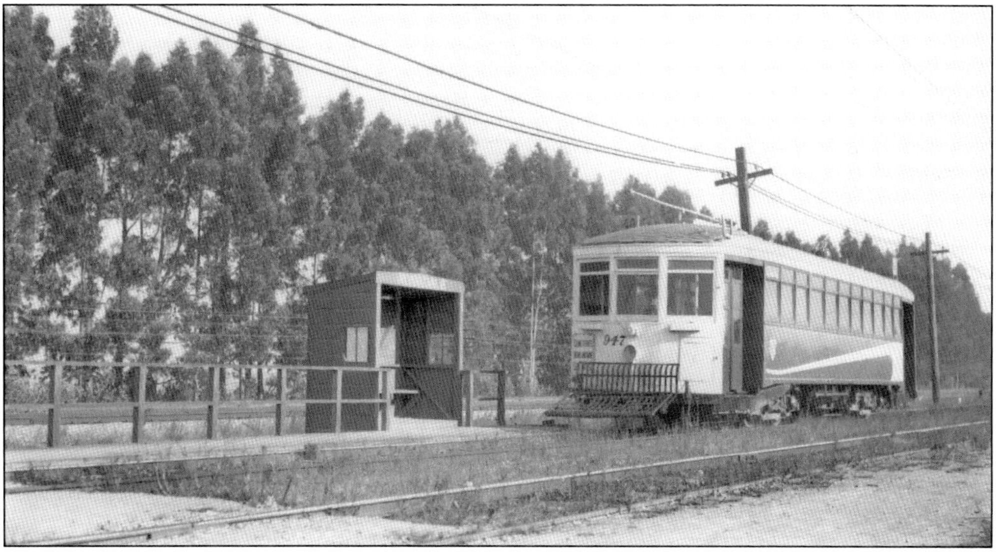

California Comfort Car No. 947, a 1931 product of the Market Street Railway's Elkton shops, is northbound at Rosedale. City cars such as No. 947 assigned to the 40 line had four folding doors, two on each platform, which enabled the car to operate in the one-man service that was legal in San Mateo County. Here No. 947 sports the post-1938 paint scheme that featured a white streamlined zip stripe on the car's sides and modernized numbering, topped with a yellow roof. None of the 1225-class cars were painted in this scheme.

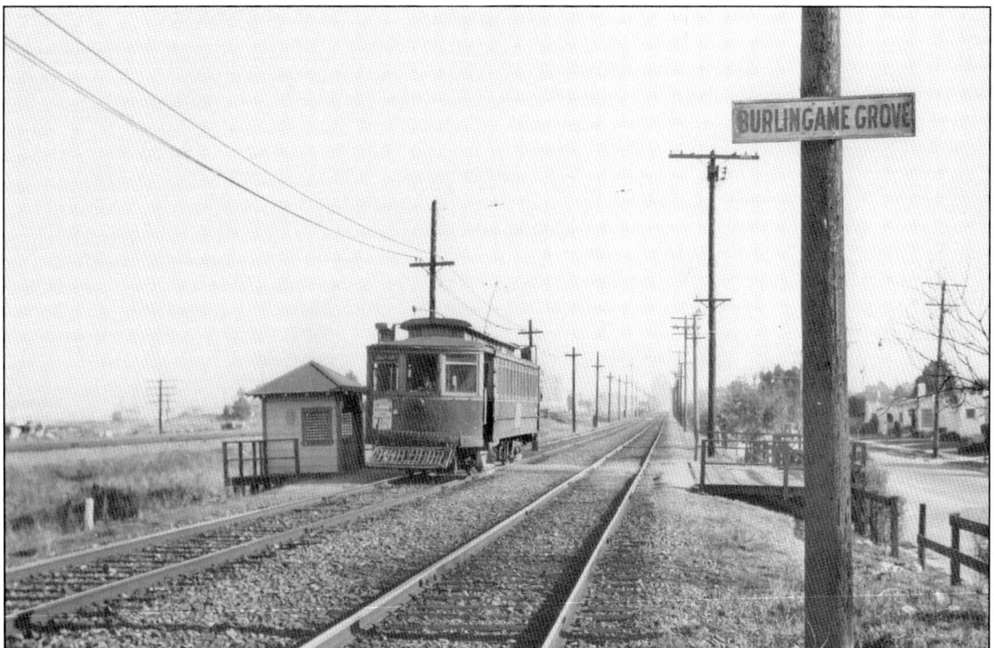

Muni car No. 1234, in that company's blue and yellow paint scheme, is northbound at the Burlingame Grove stop. Both No. 1234 and the 40 line itself would soon be history as their January 1949 date with destiny was approaching. The 1225-class was well liked by the public and was largely responsible for the line's excellent ridership even during the 1930s Depression years and in the face of significant bus and train competition. (Courtesy Robert Townley.)

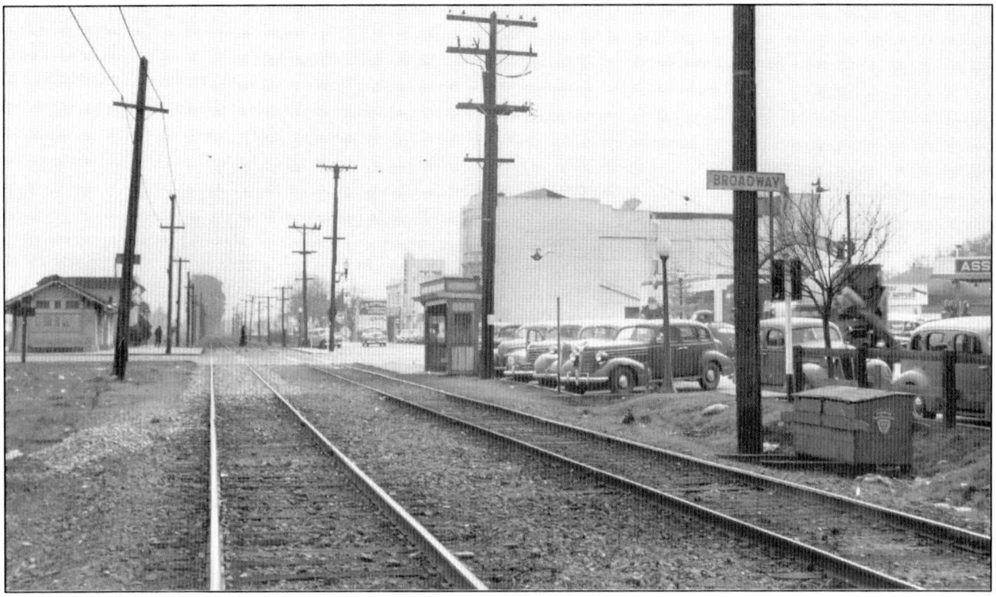

Looking south from Broadway, Burlingame, the 40 line right-of-way heads toward Burlingame's downtown. On the left is Broadway's Southern Pacific depot and on the right across California Drive is the Broadway Theatre, a Fox theatre. Originally, this area of North Burlingame was called Buri Buri, but as it developed, residents felt increasingly uncomfortable with the name because of its similarity with "beriberi," a disease and nerve disorder. Thus, in November 1915, the name was changed to Broadway. (Courtesy Robert Townley.)

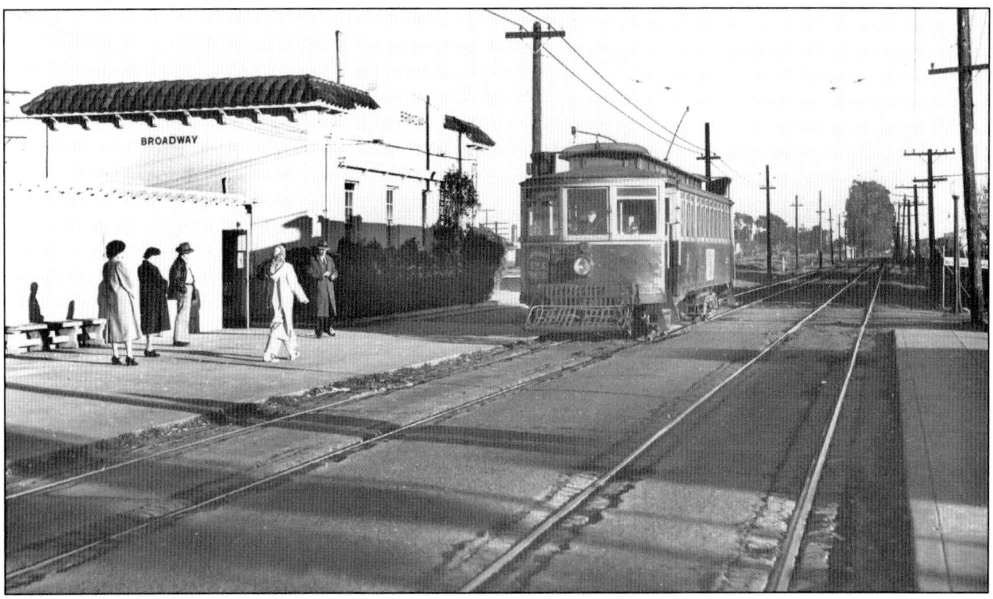

A group of five passengers will soon board No. 1232 for their northbound trip. At Broadway, Burlingame, San Francisco bound passengers had their choice of three different carriers. Besides the 40-line, riders could use a Southern Pacific commuter train (the Broadway Southern Pacific depot is on the left side of the photograph) or take a Pacific Greyhound "B" route bus. One advantage the 40 line had over its competition was that riders could get a free transfer that would take them anywhere in San Francisco on the Municipal Railway. (Courtesy Richard Brown.)

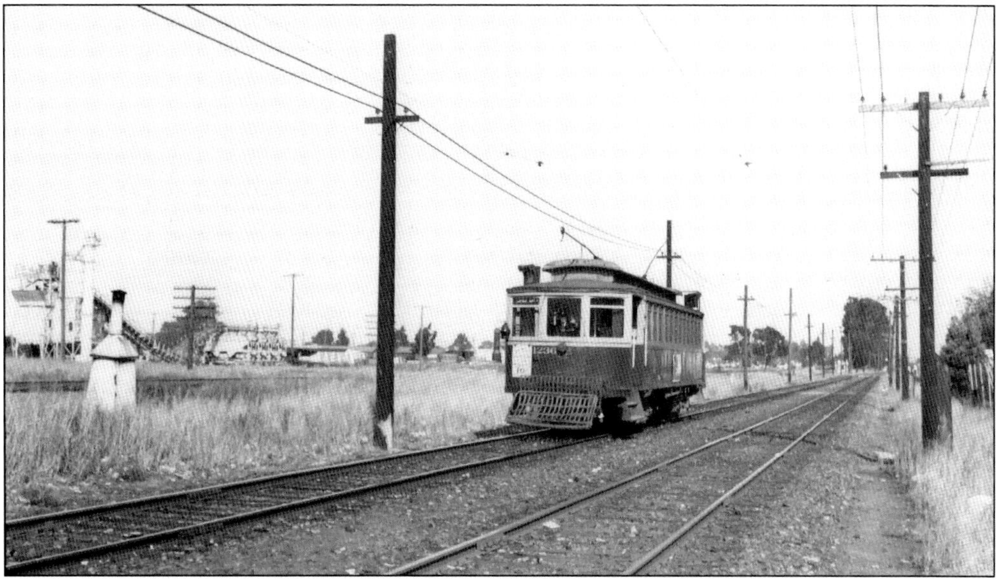

The motorman waving to coauthor Bob Townley is undoubtedly happy that he will only have to pilot car No. 1236 to Daly City Hilltop. After August 16, 1947, except for rush hour trips, the northern 40-line terminal was Daly City, instead of Fifth and Market Streets. At Daly City, No. 1236's ends would be changed and soon it would again be racing on the 40 line's private right-of-way with the "battle of Mission Street" avoided. Here, No. 1236 is just south of the Broadway stop. The sand and gravel bunkers on the left are on the site of a large apartment complex today. (Courtesy Robert Townley.)

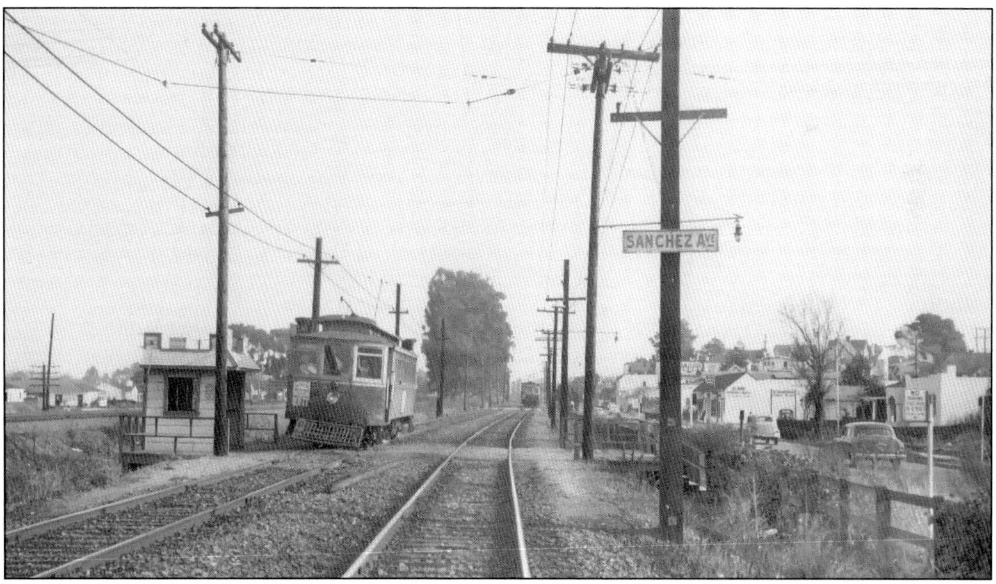

Northbound No. 1236 has stopped to board passengers at Sanchez Avenue, Burlingame. Here the immaculate 40-line right-of-way is surrounded by competition. On the left is the double-track mainline of the Southern Pacific Railroad, home of that railroad's San Francisco commuter fleet. On the right is California Drive, a roadway used by frequent Pacific Greyhound Lines buses. Greyhound's largest suburban bus operation was out of San Francisco. (Courtesy Walter Vielbaum.)

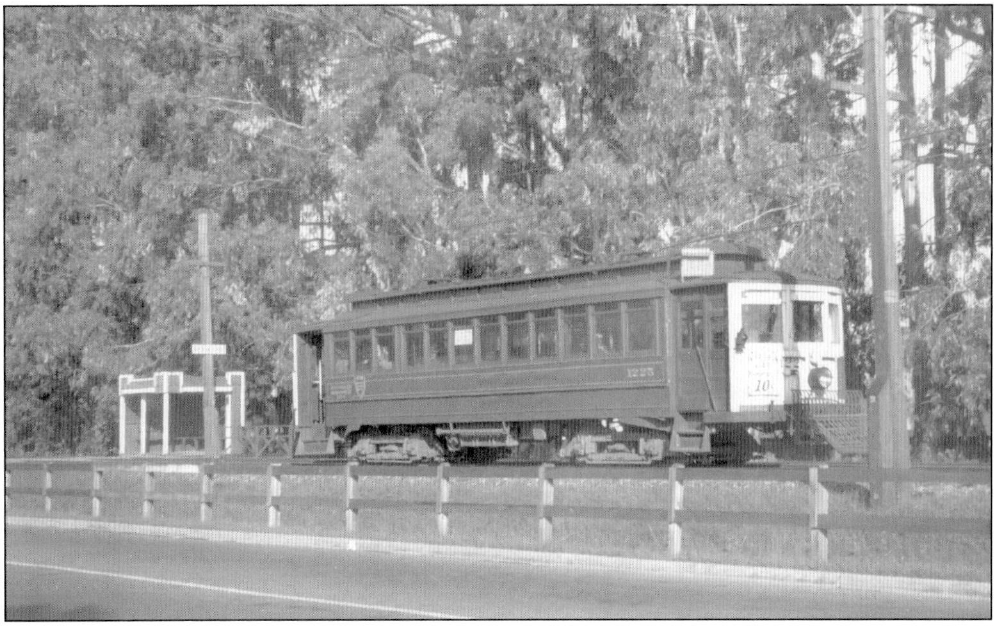

Southbound car No. 1225 at Burlingame Terrace, December 23, 1937, displays the standard post-1927 Market Street Railway 1225-class paint scheme—a medium green body with yellow numbers and the patented white front with dash lights and black numbers. The route boxes are yellow and the roof is black. Note that the shelter has been painted in the company's green and white colors. (Courtesy Will Whitaker.)

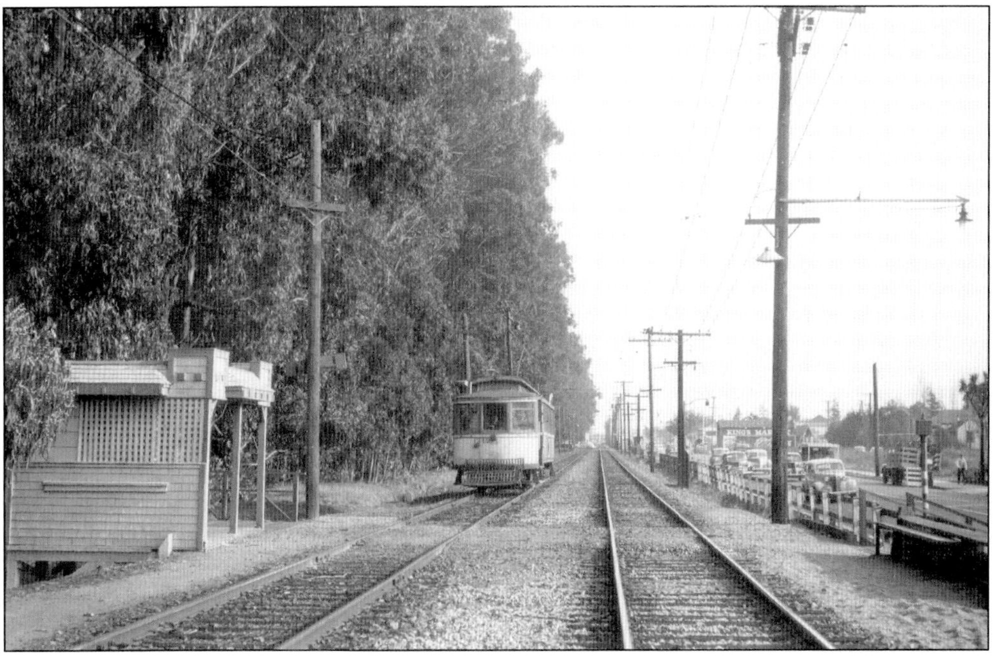

Muni era green and cream car No. 1242 will soon guide through Burlingame Terrace. The shelter has been painted tan and brown, the colors that Muni used for them. The long row of eucalyptus trees that separated the 40-line tracks from those of the Southern Pacific was characteristic of this part of the San Mateo line. (Courtesy Walter Vielbaum.)

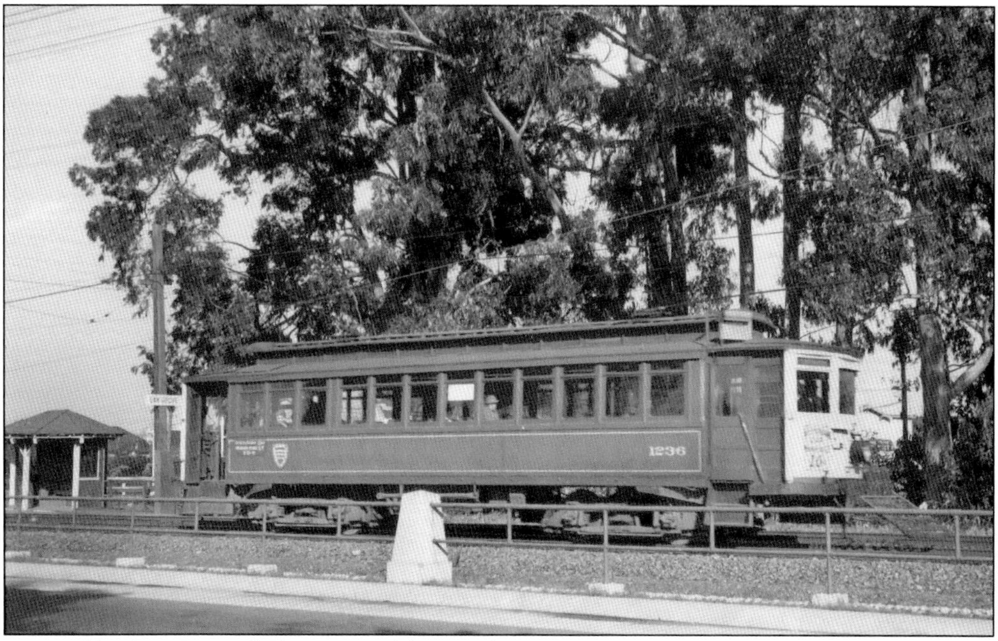

Powered by four General Electric model 57, 50-horsepower motors, car No. 1236 accelerates past the Oak Grove, Burlingame, stop two days before Christmas 1937. No. 1236's few passengers are enjoying the comfort of deeply cushioned leather seats. Despite this trip's light load, the 40 line was consistently a top moneymaker for the Market Street Railway. (Courtesy Will Whitaker.)

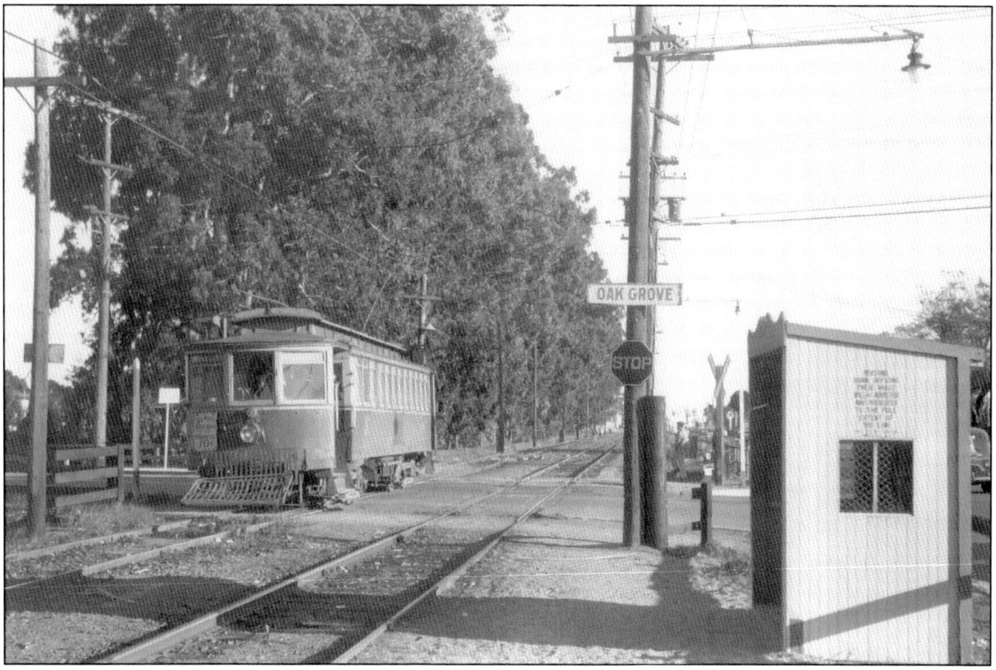

The end is near for the San Mateo Interurban as car No. 1233 crosses Oak Grove Avenue, Burlingame, on a northward journey. Graffiti artists of the period are warned by the notice on the southbound shelter that "anyone found defacing these walls will be arrested and prosecuted to the fullest extent of the law." (Courtesy Walter Vielbaum.)

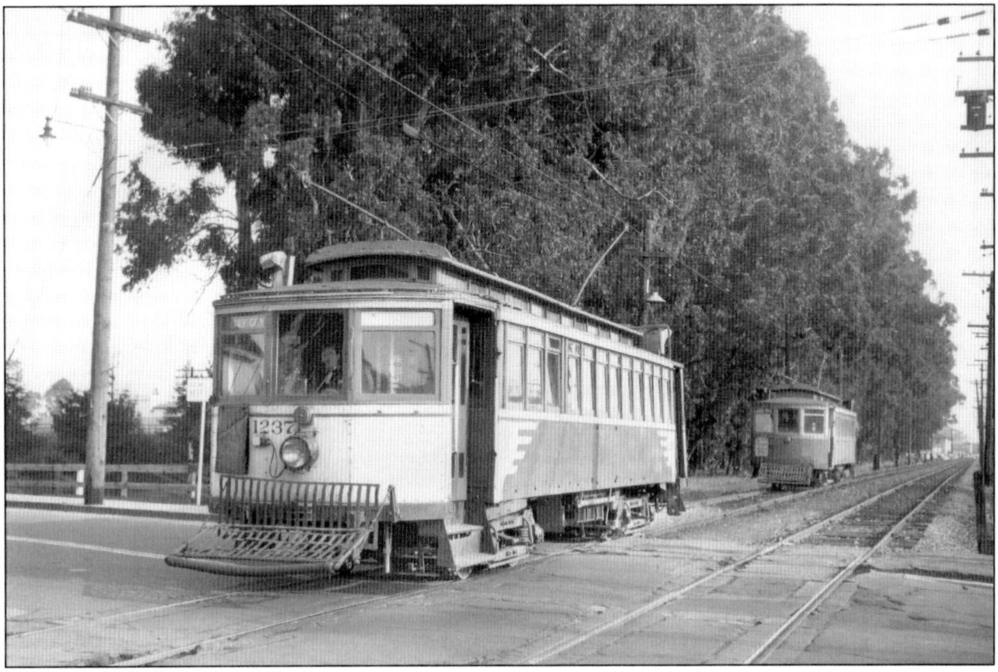

The two Municipal Railway color combinations the railway used for the 1225-class are illustrated at Oak Grove. The green and cream colors on car No. 1237 were adopted by the Muni in February 1946. The blue and yellow colors were Muni's reaction to the Market Street Railway's white zip-stripe side panel paint scheme of the late 1930s. The two cars being close together implies that at least one car is a school tripper. (Courtesy Walter Vielbaum.)

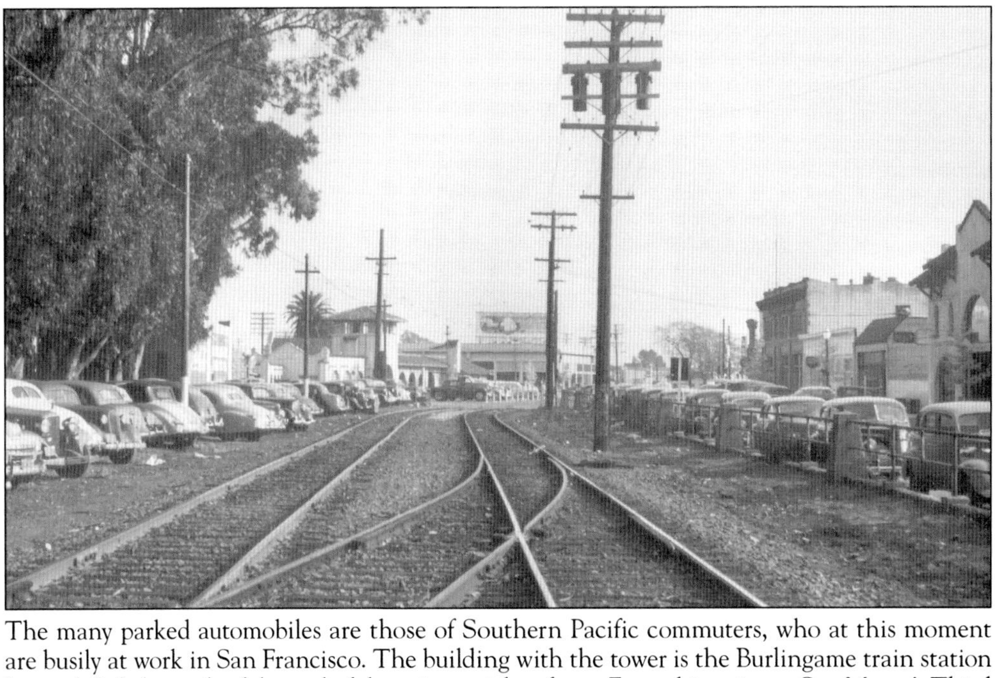

The many parked automobiles are those of Southern Pacific commuters, who at this moment are busily at work in San Francisco. The building with the tower is the Burlingame train station located slightly south of the end of the private right-of-way. From this point to San Mateo's Third Avenue terminal, it is exclusively street running. (Courtesy Walter Vielbaum.)

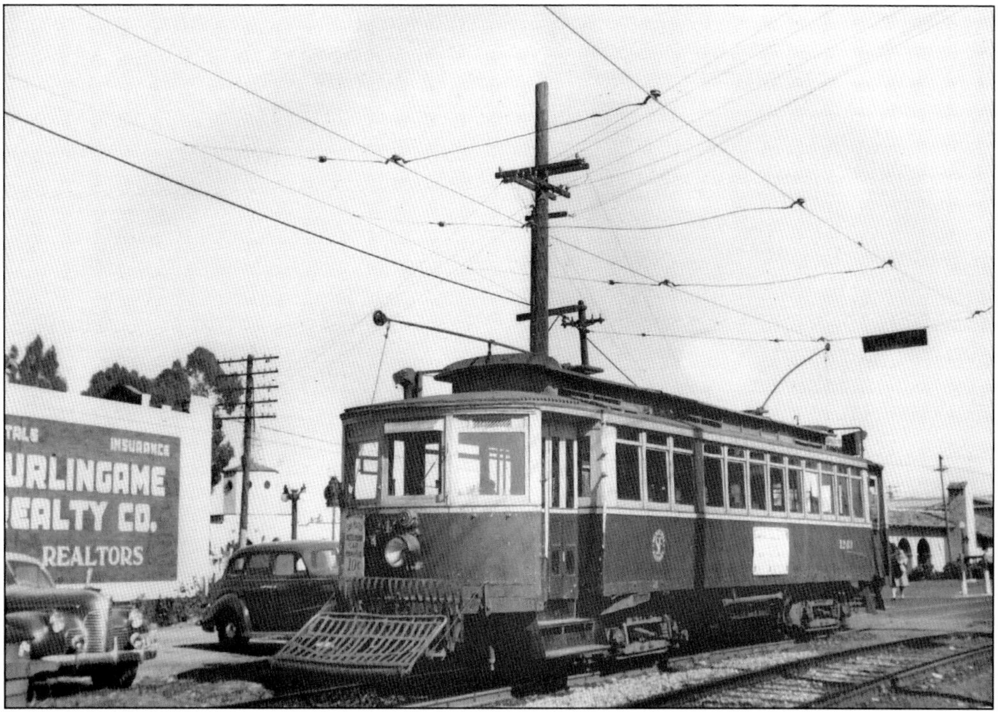

Daly City-bound car No. 1243 has just entered the private right-of-way at Burlingame, September 19, 1947. Uniquely No. 1243 still has its Market Street Railway center window visor. Typically Muni removed the window visors along with the dash light covers when they converted 1225-class cars to one of their paint schemes. (Courtesy Al Thoman.)

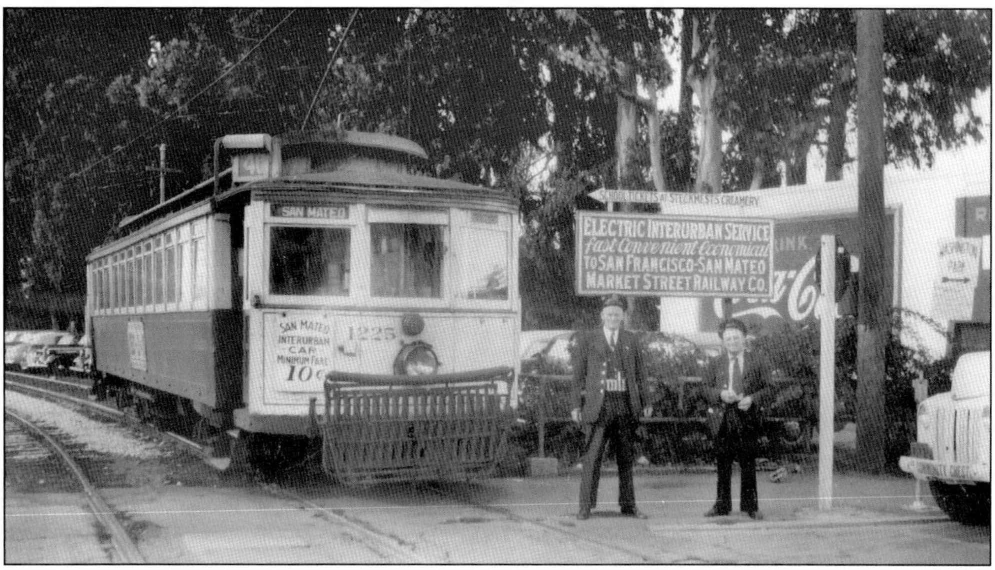

The crew of No. 1225, the first of the San Mateo cars to be painted Muni's new green and cream colors (the "wings" version of the cream and green would soon follow), is posed underneath a sign at Burlingame promoting the interurban as "Fast, Convenient, Economical." This is the point where northbound cars began the private right-of-way. School tickets can be purchased at Steckmest's creamery. (Courtesy Emiliano Echeverria.)

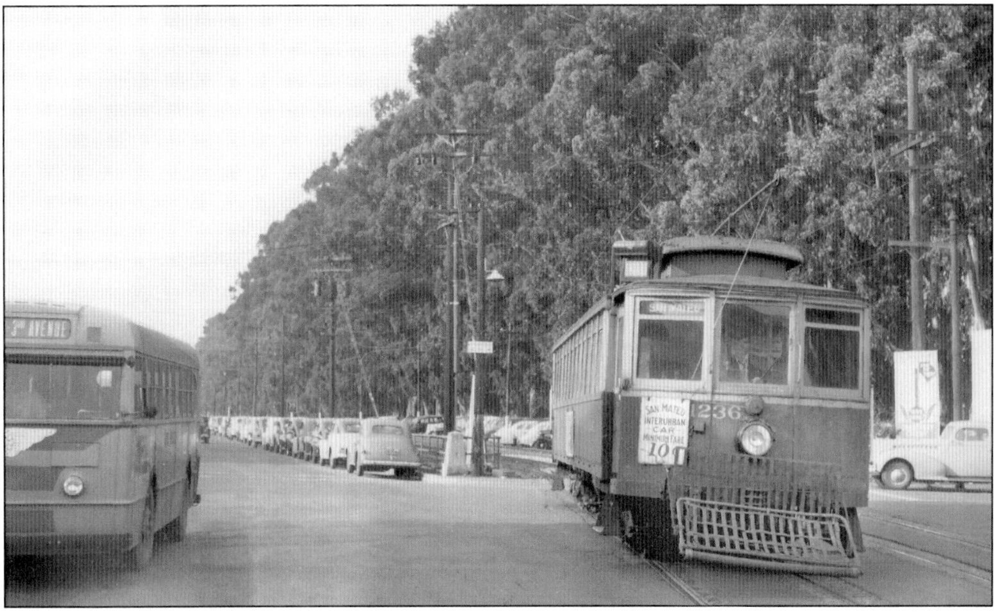

The race is on between car No. 1236, which has just started its street running at Burlingame Avenue, and the classic art deco painted San Mateo–Burlingame Transit Ford bus operating on route "A." Both the interurban and the bus are heading to a San Mateo terminal at that city's Southern Pacific depot. Route A's northern segment (from the Broadway Southern Pacific depot) essentially followed the route of the Burlingame Railway's battery car. Who won the race is lost to history. (Courtesy Walter Vielbaum.)

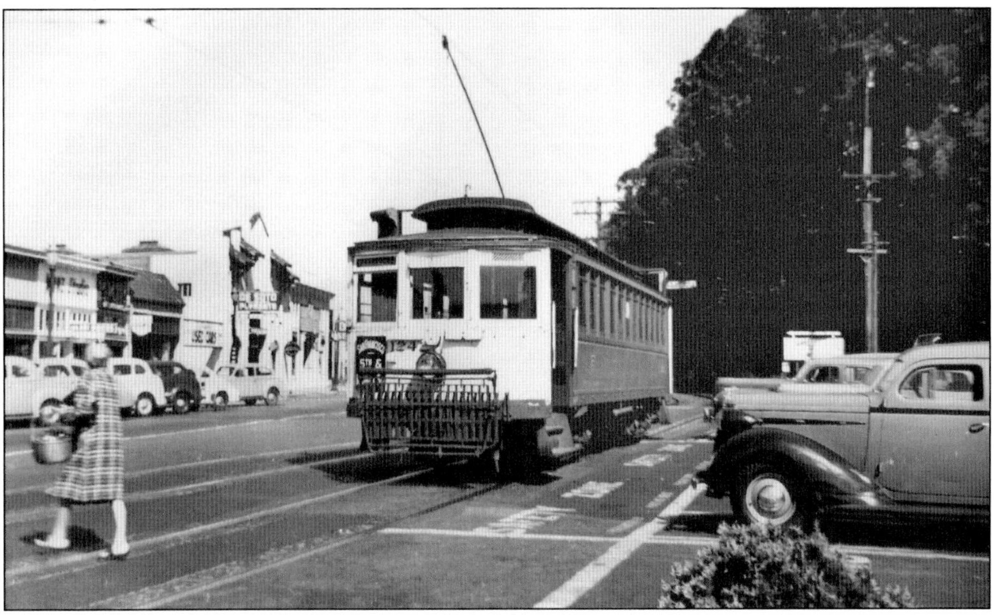

Proudly showing off its post-Byllesby era patented white front, Market Street Railway car No. 1242 leaves Burlingame's street running. The white front patent was held by Samuel Kahn, the Market Street Railway's president and by the late 1930s, the company's principal owner. A resident of nearby Hillsborough, Kahn did not use the 40 line to get to his San Francisco office, but rode the Southern Pacific commuter trains. (Courtesy Walter Vielbaum.)

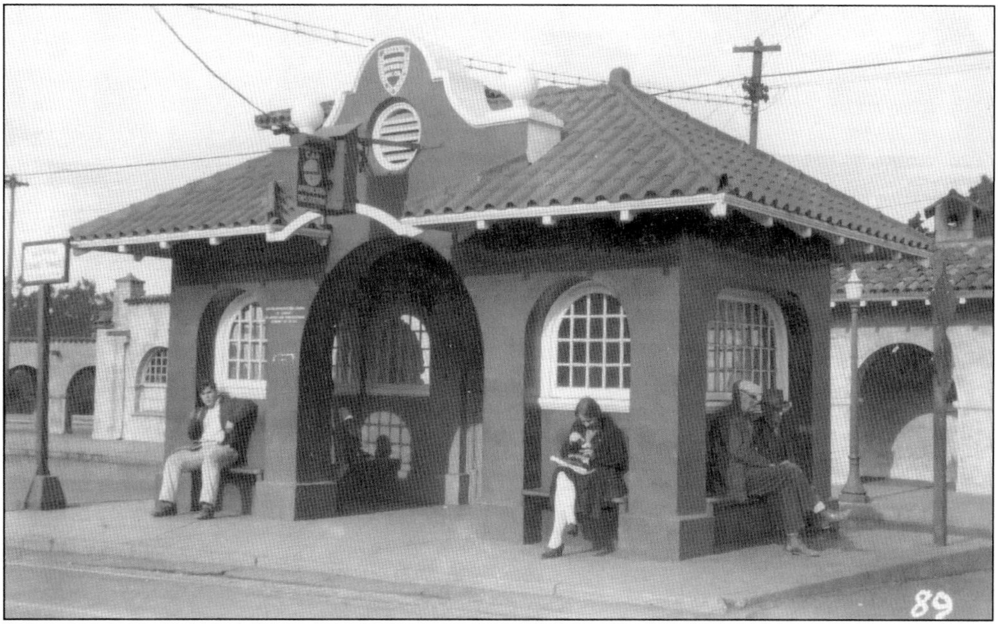

Resplendent in the green and white colors of the Market Street Railway and complete with a Byllesby shield, Burlingame's 40-line passenger shelter was the line's most impressive. The light above the entrance arch would light up went a car approached. The station was built by the Burlingame Women's Club in 1908. (Courtesy John Schmale.)

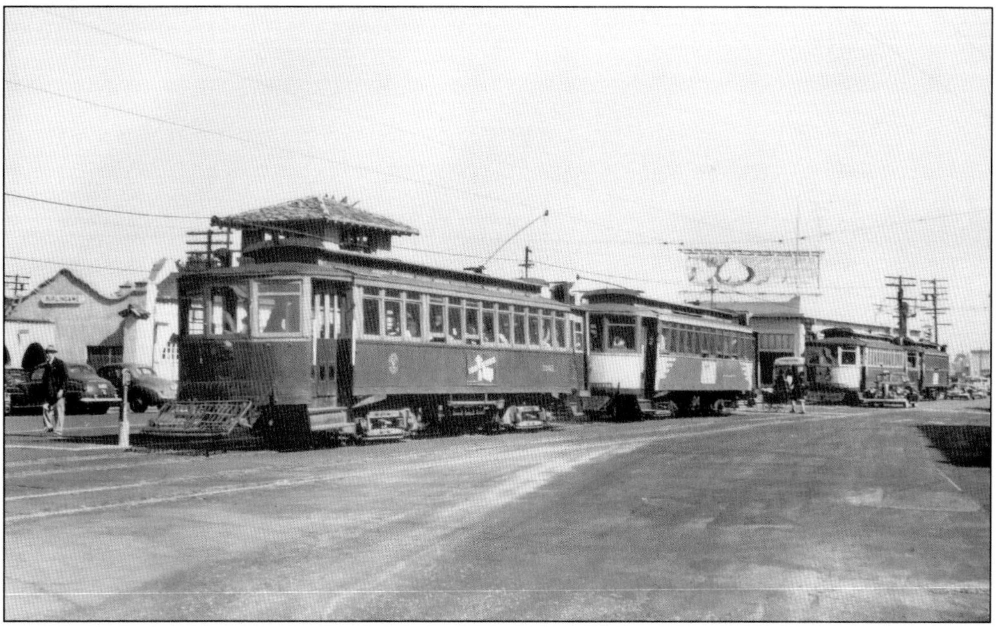

The San Mateo Union High School District boundaries started in San Bruno. However, the district's two high schools were located in the southern part of the district, at Burlingame and San Mateo. Students from Millbrae attended Burlingame and those from San Bruno went to San Mateo High School. All rode the 40 line. Four school trippers with three different Muni paint schemes are waiting on California Drive in front of the Burlingame train station for students from Burlingame High. (Courtesy Walter Vielbaum.)

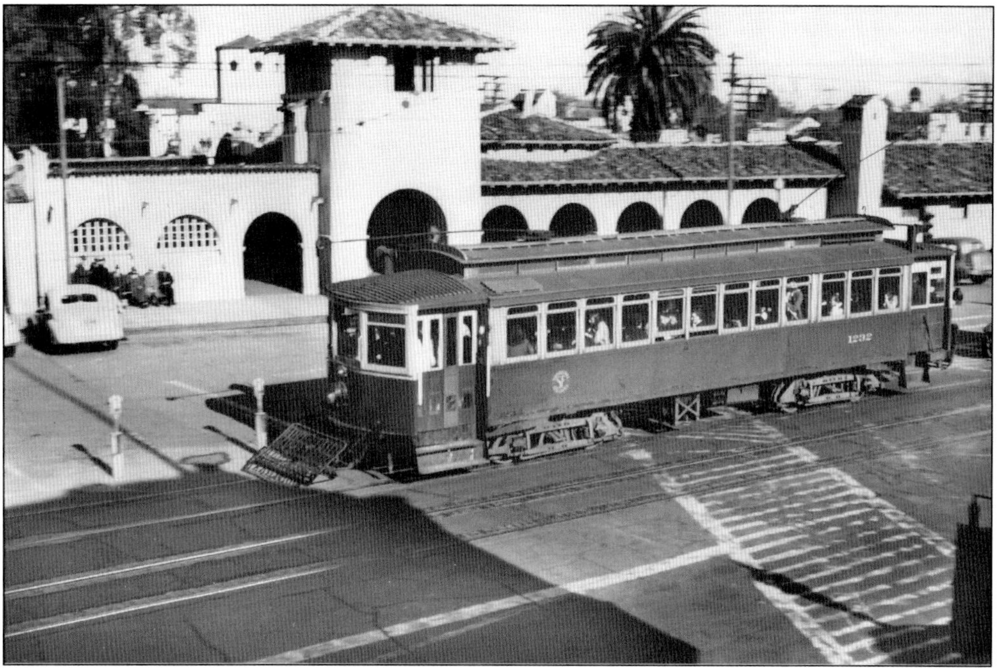

The Municipal Railway's accounting department would undoubtedly be pleased with the standing load aboard car No. 1232. The removal of the side advertising panel (to be placed on a new bus) shows abandonment is near. The Mission Revival–style Burlingame train station, which opened on October 10, 1894, is behind the No. 1232. Inspired by California's Spanish missions, the station's roof tiles came from Mission San Luis Obispo de Tolosa. (Courtesy Walter Vielbaum.)

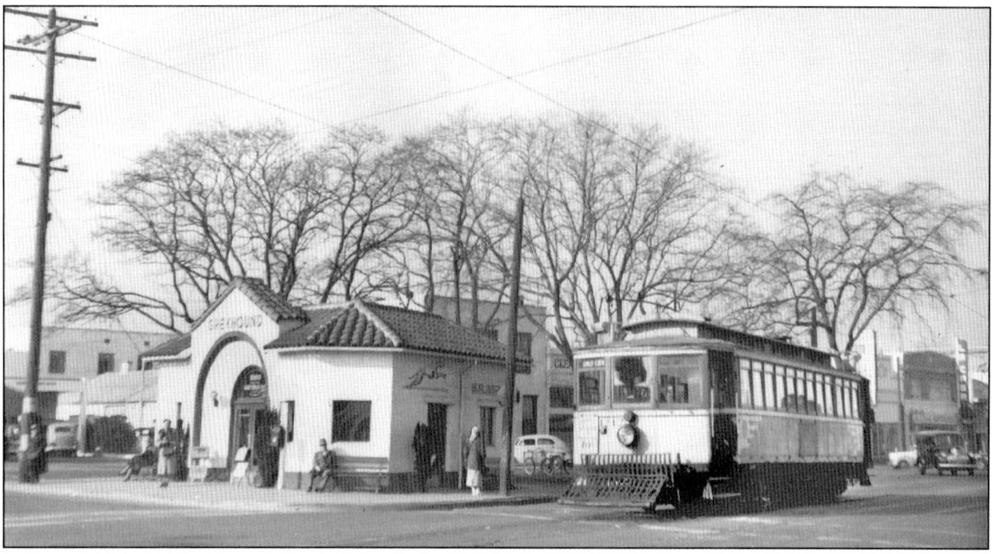

San Mateo-bound car No. 1242, signed in error for "Daly City," stops at Burlingame's Greyhound bus depot on the last day of the 40 line, January 15, 1949. In celebration of the end of the 40 line, Greyhound, which at the time operated an extensive peninsula suburban service, soon would increase its fares by 100%. Although Greyhound's service has long since been replaced by SamTrans, its Burlingame station has been restored and exists as shown today. (Courtesy Al Thoman.)

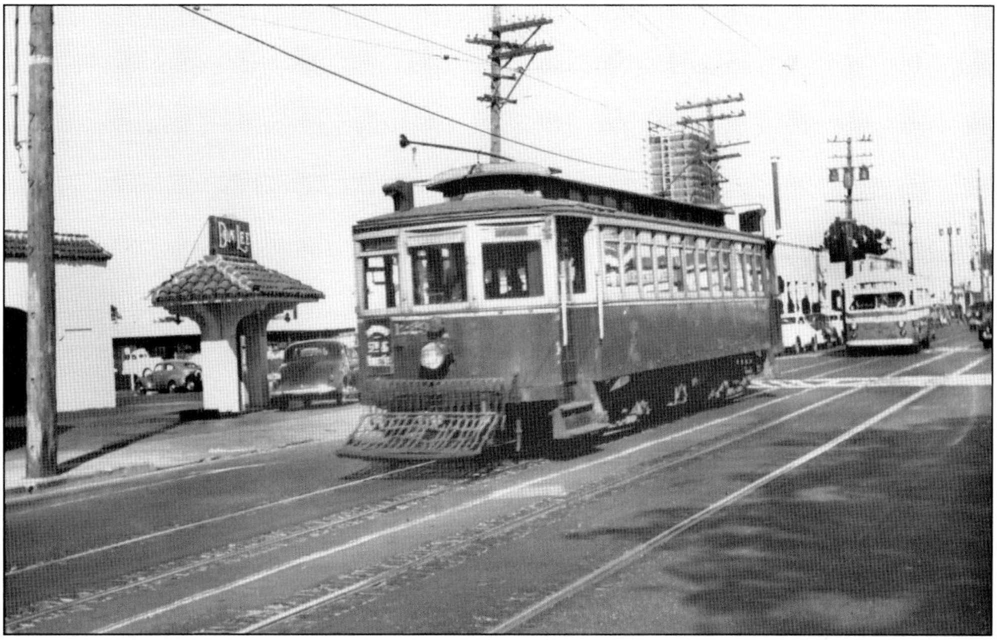

On August 13, 1947, three days before all 40-line cars—with the exception of rush hour trips—would terminate at Daly City, car No. 1229 heads for San Francisco's Fifth and Market Streets passing Burlingame's Don Lee Cadillac agency on California Drive. Immediately behind No. 1229 is a Pacific Greyhound Lines bus also bound for San Francisco on that company's "B" route. Greyhound "B" buses used the Bayshore Highway north of Broadway Burlingame. (Courtesy Jim Carpenter.)

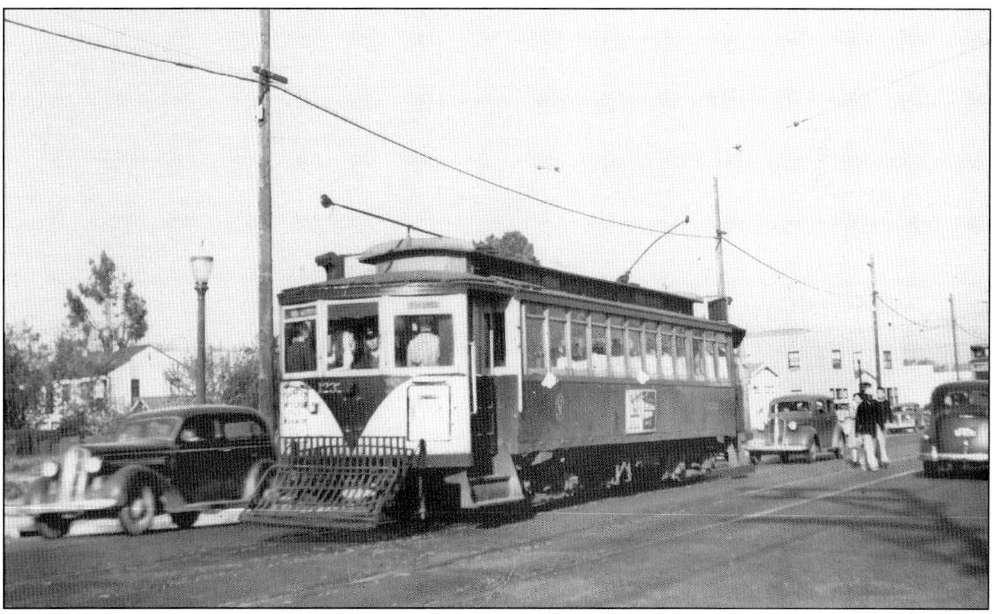

Jammed with high school students, car No. 1232, with experimental blue "Vs" on its otherwise yellow ends, rumbles along Burlingame's California Drive near the San Mateo city line, March 26, 1947. Muni would subsequently repaint No. 1232 in its standard yellow and blue scheme. Pre–World War II automobiles are much in evidence. (Courtesy Al Thoman.)

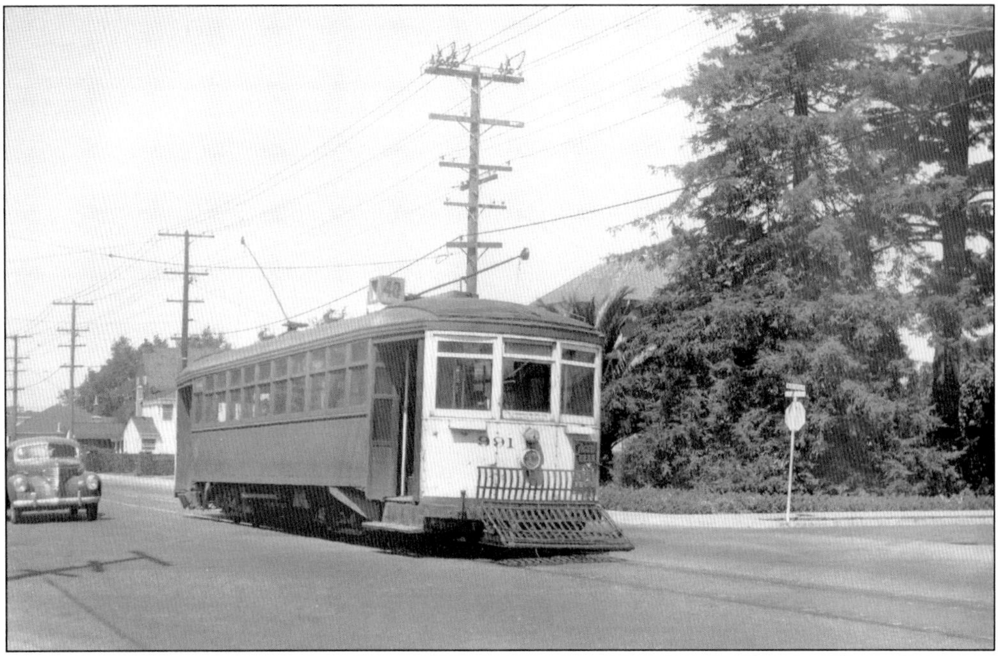

California Comfort Car No. 991, a 1933 product of the Market Street Railway's Elkton shops, has stopped at San Mateo Drive and Mount Diablo in San Mateo, September 12, 1940. Car No. 991 was one of 131 homebuilt cars that the Market Street Railway modified in 1934 and 1935 with air operated folding doors at all four corners for one-man operation. San Francisco's one-man era ended in 1939, and it would not be until 1943 that one-man cars would operate on the 40 line.

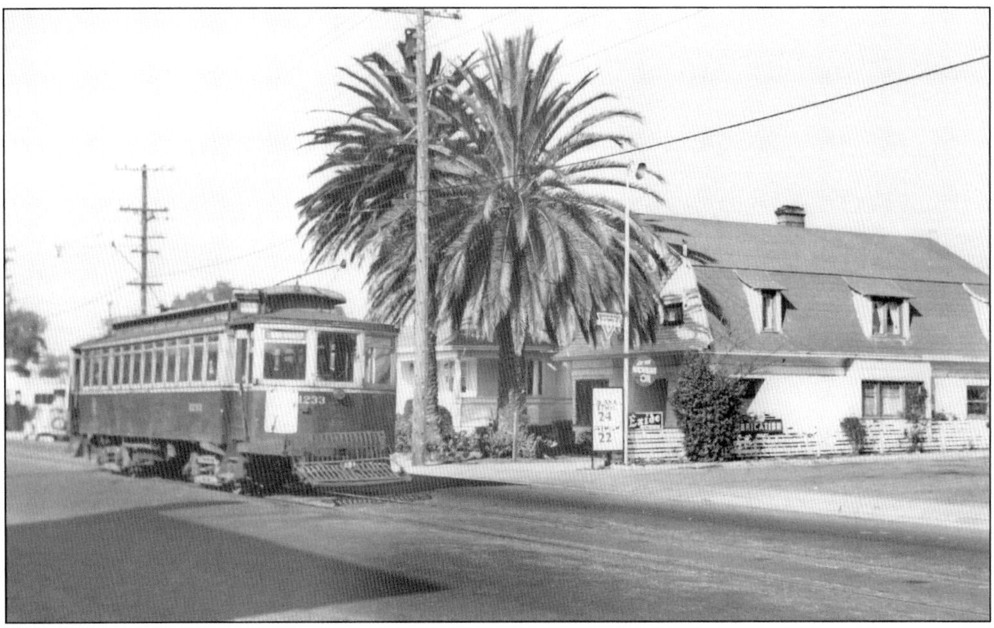

Once the 40 line entered San Mateo, California Drive became San Mateo Drive. A somewhat tired looking No. 1233 is running southbound on the single track section of San Mateo Drive south of Poplar. The gas station that No. 1233 is passing is offering "Premium" for 22¢ a gallon and "Ethyl" for 24¢. Whatever happened to ethyl? (Courtesy Robert Townley.)

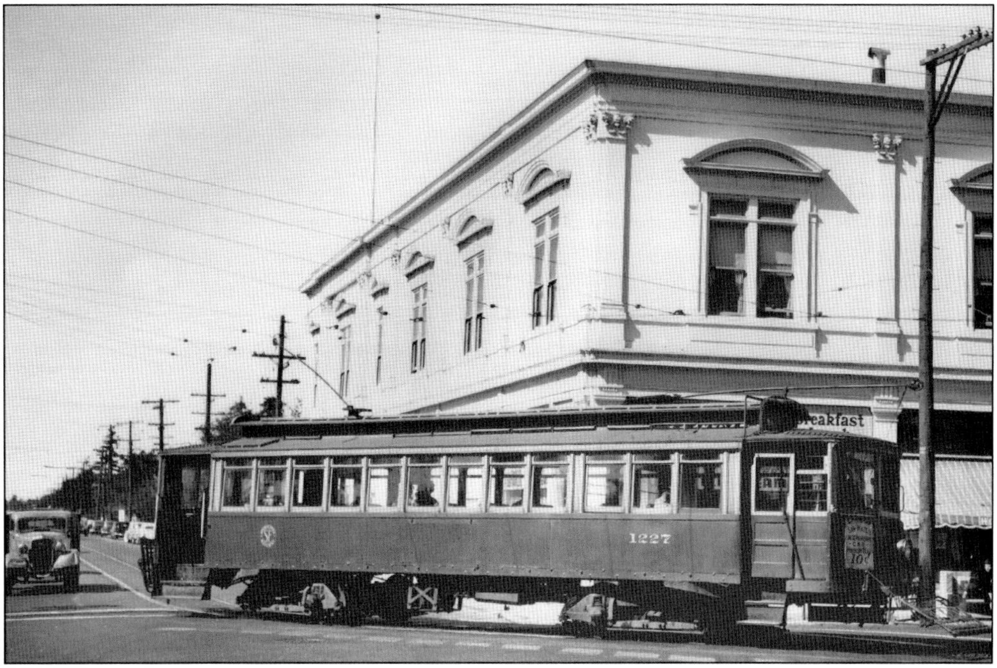

Car No. 1227 has just left the car stop at San Mateo Drive and Baldwin on its way to the San Mateo terminal. This was the car stop for San Mateo High School students from 1911 to 1927 and, after that, the stop for San Mateo Junior College students until the end of interurban service in 1949. The corner building remains today, although in a rebuilt state. (Courtesy Walter Vielbaum.)

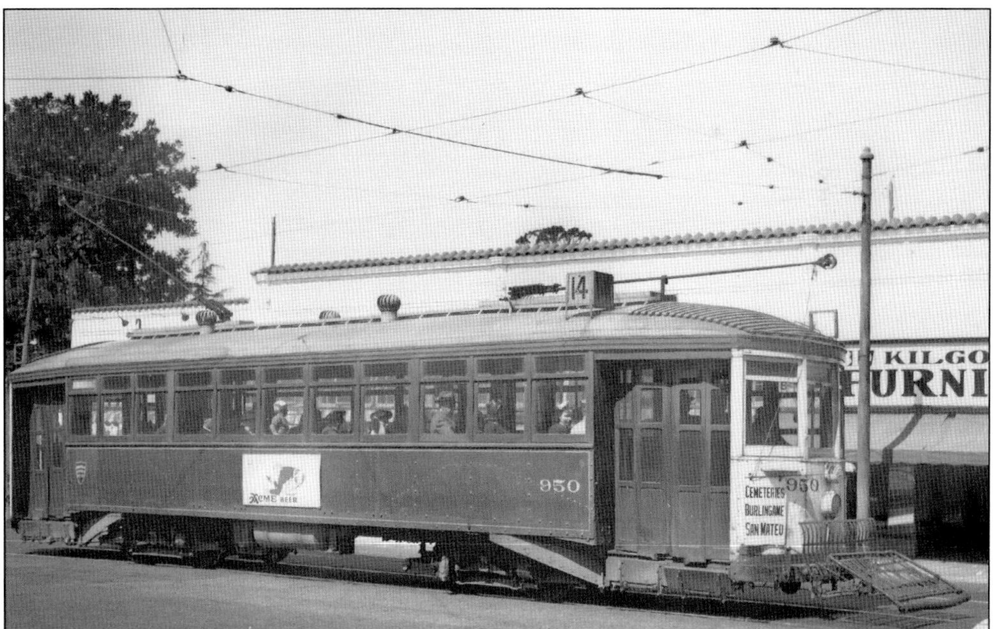

One-man car No. 950 carries a 14-route sign because someone forgot to change it to 40. Here it is turning off Baldwin onto B Street. The dash sign indicates it will go no farther than Daly City on the return trip. This was a wartime measure in September 1943. (Courtesy Will Whittaker.)

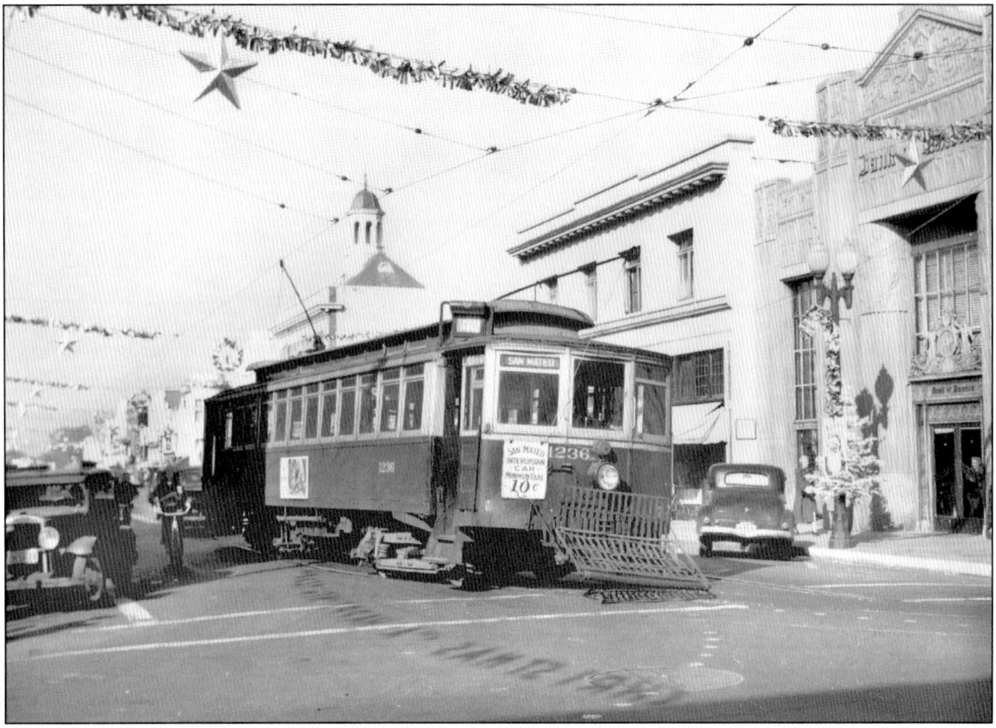

It's December 1948, and the Christmas decorations are up, bidding farewell to the 40 line. The car is turning off B Street onto Third Avenue. The building with the cupola on top behind the car is the city hall. On the corner is the art deco Bank of America. (Courtesy Robert Townley.)

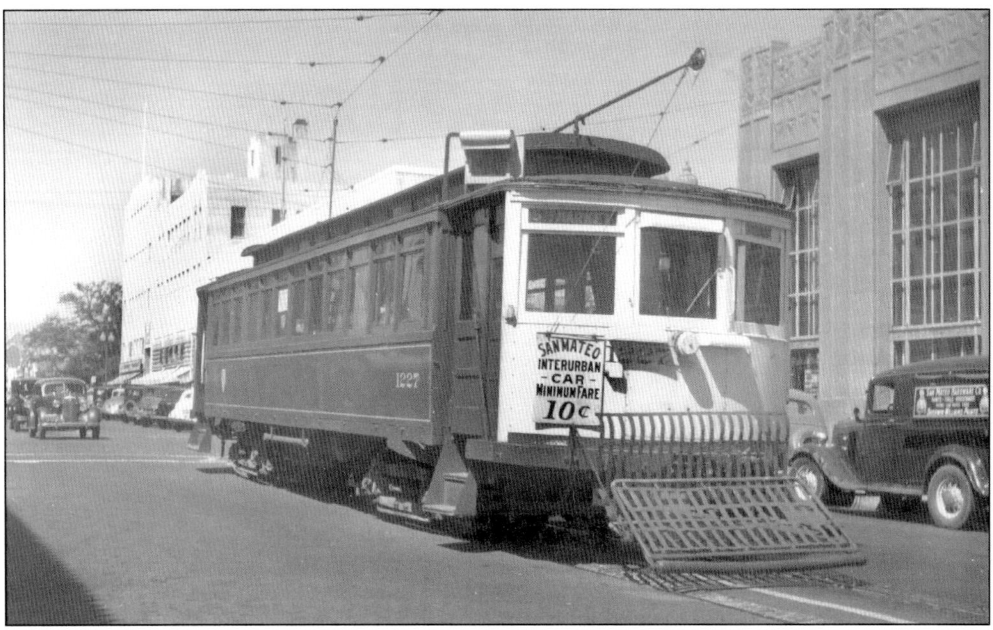

On June 24, 1939, car No. 1227 is on Third Avenue getting ready to make the left turn onto Main Street for the terminal. (Courtesy Will Whittaker.)

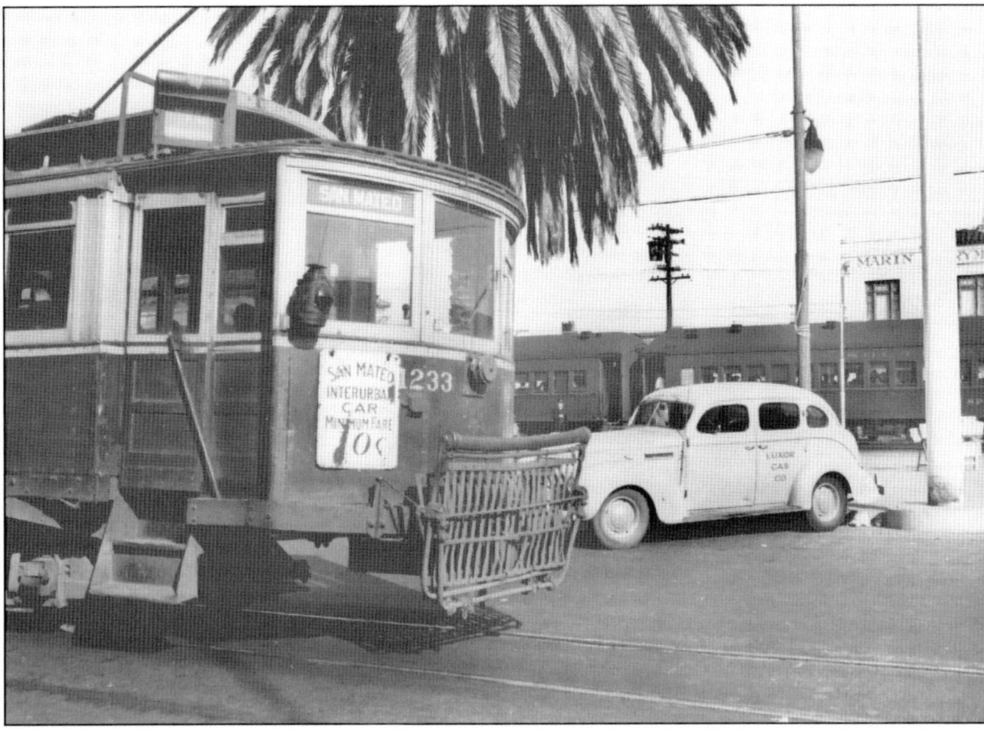

A Luxor cab waits for fares from the Southern Pacific commuters and the interurban at the San Mateo depot. This area is now the site of a theater. (Courtesy Gerald Graham.)

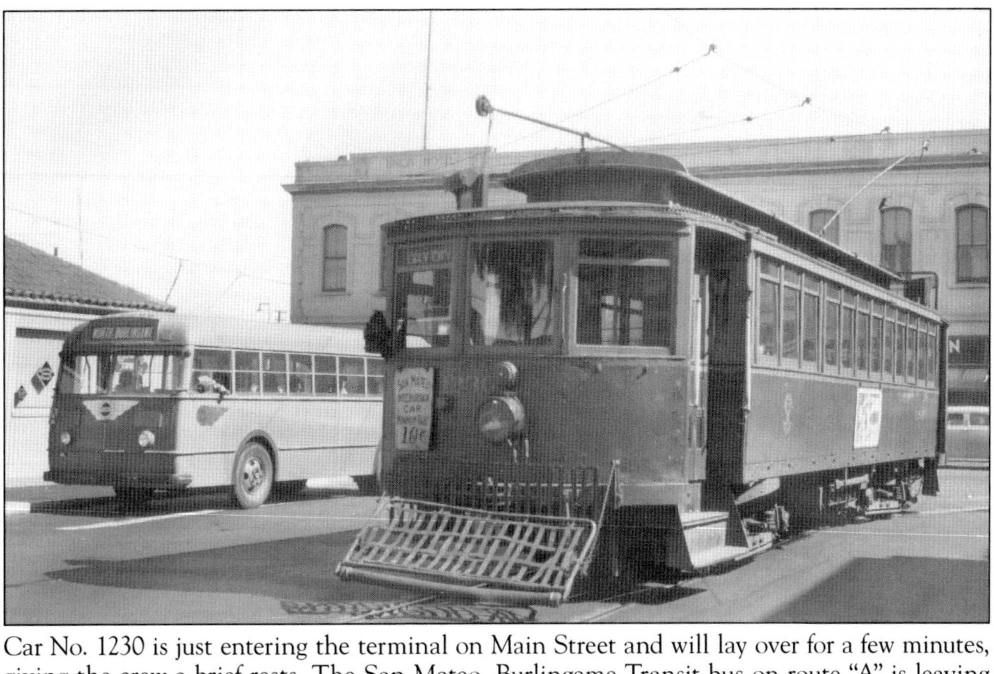

Car No. 1230 is just entering the terminal on Main Street and will lay over for a few minutes, giving the crew a brief rests. The San Mateo–Burlingame Transit bus on route "A" is leaving before the interurban to gather what fares it can get to Burlingame before the interurban leaves. The competitive edge of public transit is in a bygone era. (Courtesy Walter Vielbaum.)

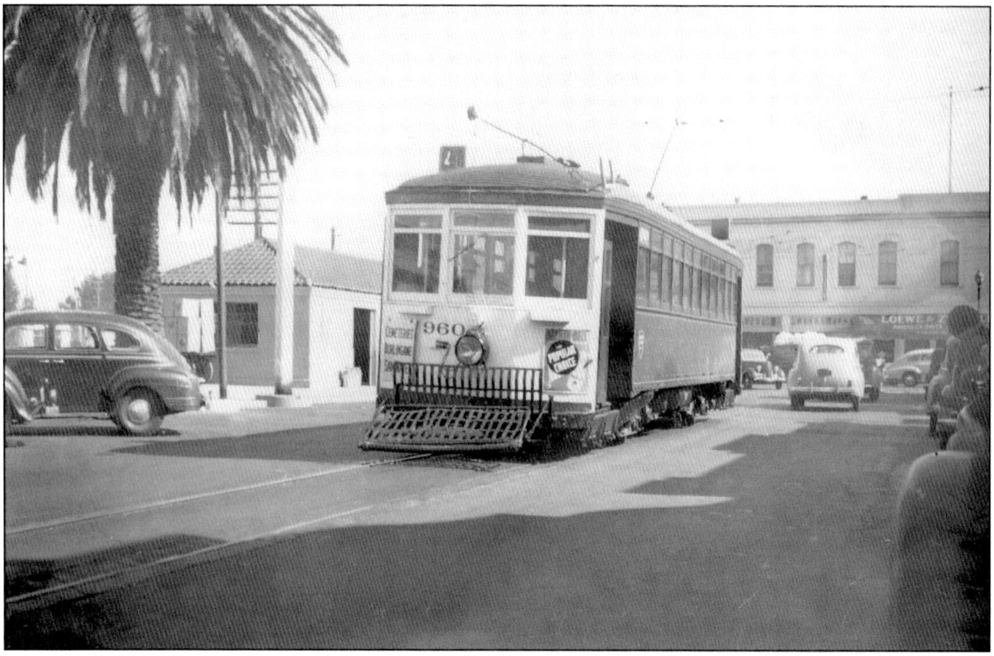

Car No. 960 rests at the San Mateo depot during the wartime era of one-man cars on the 40 line. It has been fitted with an interurban headlight for night service. The building in the rear is the Union Hotel, one of San Mateo's oldest buildings dating well before the 40-line era. (Courtesy Emiliano Echeverria.)

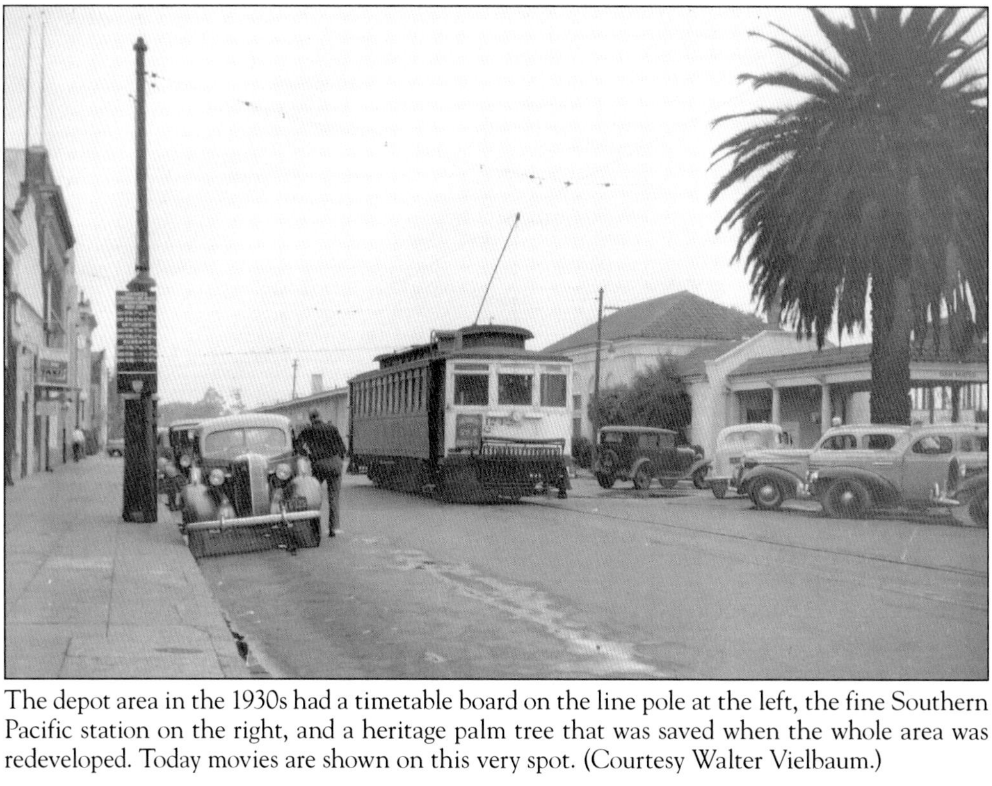

The depot area in the 1930s had a timetable board on the line pole at the left, the fine Southern Pacific station on the right, and a heritage palm tree that was saved when the whole area was redeveloped. Today movies are shown on this very spot. (Courtesy Walter Vielbaum.)

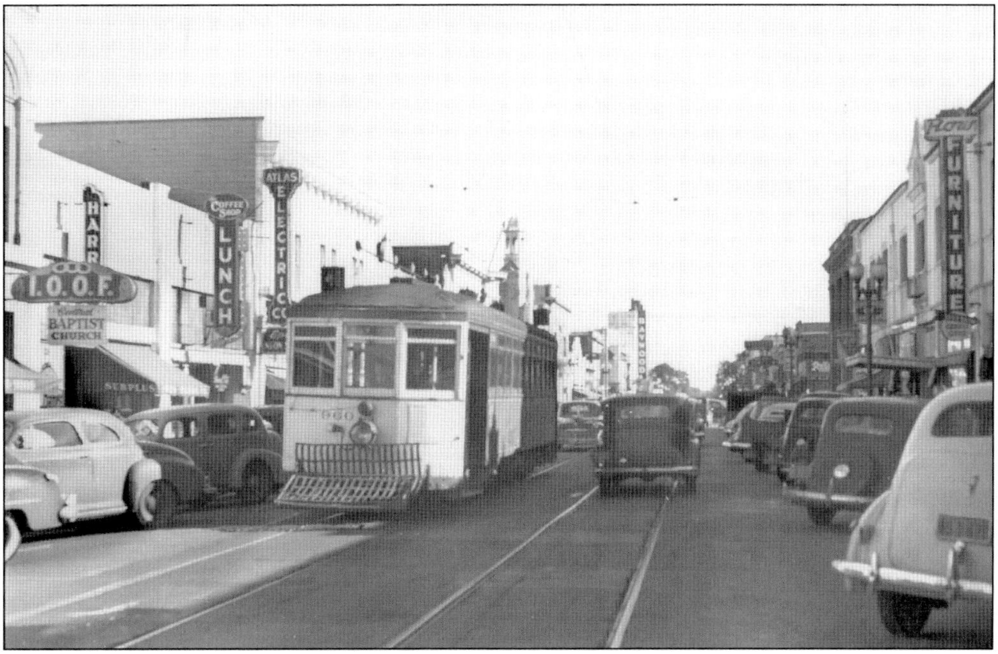

Car No. 960 heads north on B Street between First and Second Avenues in the one-man car days during the war. The passengers will have to transfer at Daly City to get to downtown San Francisco. The northbound track between Second and Third Avenues was never used as it was part of the unrealized extension to Palo Alto. (Courtesy Walter Vielbaum.)

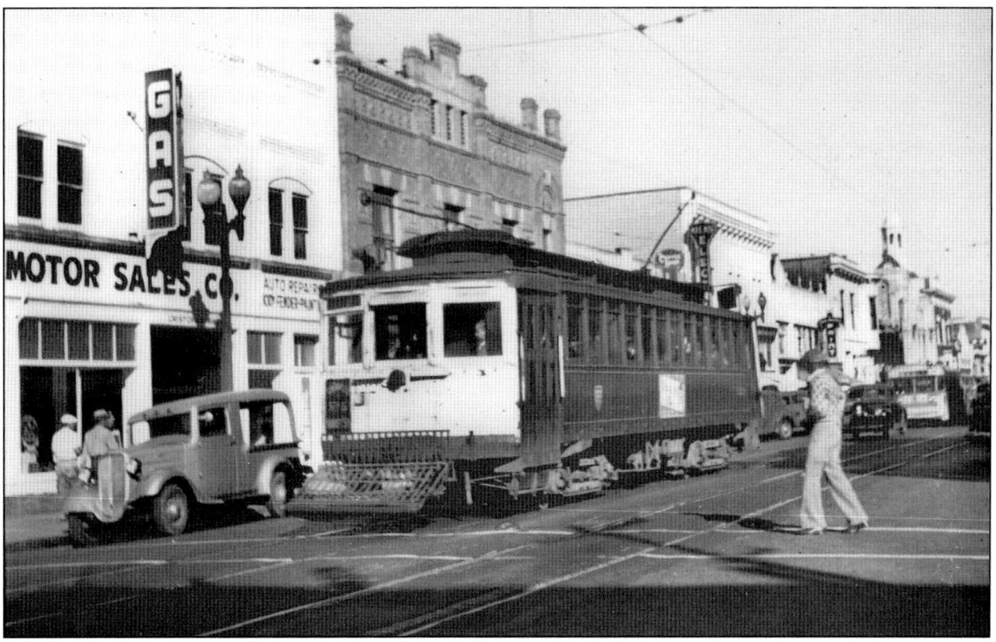

Northbound on B Street at First Avenue, car No. 1228 is followed by a San Mateo–Burlingame Transit bus. The building above the bus is San Mateo City Hall, with its cupola on top. (Courtesy Al Thoman.)

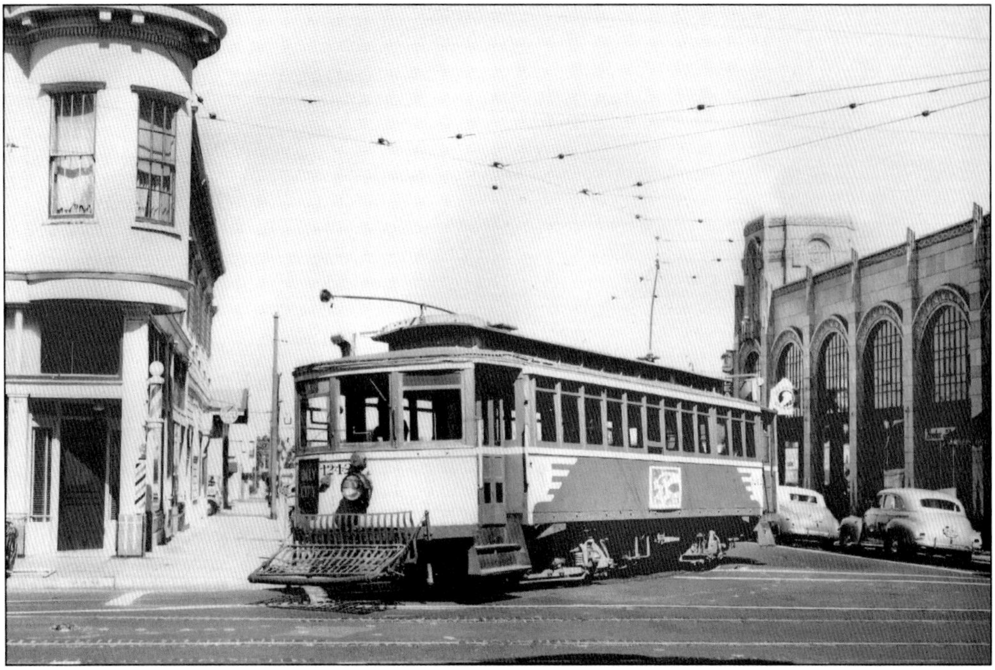

Upon leaving the Main Street terminal, car No. 1242 turned left onto Second Avenue, then turned right onto B Street by the art deco Merkel Building, which still stands. The car is painted in the Municipal Railway green and cream wings design, which it wore to its funeral. (Courtesy Walter Vielbaum.)

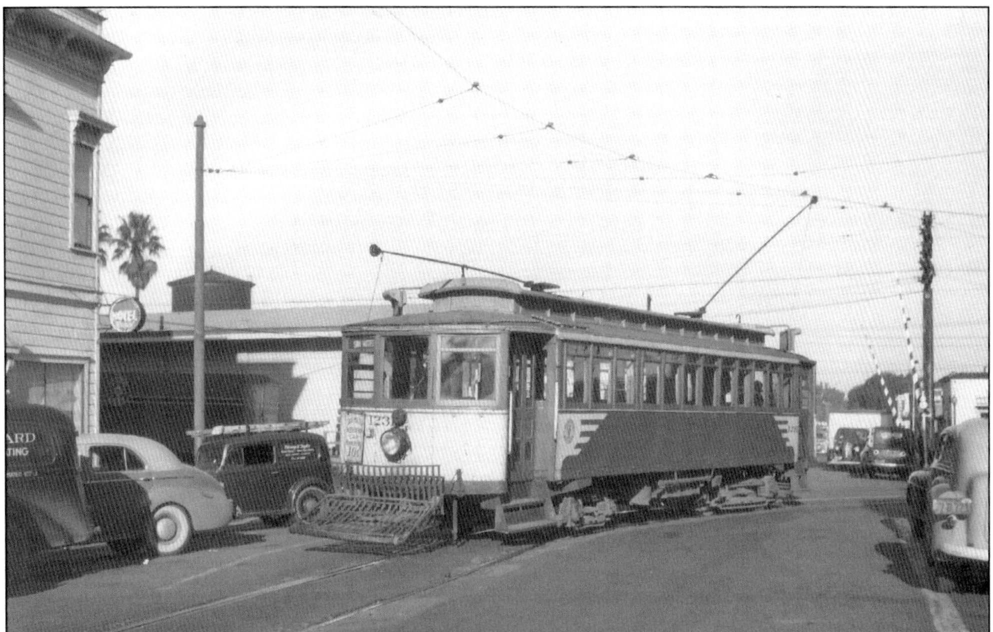

Car No. 1231 makes the left turn from Main Street to Second Avenue. The Southern Pacific freight house and water tank is on the left behind the car. (Courtesy Walter Vielbaum.)

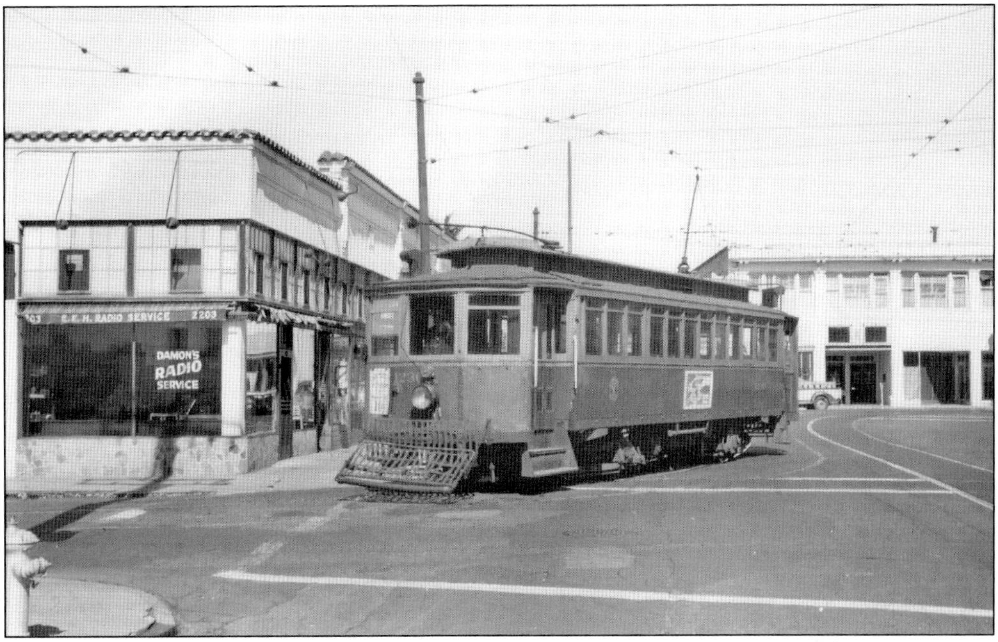

Car No. 1230, in blue and gold livery, turns onto Ellsworth Street from Baldwin on its way to San Francisco. The radio service store on the corner was the home of KVSM radio station, which recorded the final run out of San Mateo and broadcast it the next day. (Courtesy Walter Vielbaum.)

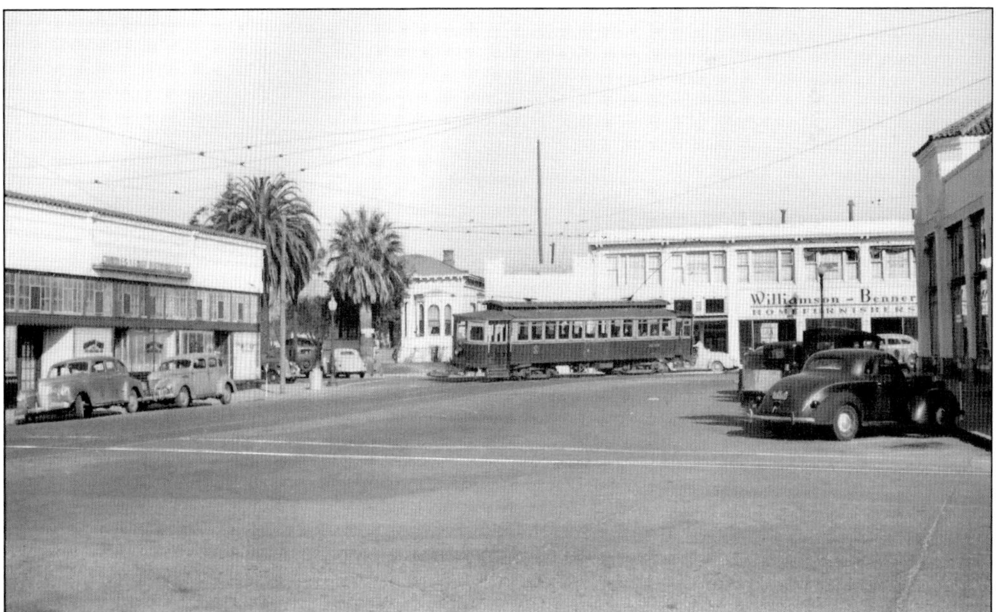

A San Francisco–bound car turns onto Baldwin from B Street. The stores on the far left occupy what is now the Trag's Market parking lot. (Courtesy Gerald Graham.)

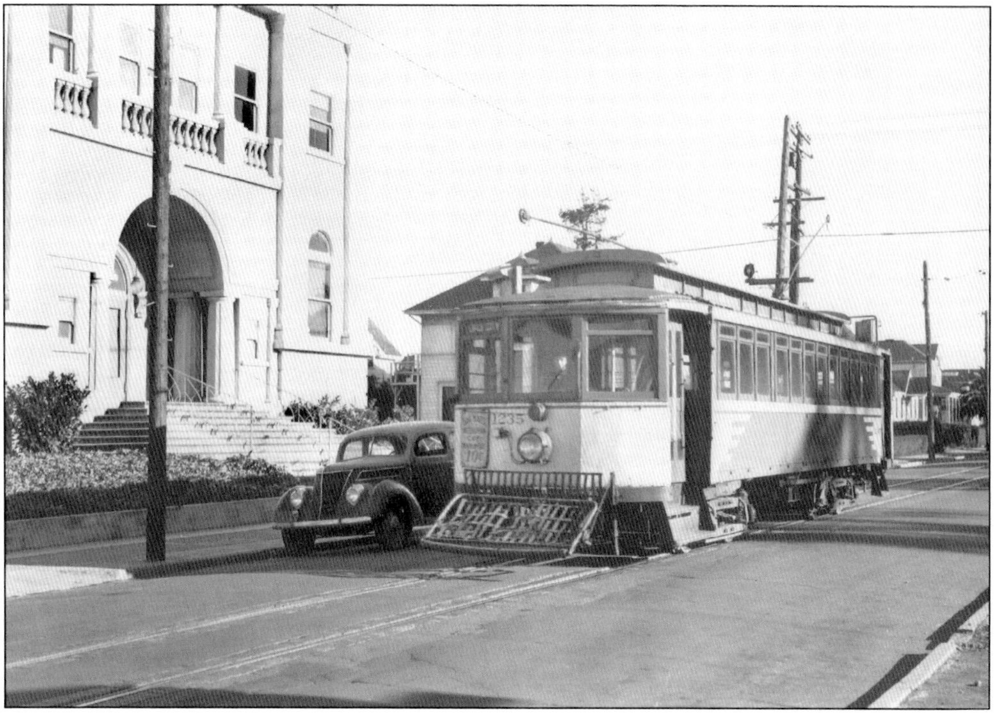

Car No. 1235 heads out on Ellsworth Street past the Masonic temple at the corner to Tilton. There were no stop signs on Ellsworth at this time and a good, fast ride was possible. (Courtesy Walter Vielbaum.)

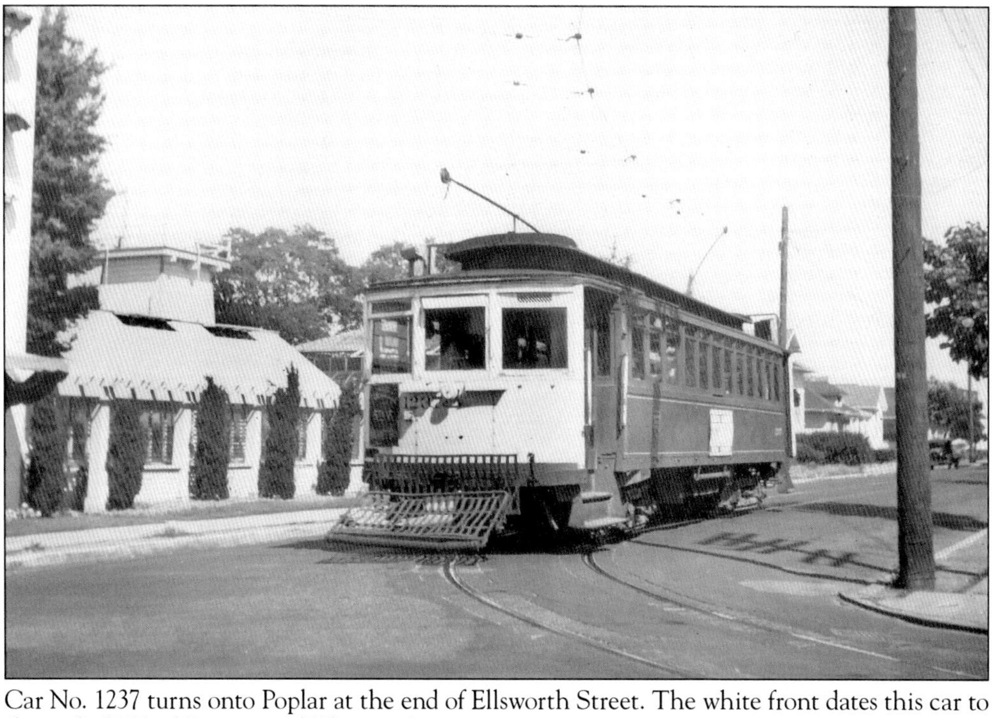

Car No. 1237 turns onto Poplar at the end of Ellsworth Street. The white front dates this car to the early 1940s. (Courtesy Al Thoman.)

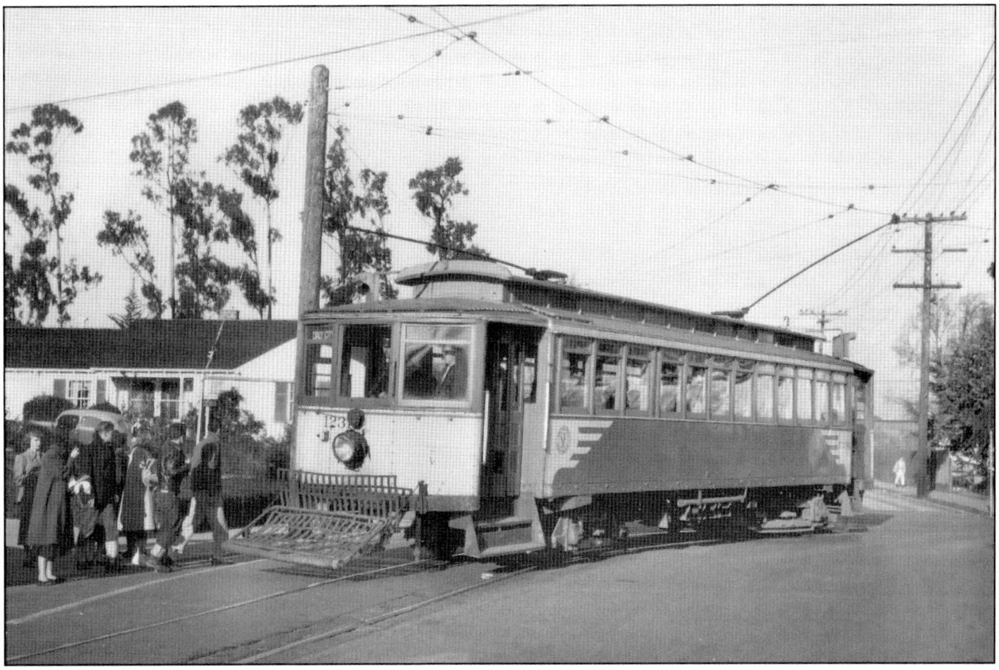

School's out! Car No. 1231 is picking up San Mateo High School students on Poplar and Ellsworth. At this time, the only high schools in the north county were Burlingame and San Mateo. Students from Millbrae and San Bruno took the interurban to school and were issued special student tickets by the school district. Jefferson High in Colma took care of the far north area. (Courtesy Walter Vielbaum.)

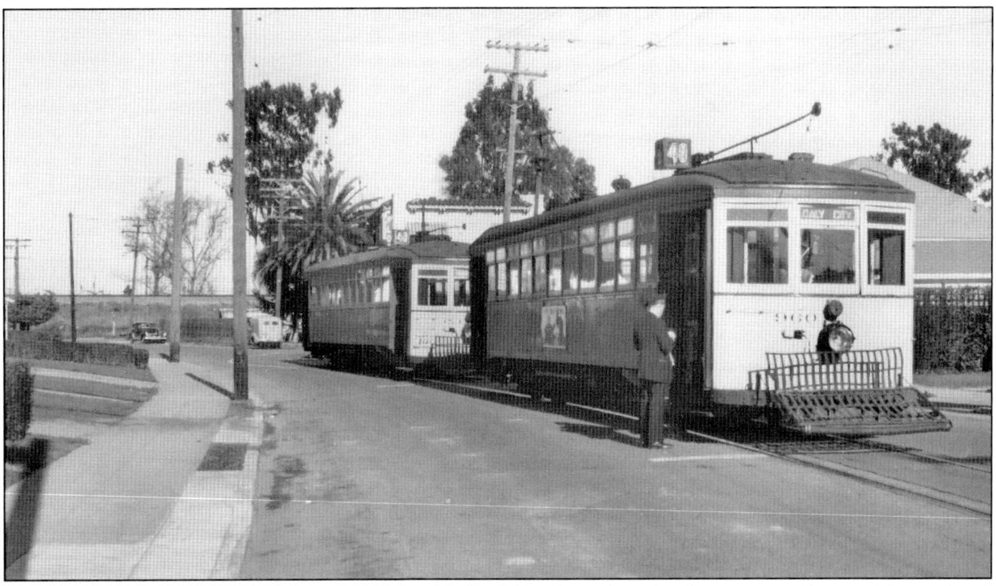

Two one-man cars await the San Mateo High School students' release to go home. The school trippers were a way of life then. It was more cost efficient for the school district to issue rail tickets instead of buying and running buses. When the interurban line closed, the students rode the Southern Pacific commuters for a short time before the school district embarked on a bus program. (Courtesy Walter Vielbaum.)

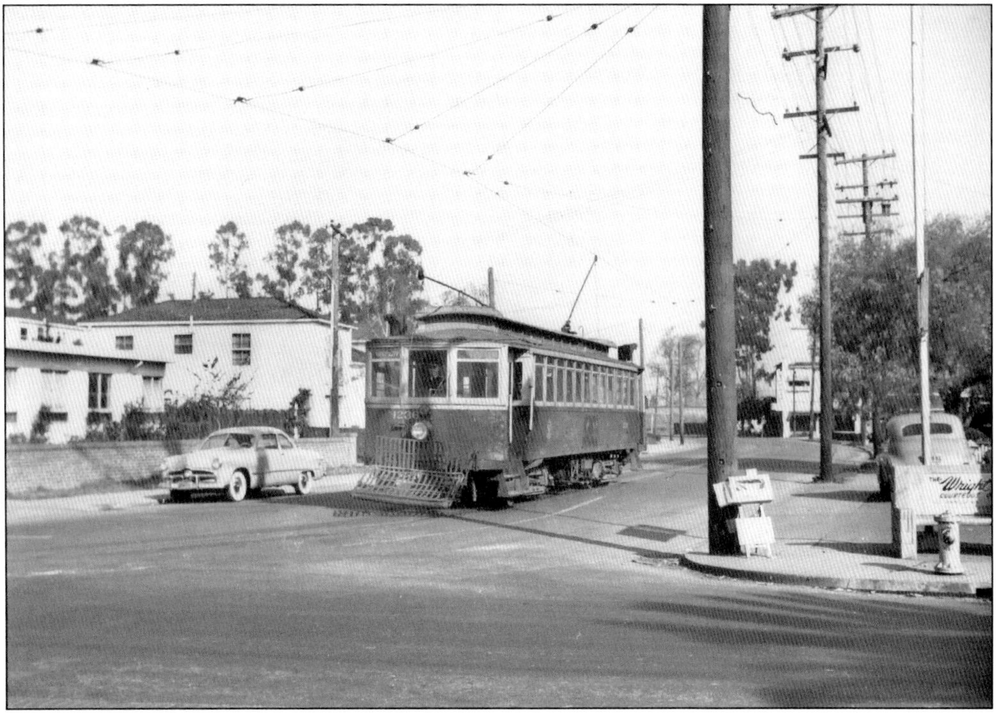

This car is at the corner of Poplar and San Mateo Drive getting ready to turn north onto San Mateo Drive to continue its journey to Burlingame. (Courtesy Robert Townley.)

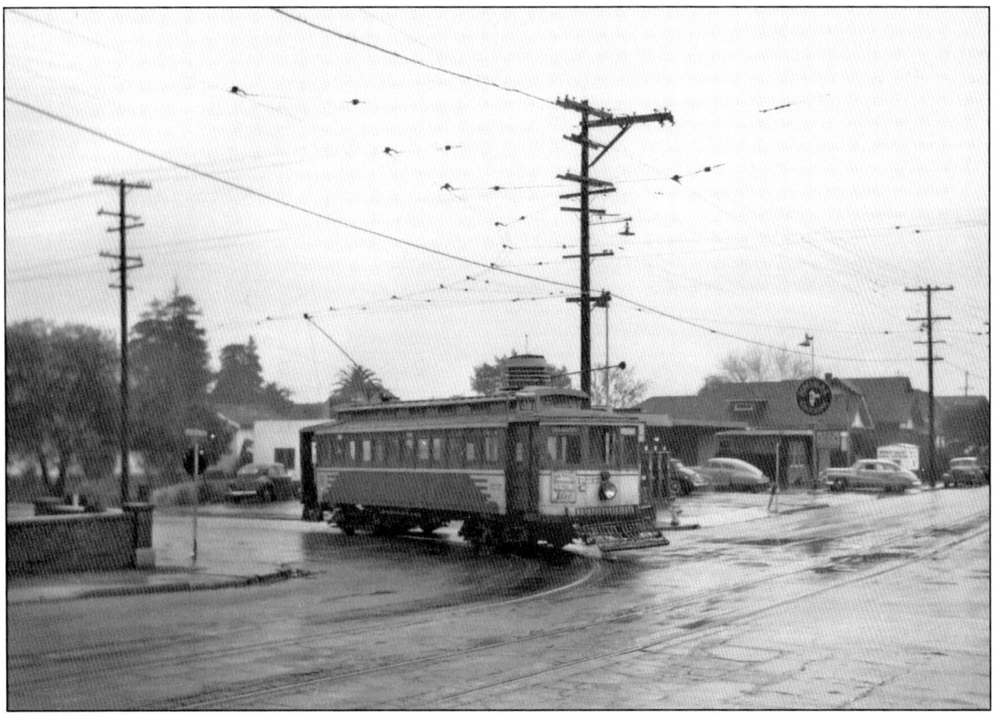

It's a cold, rainy day in late 1948 as car No. 1237 passes the long gone Signal Gas Station at Poplar and San Mateo Drive. The car is wearing its final paint job. (Courtesy Robert Townley.)

Four

Visitors from the North and Local Feeders

The interurban section of the San Mateo line was from Daly City Hilltop to San Mateo. In San Francisco, the line shared trackage with local city lines. The relatively long running time of an hour and fifteen minutes for the 20-mile trip from Fifth and Market Streets to San Mateo was attributable to the fact that one-half of the entire trip was on San Francisco, Burlingame, and San Mateo city streets. Besides interurban passenger service, the interurban section saw other operations.

The first of these was funeral car service, which the San Francisco and San Mateo management found as a new source of revenue in 1893. On September 17, 1893, the first funeral train began service to the Colma cemeteries. The principal city cemeteries were located in San Mateo County (Colma), just across the borderline of the city and county of San Francisco, and consisted chiefly of Mount Olivet, Salem, Home of Peace, Cypress Lawn, Sherith Israel, Hills of Eternity, Emanuel, and Holy Cross Cemeteries.

Express motor No. 32, pulling the trailer "Cypress Lawn," made the initial journey. Almost a year later, on August 27, funeral car service began as the SF&SM had modified the Cypress Lawn into a motor car. It was later to become funeral car No. 1. The earthquake of 1906 destroyed the Cypress Lawn at the Twenty-ninth and Mission car house.

SF&SM (and later URR) funeral cars transported mourners and the deceased to the grave sites at Mount Olivet, Holy Cross, and Woodlawn Cemeteries via connecting trackage owned by the cemeteries. The cemeteries provided still further revenue for the railways since throngs of Sunday mourners—who would often make an outing of the trip to pay their respects to the dead—had to be transported. Indeed, special schedules to carry mourners to the cemeteries lasted to the end of rail service.

After the United Railroads takeover, funeral car service was expanded. Four additional cars were added to the fleet, with the last three constructed in the URR shops being especially ornate, offering mourners deep cushion seats, carpeted floors, and drapes. San Francisco's funeral homes located their businesses on the car lines of the URR. Service was also operated from San Mateo. The basic rate for a funeral car was $20.

After their retirement, the funeral cars were placed in dead storage at the Twenty-fourth and Utah Streets carbarn, where they remained until taken to the Elkton shops to be scrapped in February 1926.

In addition, 14-line Mission streetcars were often extended on Sundays and holidays to Holy Cross to supplement interurban service. During the mid-1920s, this service was provided by the 18 line, which duplicated the 14, except that it started at Fifth and Market Streets instead of at the ferry. After the 18 line was discontinued, the 14 line once again was periodically extended to Holy Cross. Interestingly, effective April 4, 1948, Muni ran all 14-line cars on Sundays and certain holidays through to Holy Cross from 11:00 a.m. to 4:30 p.m. This routing undoubtedly was implemented because, effective August 1947, except for weekday rush-hour service, all 40-line cars only went to Daly City. The Sunday 14-line extension provided direct service for San Franciscans to the cemeteries.

Another special service that ran on the tracks of the San Mateo line was the transportation of horses and motorcycles to San Bruno's Tanforan Racetrack. Horses were picked up either at the ferry building, having arrived usually via transcontinental train, or at one of the many stables located throughout San Francisco. In order to transport horses, the URR had a motorized box car, car No. 0901, fitted with stalls. This service succumbed by 1910 to motor vehicles. Extra cars were run to carry racing enthusiasts until the line's end.

Besides the cemetery trackage and the non-revenue Daly City quarry spur trackage, a physical connection was made between the San Mateo line and the South San Francisco line. When the United Railroads built the San Mateo extension, the section of the former SF&SM line that crossed under the then Southern Pacific main line just north of Holy Cross and ran south to Baden between Mission Road and the railroad line became surplus. The new San Mateo trackage was on the west side of the Southern Pacific. The surplus tracks were turned over to a URR affiliated company—the South San Francisco Railroad & Power Company (SSFRR&P). That company built a single-track, private, right-of-way line to Grand Avenue from Baden. The single-track line continued easterly along Grand Avenue, crossing the then under construction Southern Pacific Bayshore Cutoff at grade to a terminal at Point San Bruno. Importantly, the line served Fuller Paint Company and Western Meat Packing Company (later part of Swift and Company).

Service from Holy Cross to Point San Bruno began on January 1, 1903—the same date as the start of the San Mateo shuttle. Until 1919, cars assigned to this line were marked for the SSFRR&P instead of the URR. Each winter, the underpass at Holy Cross filled with water, so that at a later date the connection was moved to Leipsic Crossing. The now Southern Pacific branch line crossing became a surface crossing. Typically, only Geneva carbarn moves crossed the railroad tracks, as connecting passengers were required to walk across the Southern Pacific track. However, certain rush hour directional schedules were operated directly to Fifth and Market Streets during limited periods of the South San Francisco line's operational history. Service ended on December 31, 1938.

From 1913 until November 19, 1917, an independent electric railway—the Burlingame Railway—connected the foothill residences of Easton, today's Broadway, Burlingame, with the URR's San Mateo Suburban line. Built and operated by the real estate developer, the line operated a single storage-battery car to the developer's housing development located in the Burlingame foothills, which then was known as Easton's Hills. The one-and-a-half mile line reached Easton's Hills (Burlingame Hills) via Easton Drive (today's Hillside Drive). Although the streetcar line was not financially successful, the line helped trigger "remarkable growth." The development combined with the car line proved a lure for many San Franciscans.

Continual visitors from the north were a variety of work cars used for building and maintaining the line. Indeed, the first car to arrive in San Mateo was line car No. 0301 on December 26, 1902.

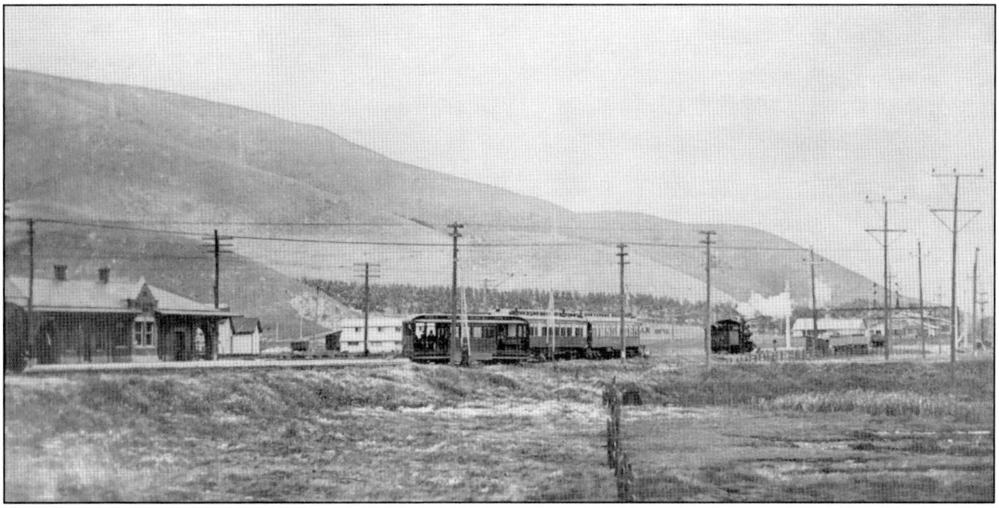

The original Southern Pacific depot at South San Francisco has a visitor; a diminutive South San Francisco Railroad and Power car is just about to cross the Southern Pacific main line at the depot heading for downtown South San Francisco. Just visible to the far right is the signal bridge over the Southern Pacific main line. This bridge remains in place today. The line served South San Francisco's residents and the industrial areas on the bayside of South City until the end of 1938. (Courtesy Charlie Smallwood collection.)

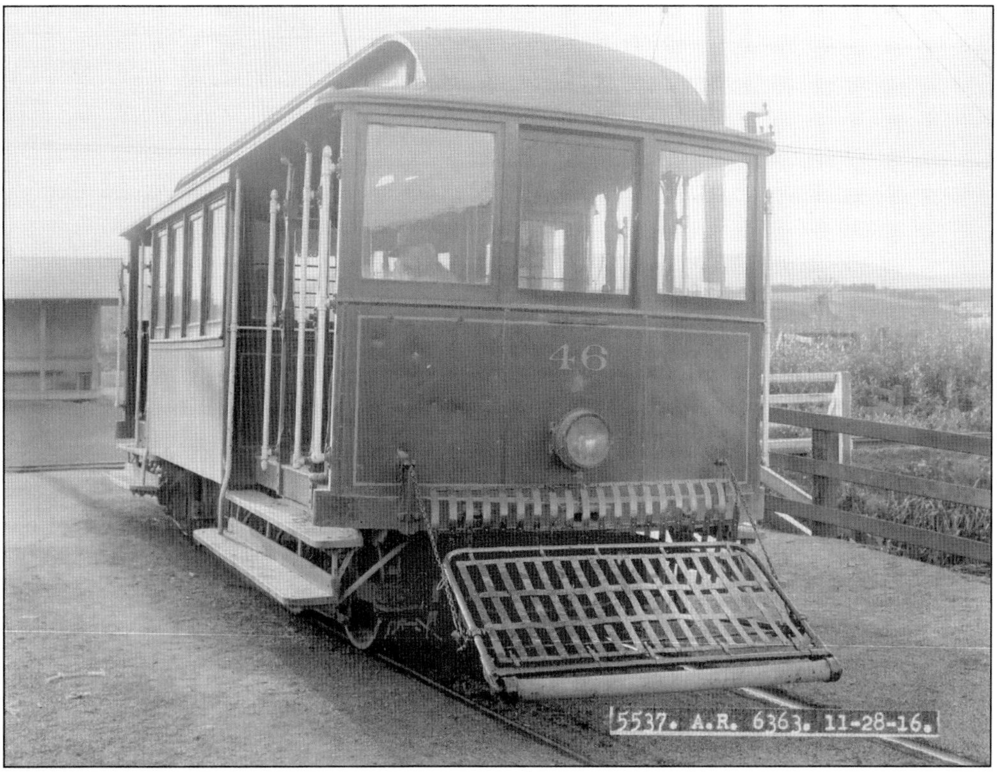

South San Francisco Railroad and Power car No. 46 lays over in South San Francisco on November 28, 1916, awaiting transfer passengers from the San Mateo line. The view shows how rural this part of the line was. (Courtesy Rudy Brandt.)

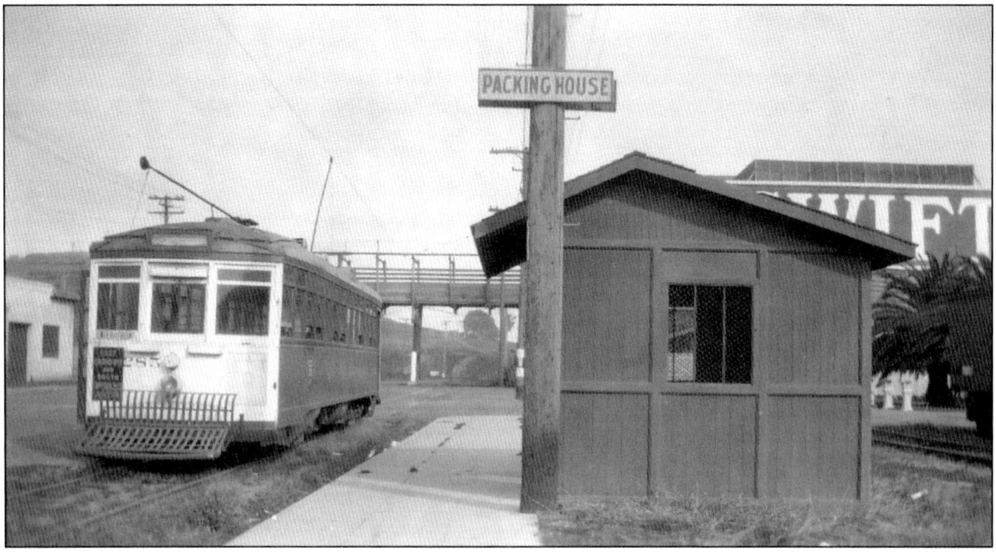

One-man car No. 285 lays over at end of the line near the Swift Packing Plant awaiting it's time to return to Leipsic Junction. This car, which had no rear door, was regularly assigned to the South City Line. (Courtesy Bill Billings/Western Railroad Museum.)

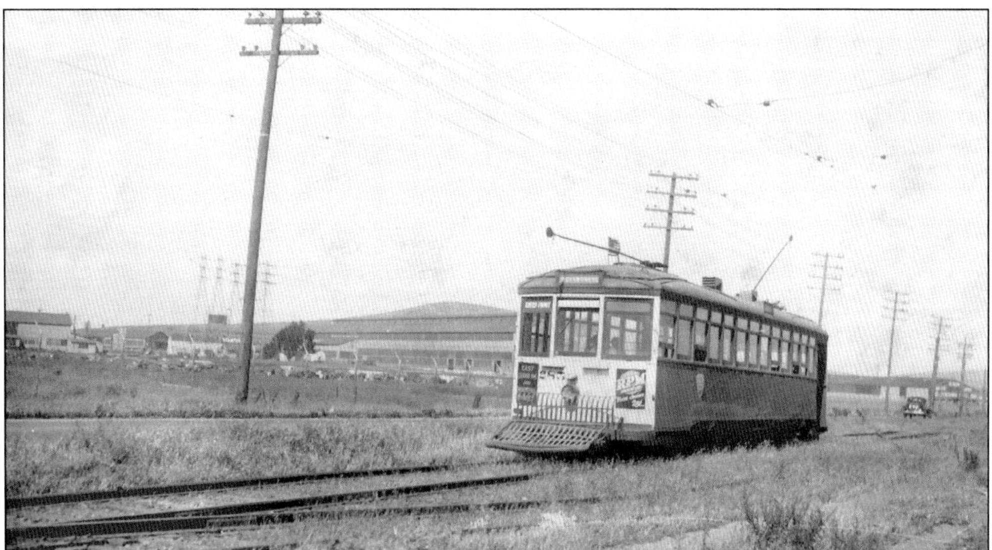

Car No. 285 speeds along the side-of-the-road section in 1935 past a passing track on the single-track line to the meatpacking houses and Fuller Paint Company. The narrow two-lane road on the left of the car is Grand Avenue. (Courtesy Emiliano Echeverria.)

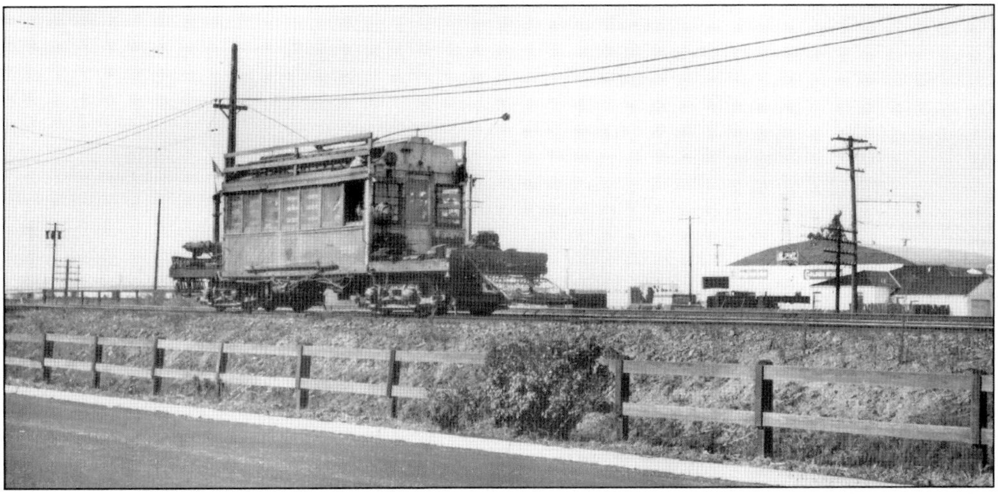

Here's No. 0507, the Geneva Wrecker, speeding south of Sanchez Station on the way to the crossover at Burlingame to rescue No. 1228, a school tripper, that decided it didn't want to stay on the track. No. 1228 went on the ground in the middle of the crossover loaded with high school students. (Courtesy Walter Vielbaum.)

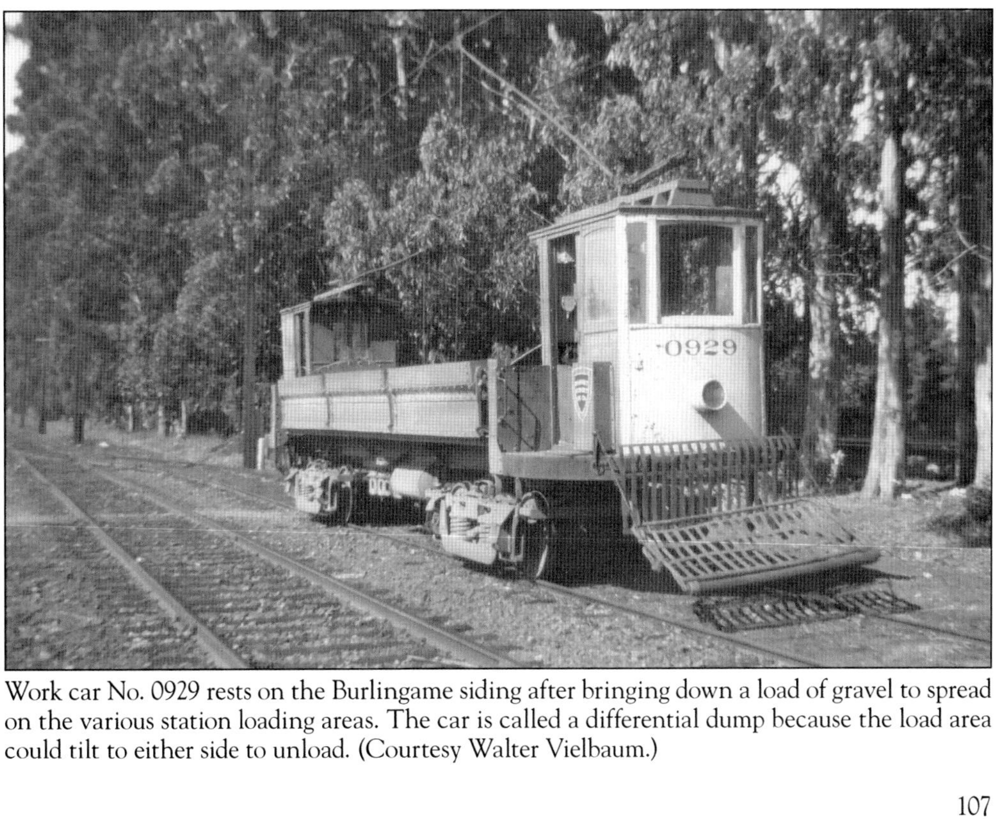

Work car No. 0929 rests on the Burlingame siding after bringing down a load of gravel to spread on the various station loading areas. The car is called a differential dump because the load area could tilt to either side to unload. (Courtesy Walter Vielbaum.)

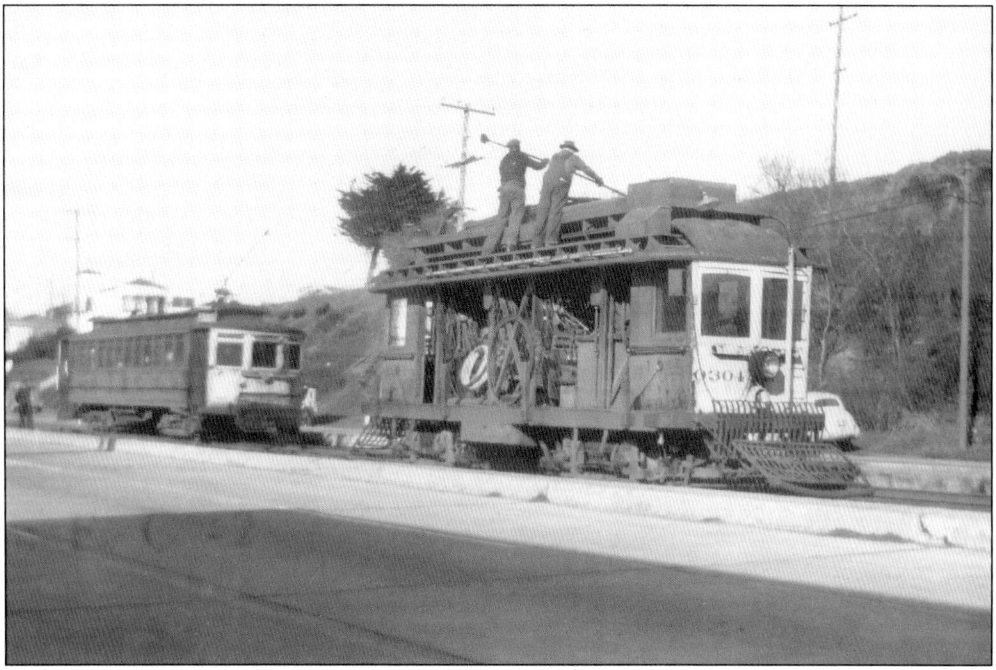

The line crew is busy at work on No. 0304 in the Colma area. The single trolley pole had to be manually positioned for the direction of travel. The car was mostly used on non-street trackage. (Courtesy Emiliano Echeverria.)

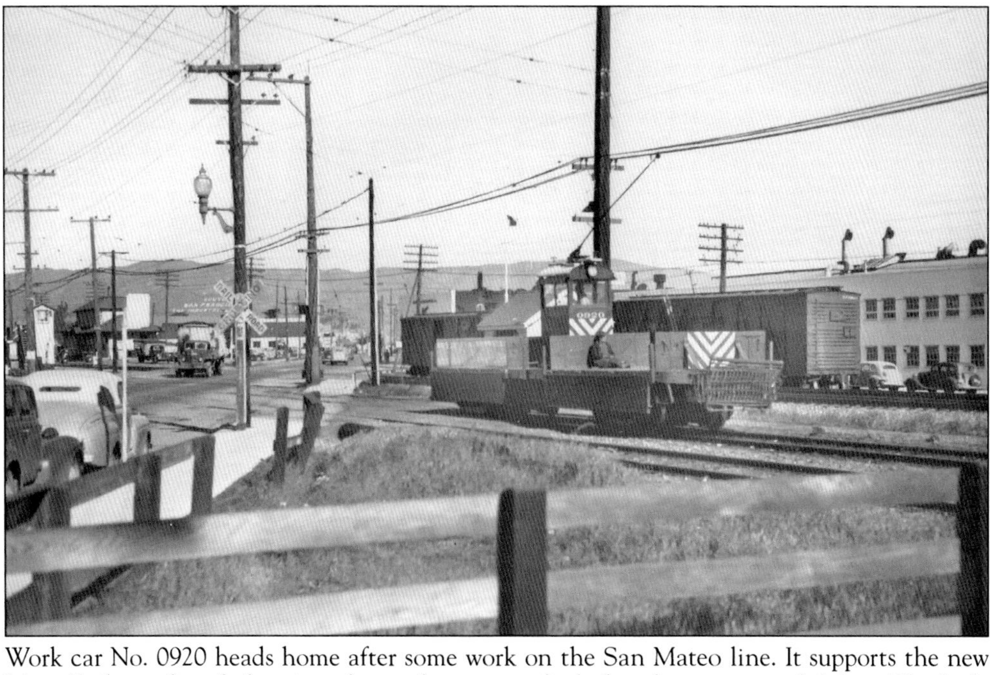

Work car No. 0920 heads home after some work on the San Mateo line. It supports the new Muni Railway olive drab paint scheme that was applied after the merger with Muni. The little tower on the far left was the gate man's tower for the crossing gates on San Mateo and San Bruno Avenues for the Southern Pacific. The Southern Pacific San Bruno depot is also visible next to the tower. (Courtesy Walter Vielbaum.)

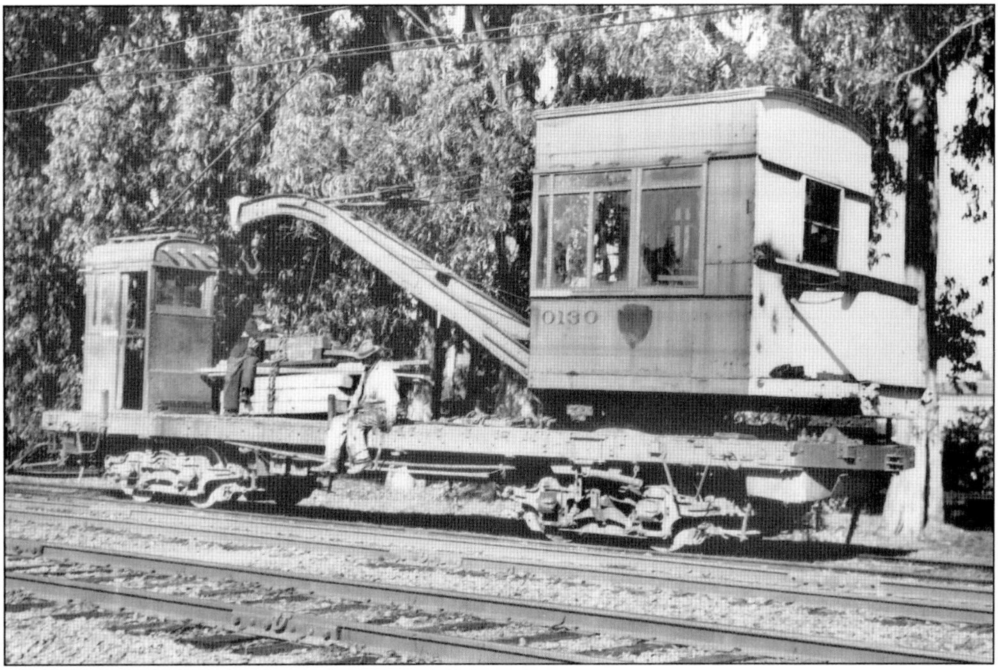

The crane, No. 0130, takes a lunch break on Burlingame siding after bringing down a load of crossties. The siding retained its original rail and cast weld joints that were installed in 1902. (Courtesy Walter Vielbaum.)

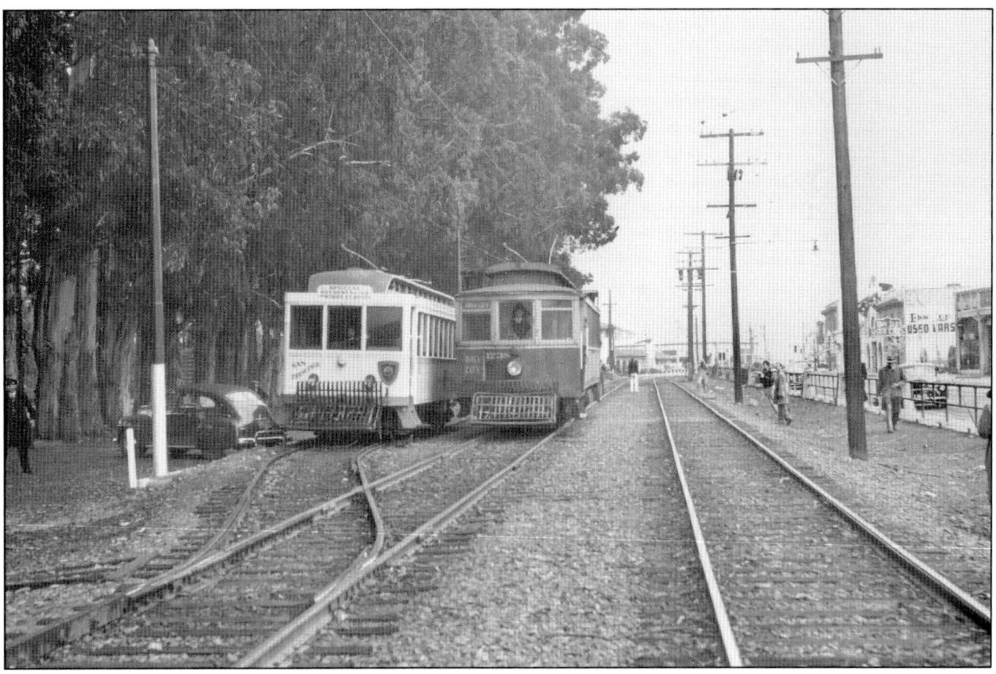

On December 12, 1948, the private party car San Francisco rested on Burlingame siding during a tour of the 40 line. The siding was always a favorite spot with railfans. Today this right-of-way is the northbound lanes of California Drive. (Courtesy Richard Brown.)

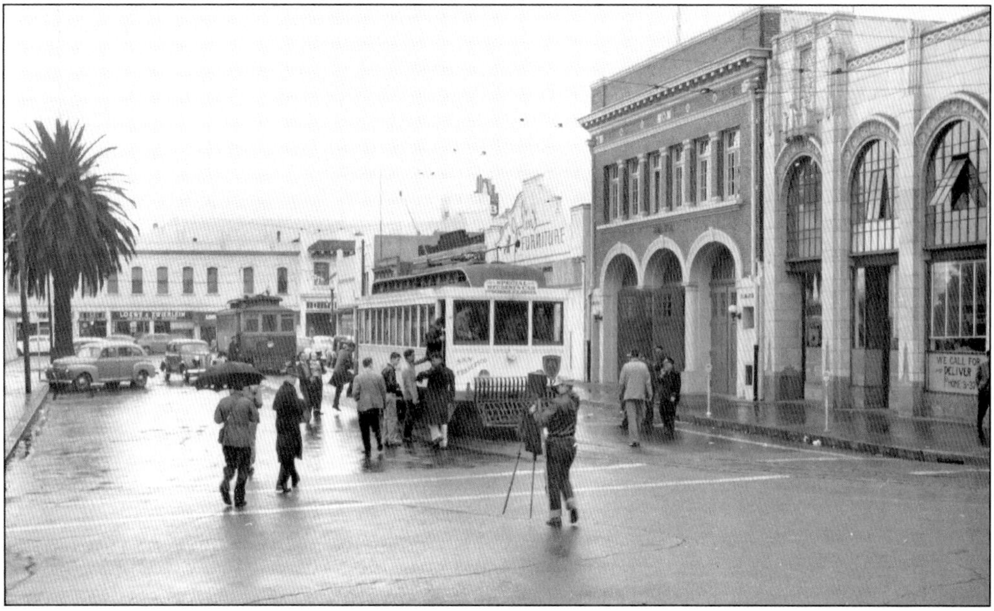

This is the way Railroad Avenue, in front of the Southern Pacific depot in San Mateo, used to look. The fellow with the view camera was Emanuel Mohr. That's the fire station on the right. The body of the San Francisco rests at the Western Railway Museum awaiting restoration. (Courtesy Gerald Graham.)

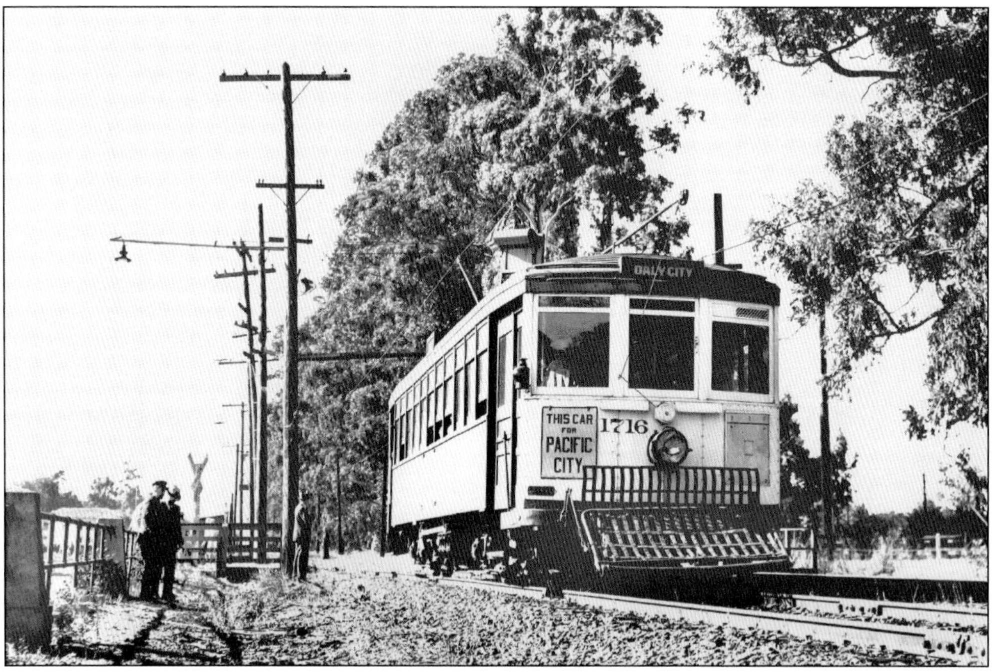

On October 5, 1941, car No. 1716 was chartered for a trip to San Mateo. The group chose to display one of the old dash signs from the 1920s that was used for Pacific City, an amusement beach and park on Coyote Point. No. 1716 was one of several cars upgraded from city service to use on the 40 line on heavy days of ridership. The car is southbound at Oak Grove. (Courtesy Jim Carpenter.)

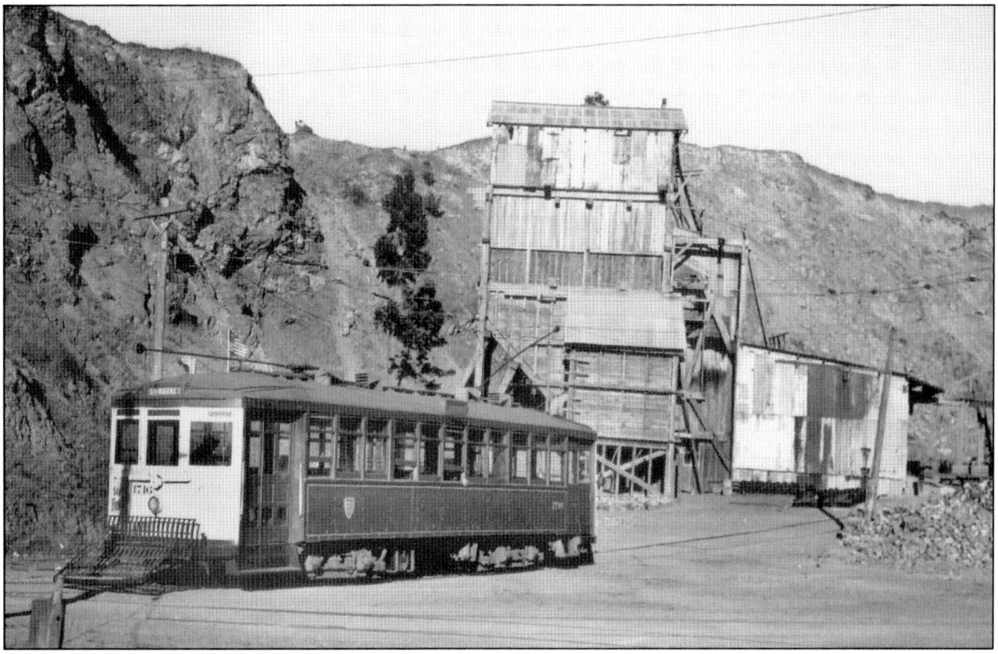

Car No. 1716, an excursion car, visits the quarry at the top of the hill in Daly City. This quarry furnished the track ballast for the private right-of-way sections on the 40 line and other lines in San Francisco. Very few pictures of this quarry with rail equipment exist. In less than two months, World War II would commence, putting excursions on hold for the duration. (Courtesy Jim Carpenter.)

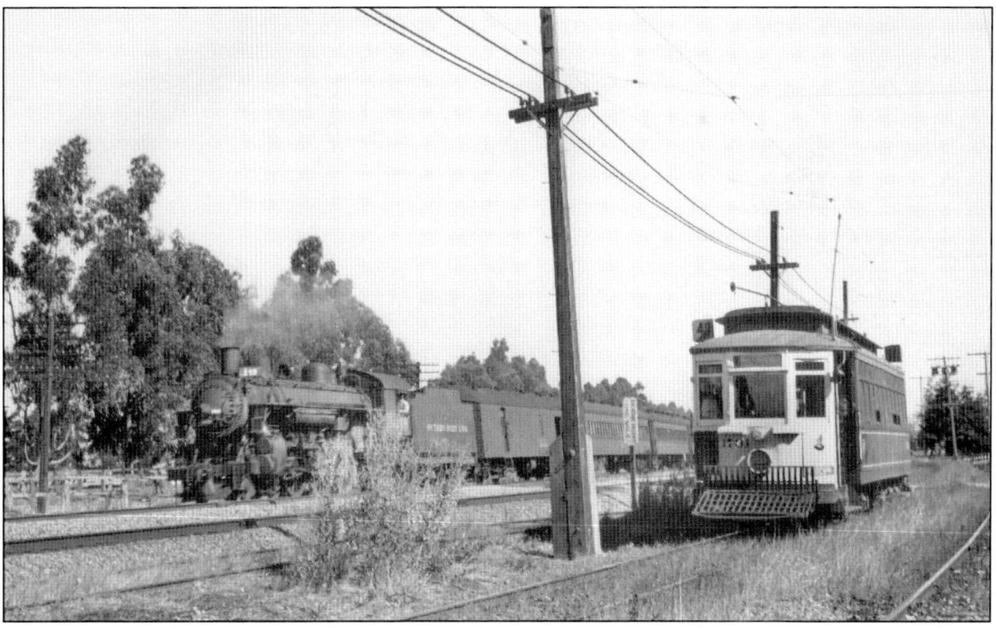

Car No. 1731 was used on the very last excursion to San Mateo until the war was over. Here the car is northbound at Millbrae Dairy racing a Southern Pacific commuter train. One of the original square-tapered redwood line poles from 1902 still supports the trolley wire. The sign between the streetcar and the train states "Burlingame-Broadway one mile." (Courtesy Jim Carpenter.)

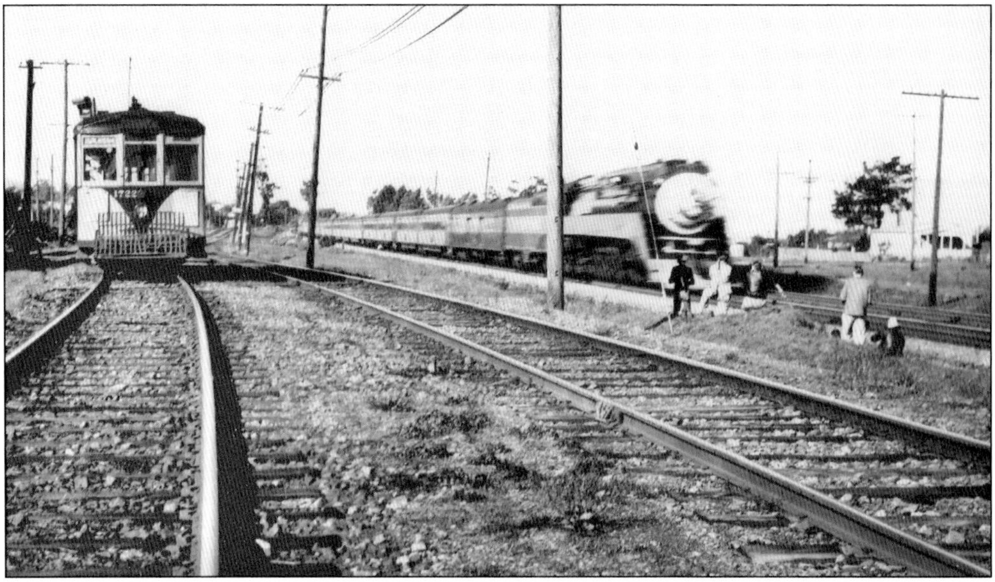

It's December 27, 1946, and the California Railfans Association has chartered the No. 1722 for a trip to San Mateo. The train was stopped to get a photograph of the "Noon Daylight" as it sped past the group, which included the authors, at 16 Mile House Station. The CRA was a teenage railfan group that was formed because the established groups didn't admit teenagers. The group disbanded when the members grew older. (Courtesy Richard Brown.)

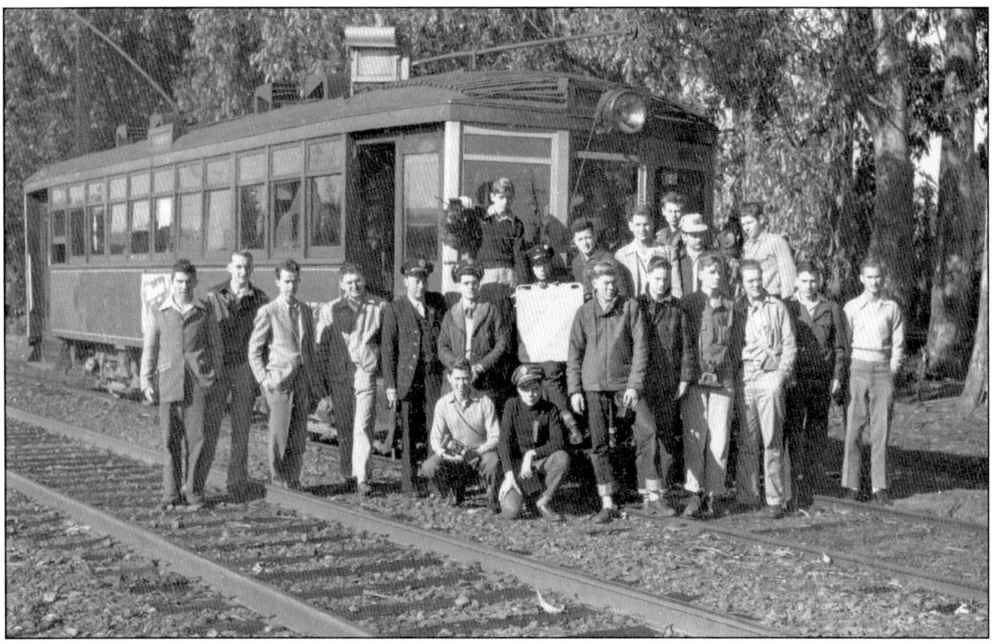

The No. 1722 pulled into Burlingame siding for a group photograph. Emanuel Mohr, top row second from right, is followed, from right to left, by Bob Townley, Walter Vielbaum, Jack Perry, Val Golding holding the CRA dash sign, and Bob Croset. In the middle row to the far left is Tom Gray, and in the middle is Lorin Silleman in a conductors uniform next to Bert Ward, the motorman. The interurban headlight was hung up over the front window because the group thought it looked neat. Every generation has their "thing". (Courtesy Richard Brown.)

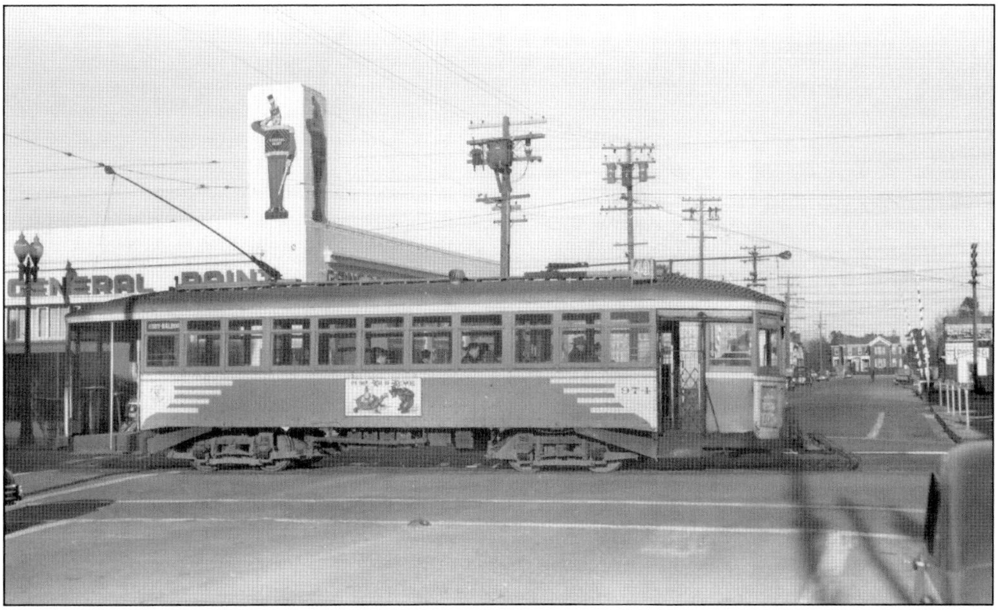

Car No. 974 made one of the very last fan trips to San Mateo. Here it is on B Street crossing First Avenue on its way to the terminal at the Southern Pacific depot. This car was saved by Bay Area Electric Railroad Association, only to have it burned by vandals. (Courtesy Richard Brown.)

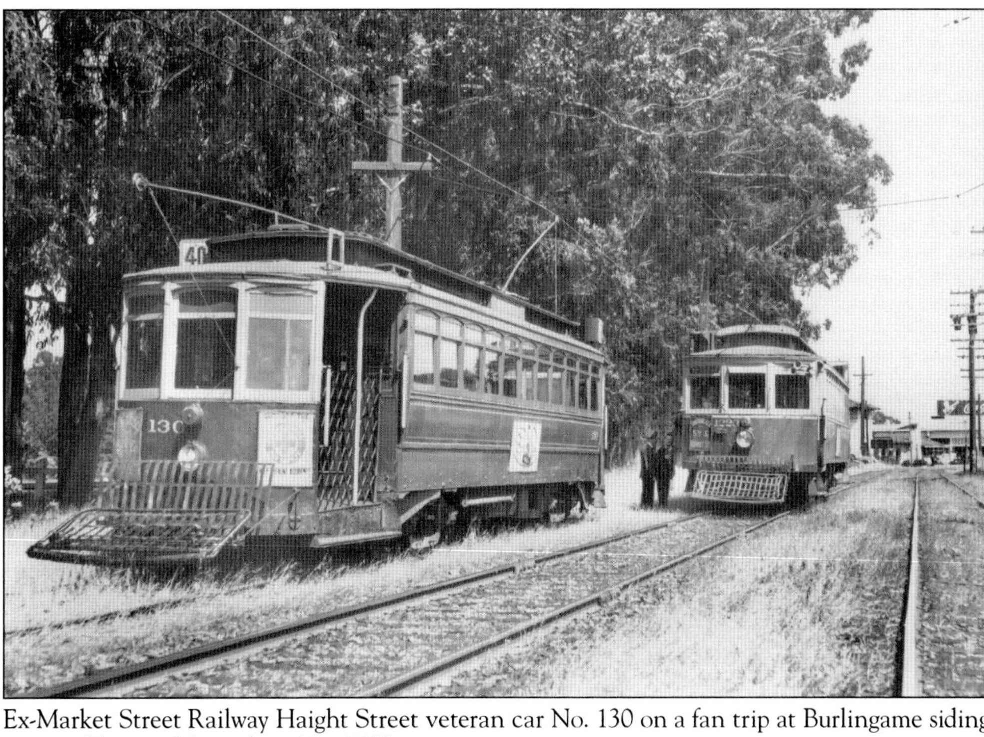

Ex-Market Street Railway Haight Street veteran car No. 130 on a fan trip at Burlingame siding is passed by northbound car No. 1229.

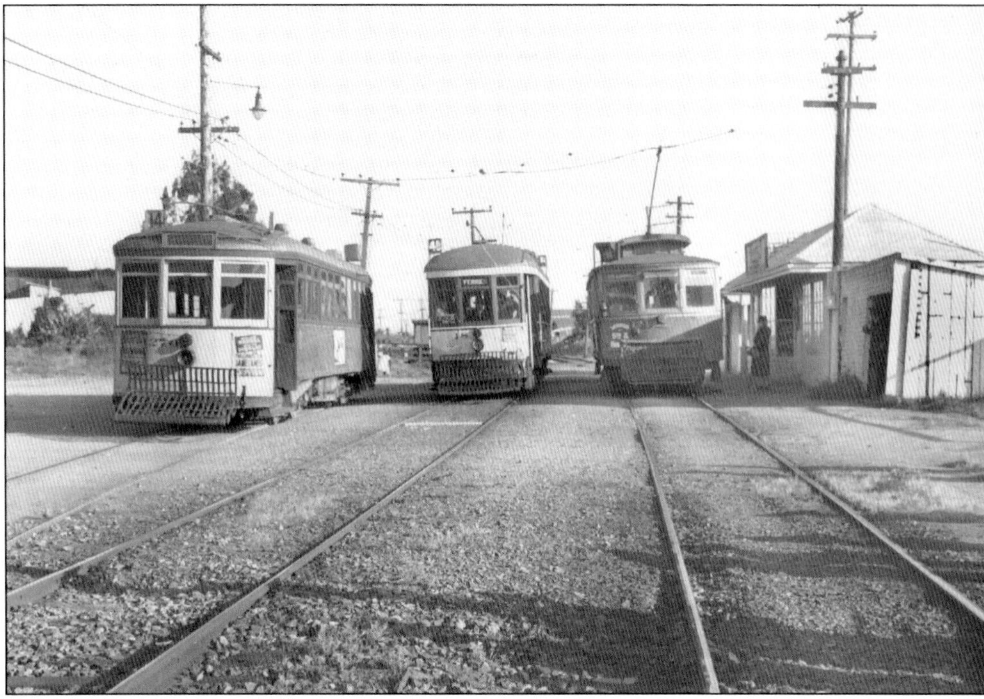

These three cars, lined up at Holy Cross with car No. 18, are on a fan trip.

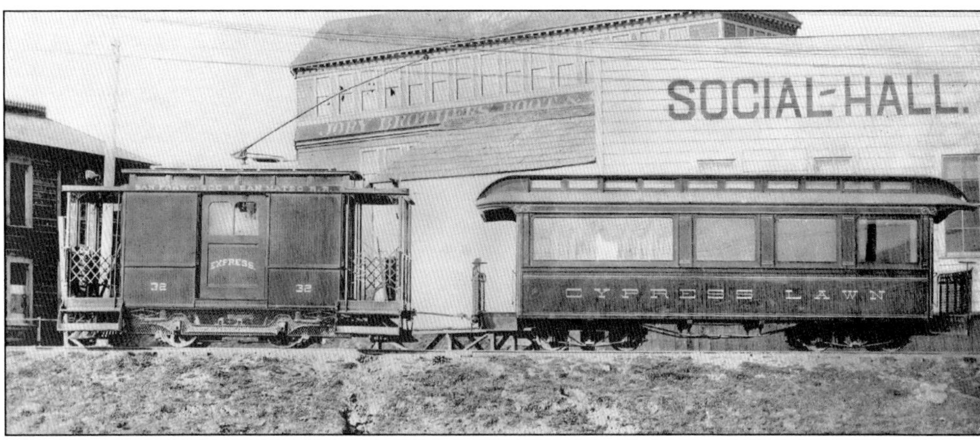

Southern Pacific had been running funeral trains to Colma since the mid-1880s. Enter SF&SM's new electric funeral train consisting of an express motor and a car named Cypress Lawn. Exit the Southern Pacific service. Soon after, Cypress Lawn was motorized and ran under its own power until around 1906. It was destroyed in the earthquake of 1906 when a portion of the Mission and Twenty-ninth Streets car house's facade collapsed onto the unlucky car stored inside. (Courtesy Rudy Brandt.)

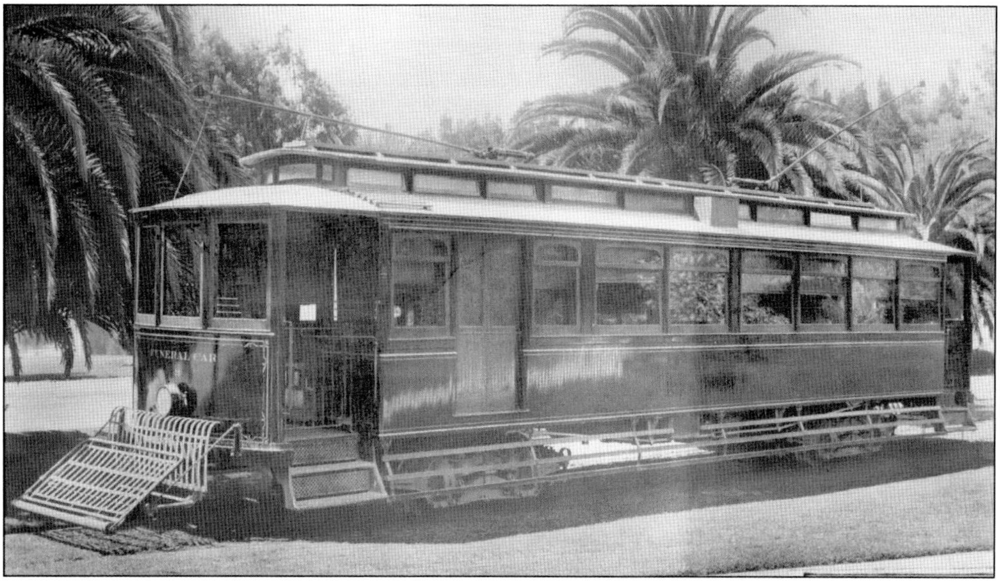

Funeral car No. 3 poses for its formal portrait at Cypress Lawn. URR continued in the business of transporting the remains of San Francisco's dead and, indeed, expanded it to the regular use of four cars. These cars replaced smaller, older cars. URR maintained the trade throughout its existence, although after 1915 it catered to a declining clientele. The three cars of this class were scrapped early in 1926. (Courtesy URR.)

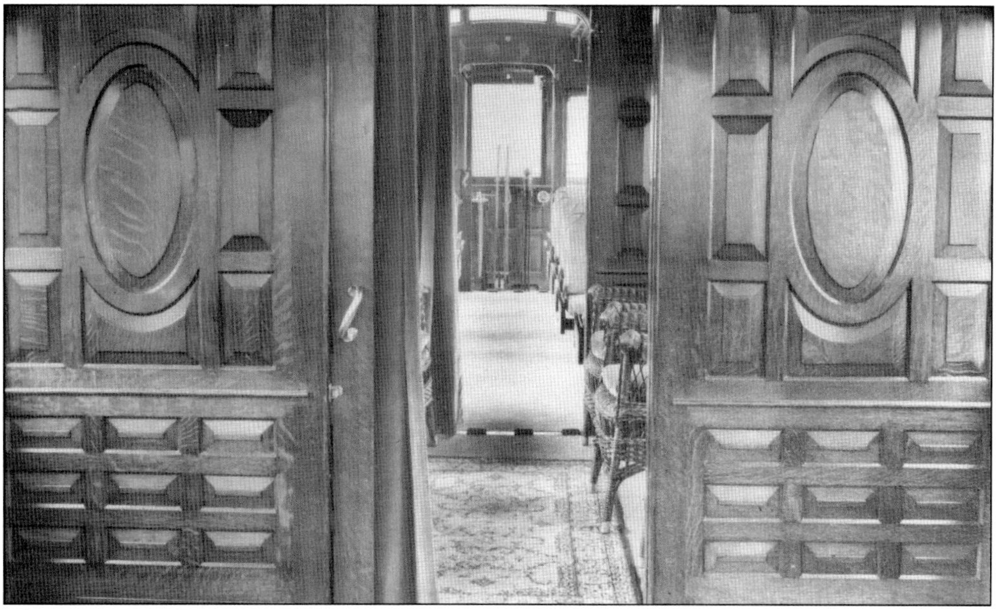

This view from the casket compartment looks toward the wicker chairs of the immediate family compartment and finally the regular seats in the last compartment for the mourners. URR spared no expense in making its homebuilt funeral cars the most elegant in the fleet. Appointments included fine paneling, wicker and rattan seats, and a special table for the casket that extended outside the car for easy placement and removal of the remains at the funeral home and cemetery respectively. Additional regular cars could be chartered if there was a large crowd. The funeral car service ceased in the early 1920s. (Courtesy Richard Schlaich.)

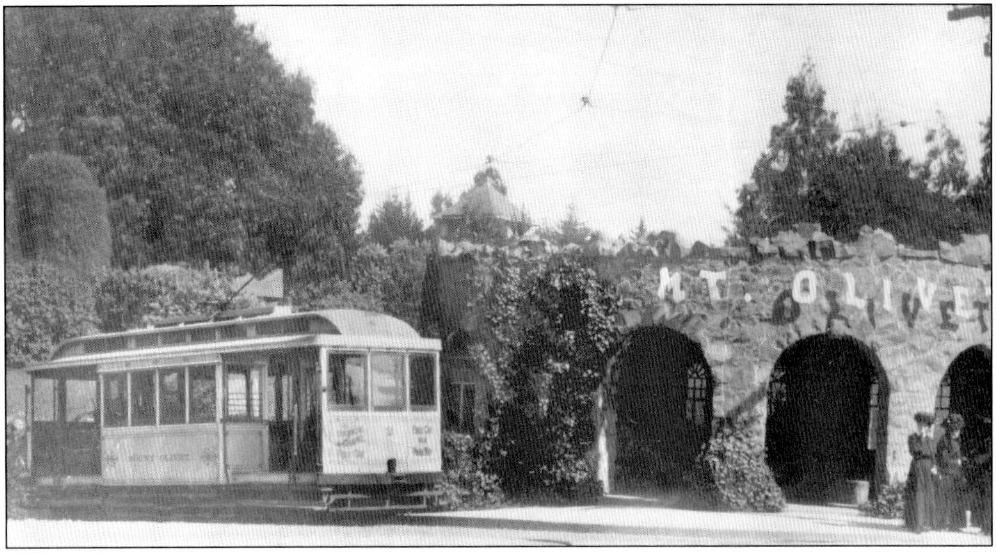

Mount Olivet Cemetery had its own line connecting the cemetery with the 40 line. This car was identical to the old South San Francisco Railroad and Power Company cars and was an ex-SF&SM car of the 41–50 series. At the cemetery entrance, Mt. Olivet awaits passengers to transport them back to the San Mateo line. When out of service, it was replaced by similar car URR No. 45. (Courtesy Emiliano Echeverria.)

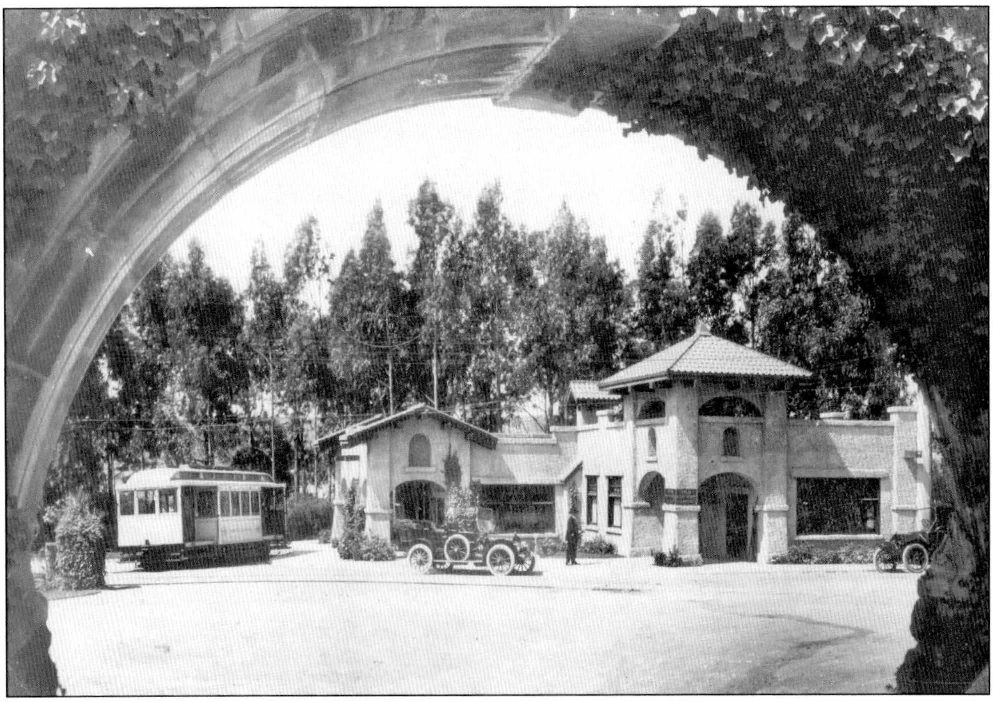

Shown here are the offices of the Mount Olivet Cemetery on the old county road, this car is ready to depart down the hill to the lower station to connect to the San Mateo line. A free service for Mount Olivet patrons, this private line ran until the mid-1920s. The car was serviced under contract by URR/MSR at the Geneva car house. In 1927, the car was scrapped and the line taken up. (Courtesy Emiliano Echeverria.)

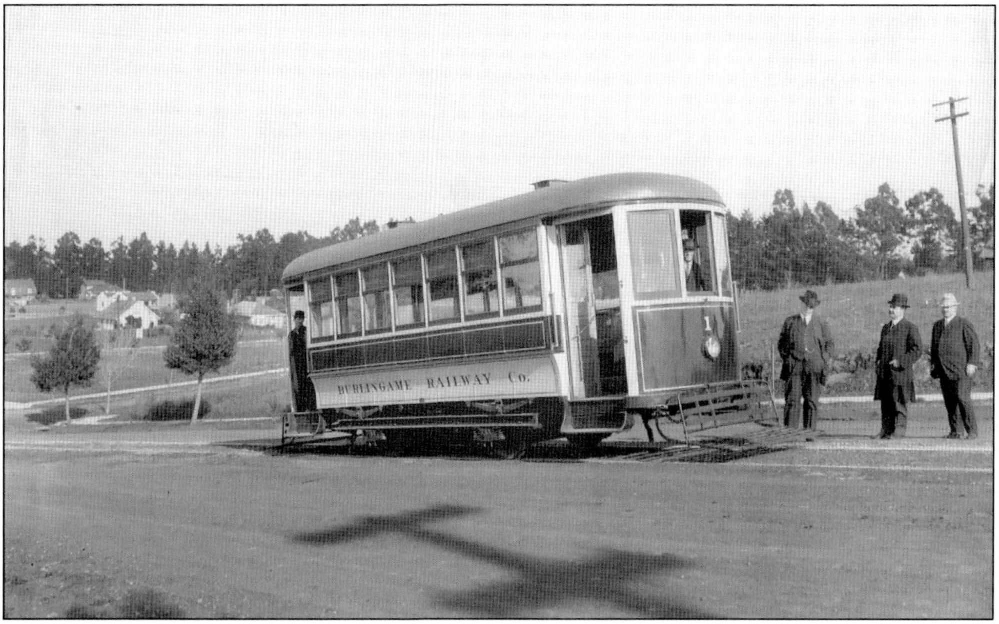

The official party is seated on the car ready to go downhill. The cross street at the top of the hill is Vancouver, which at this time supported large entrance columns to Burlingame Hills. From Vancouver to Alvarado, the line was on a center strip right-of-way. There was only one car and the operator did all maintenance in the street as there was no carbarn. Easton filed for a franchise to extend the line south to Burlingame Avenue, the location of Burlingame's Southern Pacific depot, but never executed it. (Courtesy Rudy Brandt.)

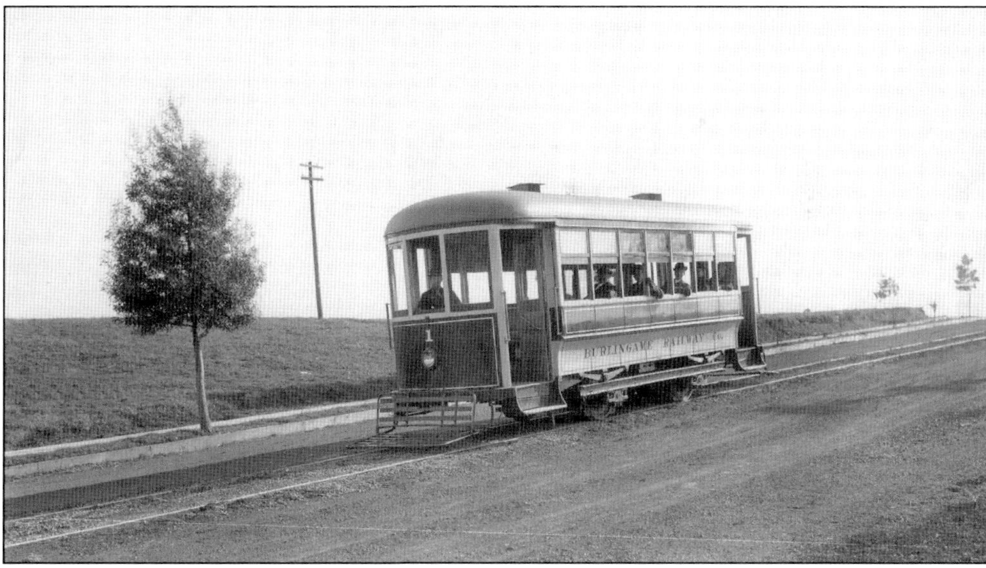

On opening day of the battery car line up on Burlingame's Hillside Drive on Saturday, February 22, 1913, the officials stopped on the 12.76 percent grade between Baden at the bottom and Vancouver at the top to show off the car's ability to make the hill. After crossing Vancouver, the car entered the new Easton subdivision, known as Burlingame Hills. The line was a real estate promotion. The car was purchased from the Federal Storage Battery Company and seated 26 passengers. (Courtesy Rudy Brandt.)

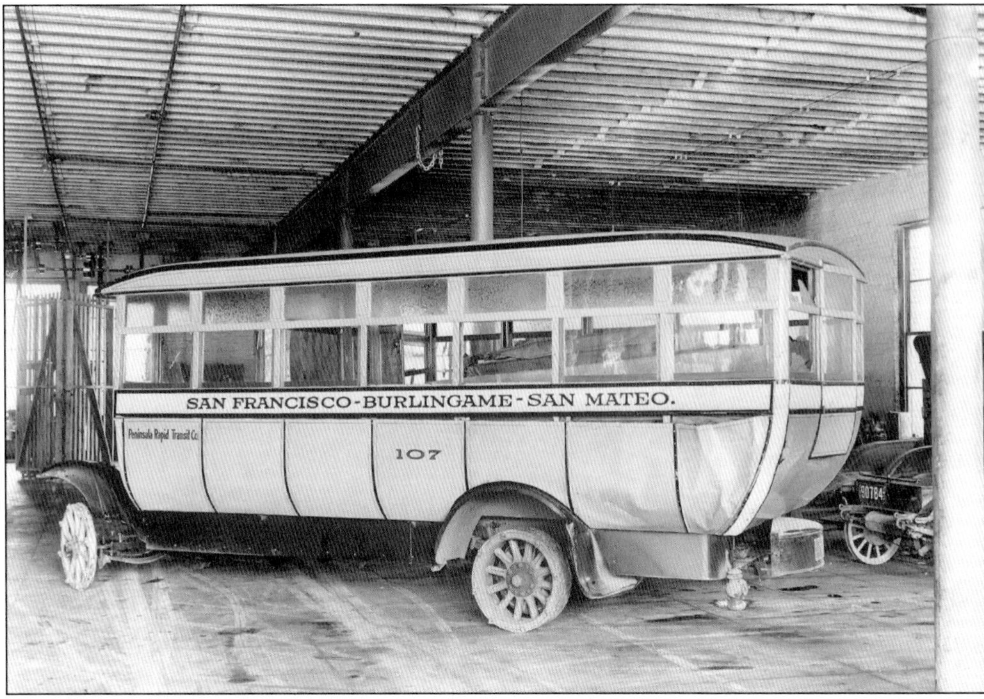

Here was the motor coach competition in July 1915. We don't know the circumstances which led to the altercation damage in the photograph, but Peninsular Rapid Transit bus 107 is hurting, and URR was there to document the damage for the claims department. Peninsular Rapid Transit was a predecessor of the service operated by Greyhound, which eventually became a part of today's SamTrans services. (Courtesy Rudy Brandt.)

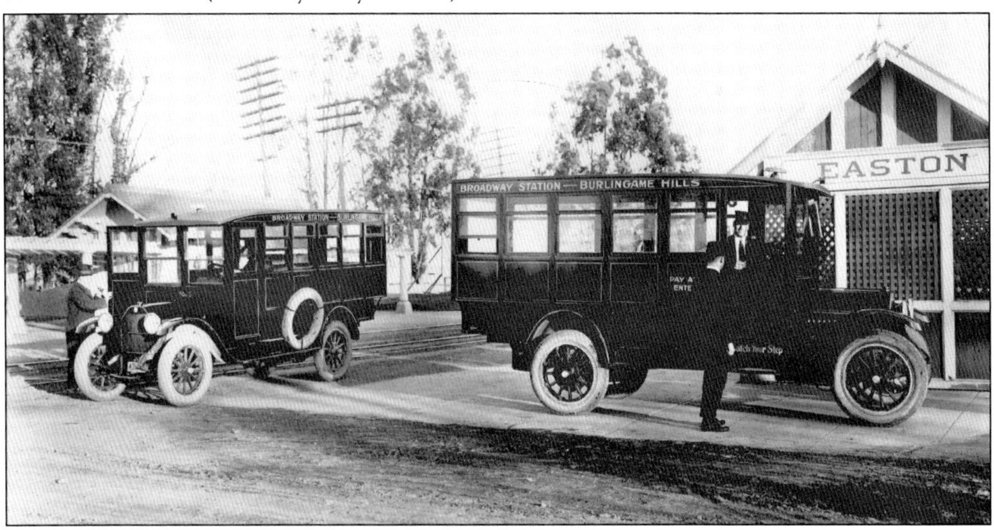

The Burlingame Railway started in 1913, but by 1917, losses prompted its discontinuance. Permission to abandon was granted only if another type of service could be maintained. This brought about the introduction of two Studebaker buses with 40-horsepower engines and 15-passenger capacity to take over the route on November 19, 1917. These buses could be chartered on Sundays for outings by families. Here the buses are posing on opening day at Broadway, or Easton Station. Ansel Easton finally got out if the transit business. (Courtesy Rudy Brandt.)

Five

THE RIDE IS OVER

The January 16, 1949, demise of the 40 line was considered important enough for San Mateo's 5,000-watt radio station KVSM to send two reporters to chronicle the last trips. August Stokes was the motorman on No. 1241, the last revenue car. Stokes, Muni's only veteran of the Spanish–American War, had worked on the 40 line for 26 years. When asked by the radio reporter for his thoughts, Stokes replied without a tone of remorse in his voice, "Don't like them to take it off." Conductor Frank Pattee, with a quarter-century of 40-line service, told the radio audience "it was a swell run."

Mrs. Harrington of Burlingame imparted that Pattee was her "favorite conductor, the best one who had been on the line, so courteous and nice." She gave him a big kiss. Harrington gleefully also informed everyone when she boarded No. 1241 that as a little girl in 1903, she rode the first car to San Mateo. With a clang of the bell and Pattee's cry of "goodbye," No. 1241 left San Mateo forever, as the KVSM announcer reported, "the special charter line of the railfans" is in its wake.

Excited railfans were eager to denounce the folly of the abandonment. The railfans quickly surrounded the radio announcer upon his boarding of the special. "It has the potential for rapid transit." "A sad affair." "You can't even smoke on buses." The sole counter comment came from Francis Guido, a San Mateo lawyer, founder and longtime publisher of *The Western Railroader*. Guido stated that it was a "sad shame it has to go out, but it's something everyone wanted, wasn't it?" He was soundly booed.

Unfortunately, Guido accurately mirrored the temperament of the times. As America's streetcar and interurban mileage shrunk, few complained. To the majority, "progress" had been served. This was the era when streetcars were regarded as an obsolete mode of transport. The public and most of the railfans knew that such abandonments were part of the natural economic order.

Following shortly behind No. 1241 was a Northern California Railroad Club fantrip with car No. 1235 under the command of motorman Lorin Silleman and conductor Dick Biermann, both railfans of long standing. For the railfans aboard No. 1235 a source of excitement was the night's unusual routing, which was different from any prior 40-line routing. Cars on their last trip would operate directly to Muni's streetcar cemetery, Funston Yard ("the boneyard"), on Lincoln Way. Once in San Francisco, after stopping at the Geneva barn, No. 1235 and all 40-line cars would head down Mission Street that fateful night.

Amid much whistle-blowing and clatter-gong ringing, the 46-year-old No. 1235 departed San Mateo for the last time at 1:30 a.m. The routing was to be Mission Street to Second Street, Second Street to Market Street, and then west on Market Street to Eddy Street, over the Eddy Street trackage of the 31 line to Divisadero, and then over parts of abandoned tracks of the 20, 7, and 17 lines on Divisadero, Oak, Stanyan, Frederick, and Lincoln Way to reach the Funston Yard. Before going north on Second Street, however, No. 1235 continued down Mission Street to the ferry, thereby becoming the very last car to use that trackage.

When No. 1235 arrived at the boneyard, the era of the San Mateo Interurban, which had begun as San Francisco's first trolley line, was over. Motorman Lorin Silleman was given a construction plate from No. 1235's 1923 rebuilding accompanied with the following text: "From 40 Line Car 1235 /The last special car whose final dawn was seen January 16, 1949/With love and admiration this plate is given to Motorman Lorin Sillerman [*sic*], by whose hand the San Mateo Interurban was safely guided to the Great Carbarn in the Sky. Charles R. Ward."

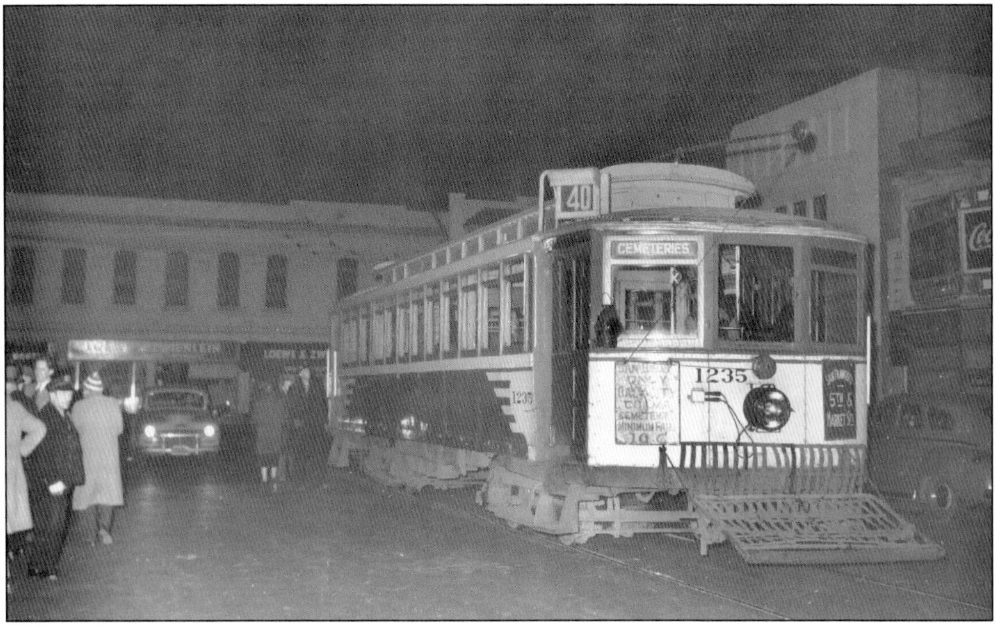

The Northern California Railroad Club chartered car No. 1235 for the last trip on the 40 line following the last regular service car. Here it is at the San Mateo depot late at night on January 15, 1949. It was a sad occasion. The appropriate destination ("Cemeteries") was displayed on the route sign box. This was the end of the line for these cars as well as the route. (Courtesy Robert Townley.)

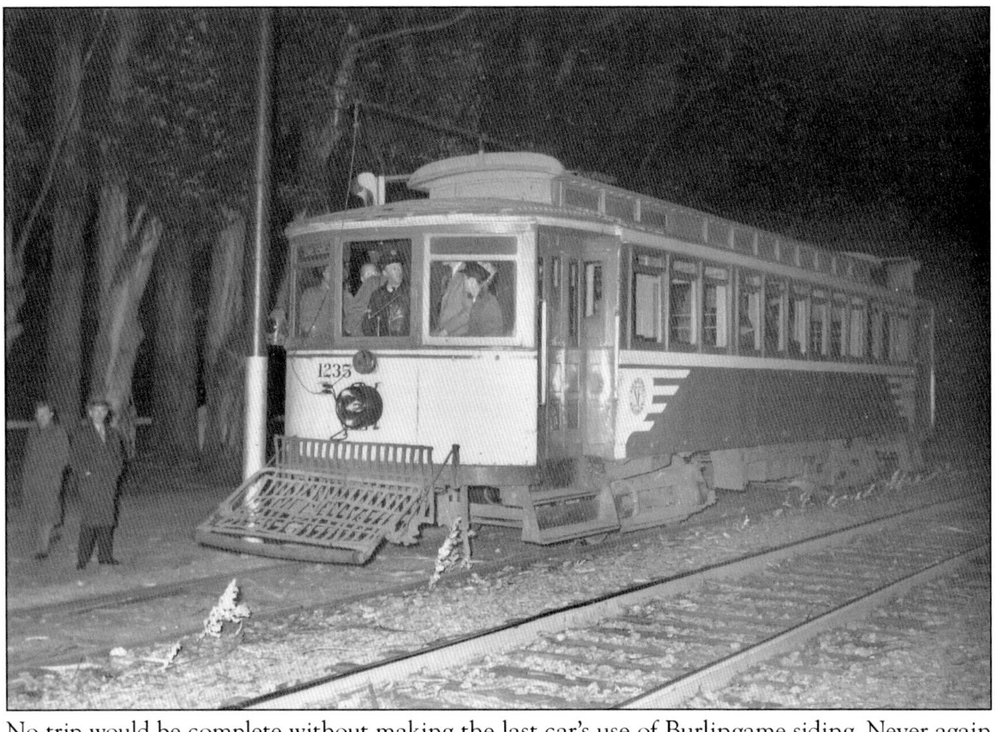

No trip would be complete without making the last car's use of Burlingame siding. Never again would a car rest on the siding. (Courtesy Robert Townley.)

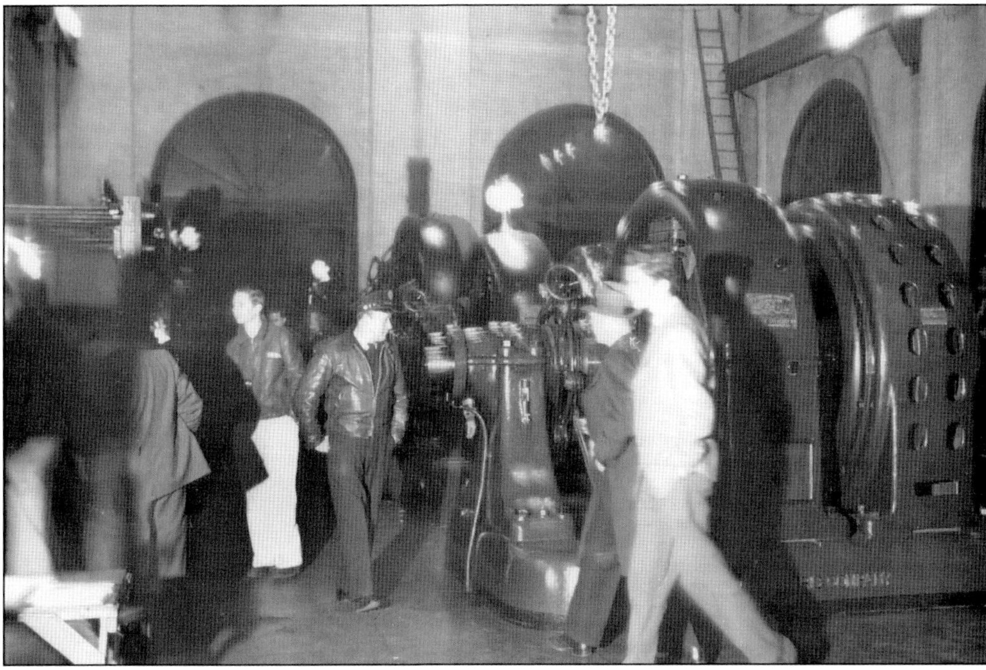

The "funeral party" stopped at the Millbrae substation for a final farewell to the crew. Lorin Silleman, wearing the leather jacket, is shown inspecting one of the rotary converters and taking a last look at the machine that powered the line he worked on. This site today is directly in front of the Millbrae Cal Train-BART depot. (Courtesy Robert Townley.)

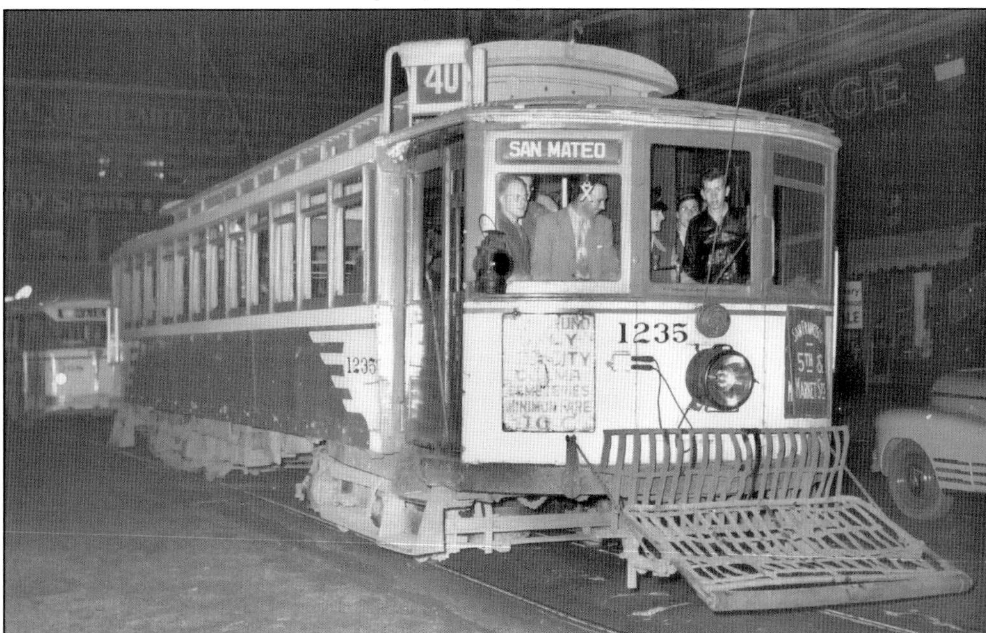

When the party, which included the authors, returned to San Francisco, it made one last trip to Fifth and Market Streets, the line's terminal since 1904. An era in transportation was closing. (Courtesy Robert Townley.)

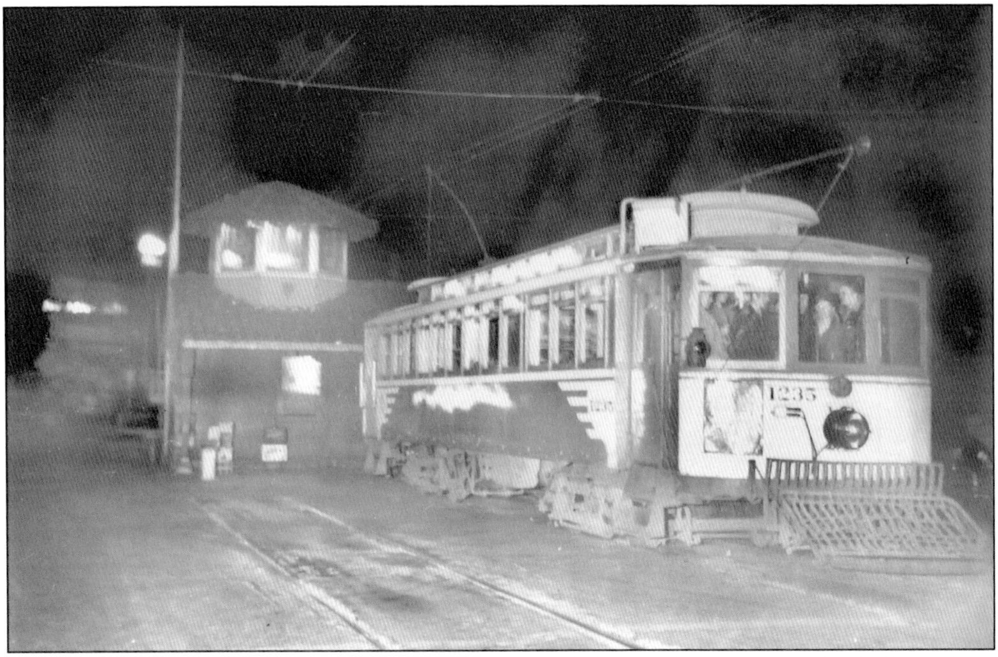

The group made one last trip to the Mission Street line's ferry stub terminal at the Embarcadero. When the 40 line closed, the Mission Street lines also closed. In 1902, the precursor to the 40 line started near the ferry building. (Courtesy Robert Townley.)

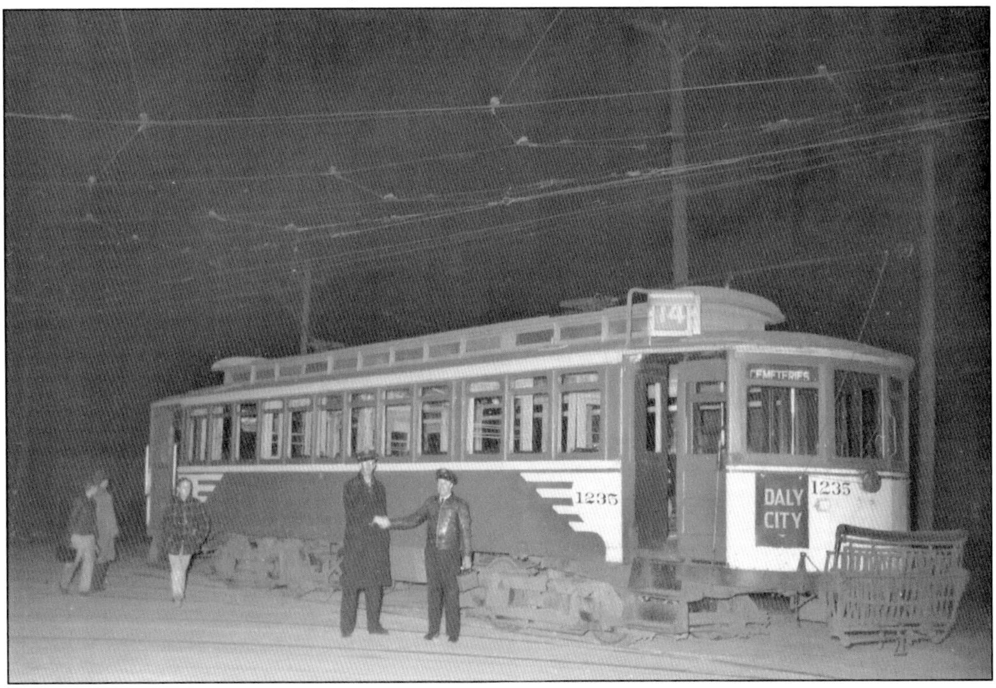

At about 2:00 a.m. the next morning, on the 16th of January, 1949, the group pulled into the boneyard on Lincoln Way. Lorin Silleman shakes hands with Richard Bierman, the conductor. Both have operated car No. 1235 for the last time. Number "14" is displayed in the route box for the final trip out Mission Street from the ferry terminal. (Courtesy Robert Townley.)

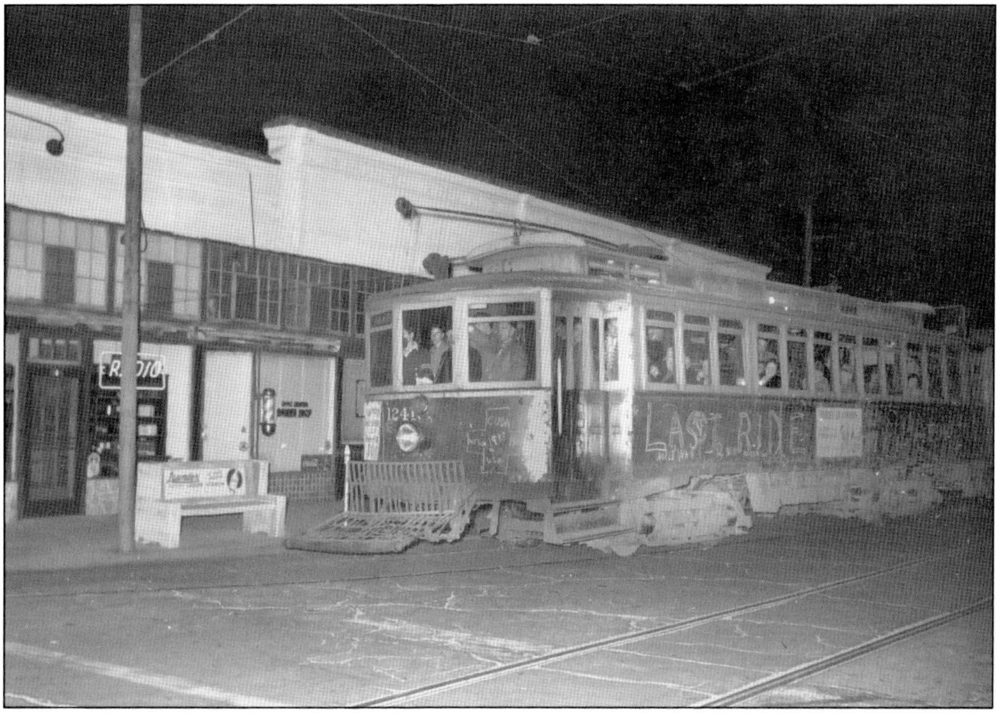

No. 1241 was the last regular service car. Here it is turning onto Ellsworth from Baldwin. Today the stores behind the car are gone, and the space is a parking lot for a grocery store. (Courtesy Al Thoman.)

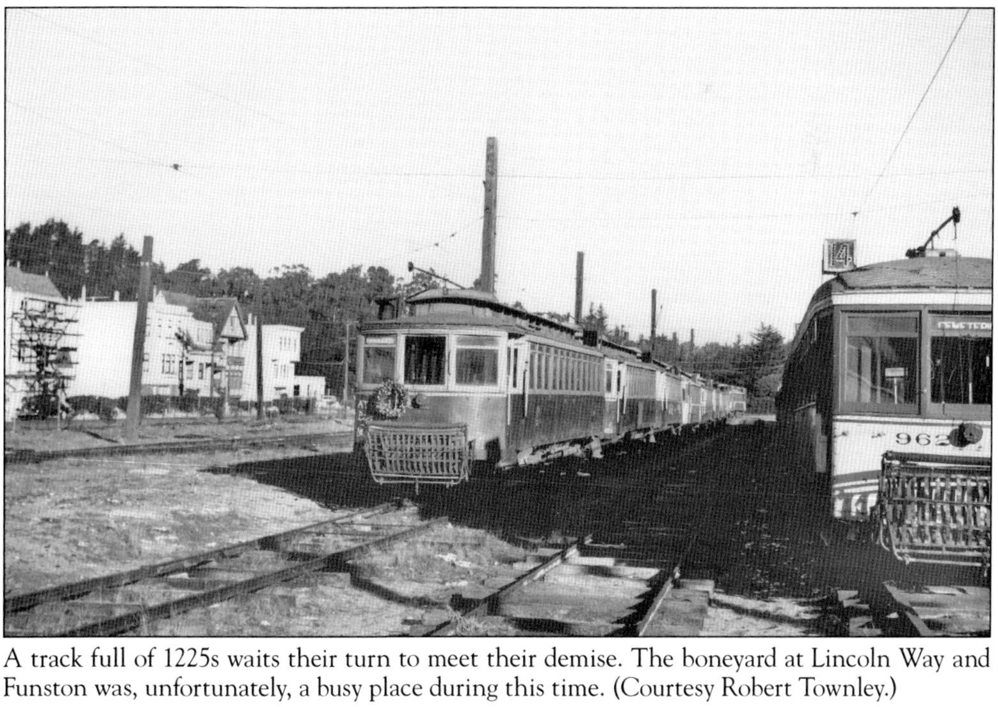

A track full of 1225s waits their turn to meet their demise. The boneyard at Lincoln Way and Funston was, unfortunately, a busy place during this time. (Courtesy Robert Townley.)

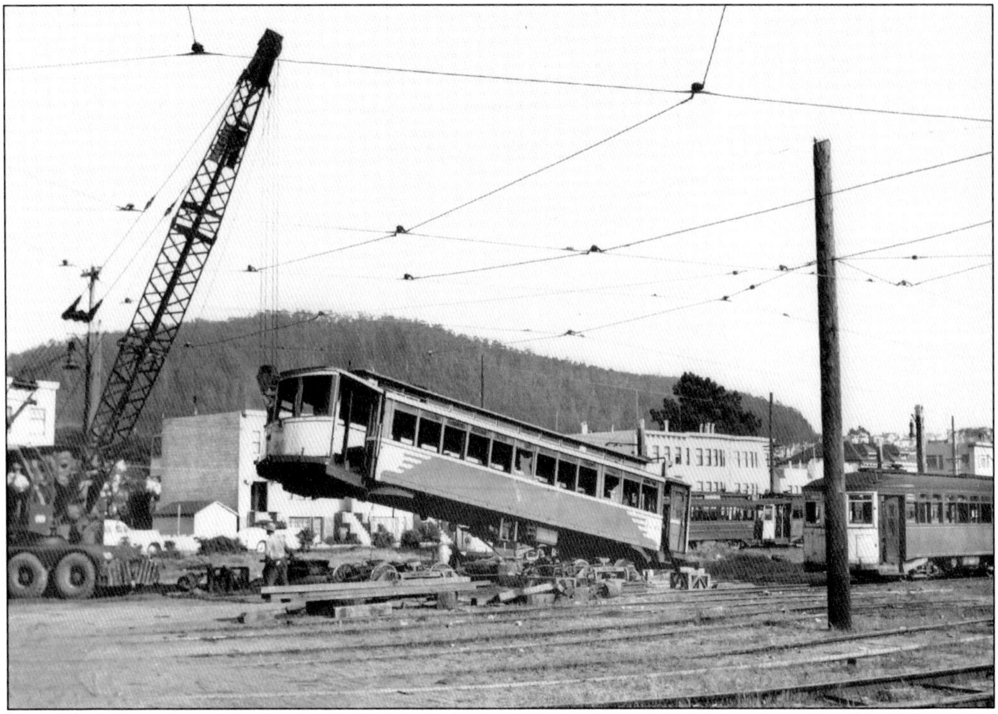

Car No. 1242 is being lifted by the end of the platform. Because the platforms were not designed for load stress in an upward direction, more than one car had its platform torn off and fell to the ground. The scrapper apparently didn't realize this design function. It's a wonder no one got hurt in the process. (Courtesy Robert Townley.)

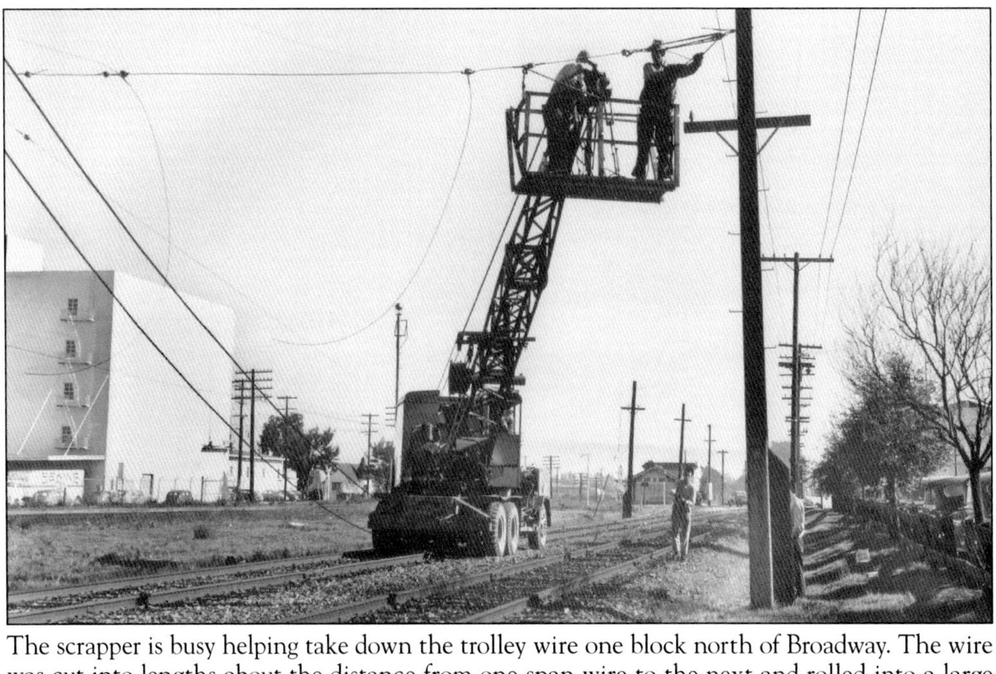

The scrapper is busy helping take down the trolley wire one block north of Broadway. The wire was cut into lengths about the distance from one span wire to the next and rolled into a large coil for easy handling. (Courtesy Walter Vielbaum.)

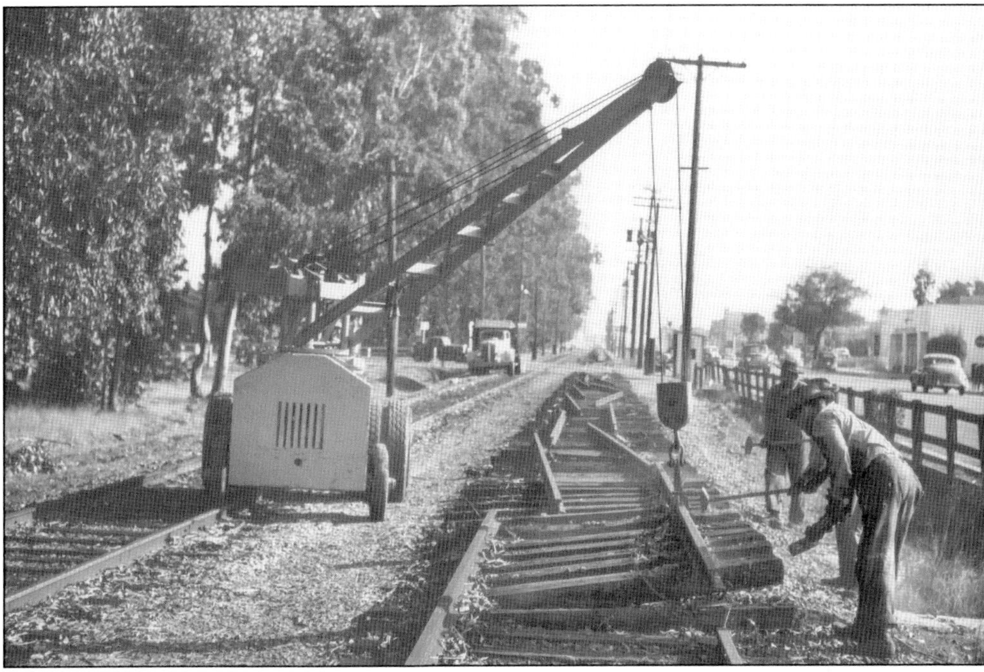

The scrapper is busy knocking off the redwood crossties just north of Oak Grove. The scrapper complained bitterly about people stealing the crossties, as the plan was to sell the good ones to other railroads and the rejects to gardeners and firewood seekers. (Courtesy Walter Vielbaum.)

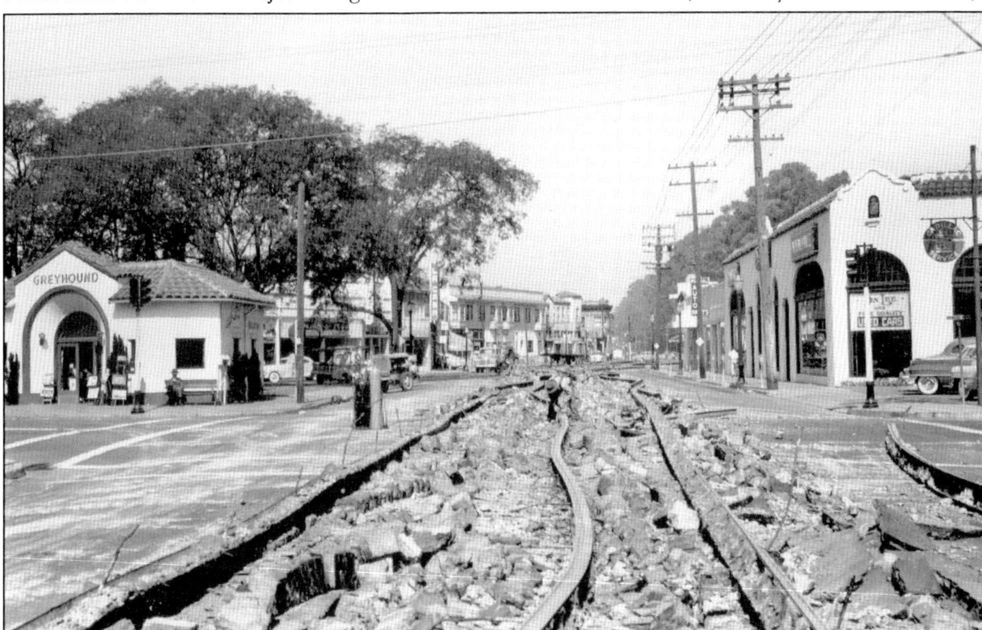

No, it's not a war scene. Ripping up the girder rail on California Drive put a serious crimp in the use of the street. The Don Lee Cadillac distributor, right, on the corner of Howard Avenue and California Drive had been the home of the main shop and building facility of the Peninsula Rapid Transit buses. Burlingame built and owns the Greyhound depot, which survives today. (Courtesy Walter Vielbaum.)

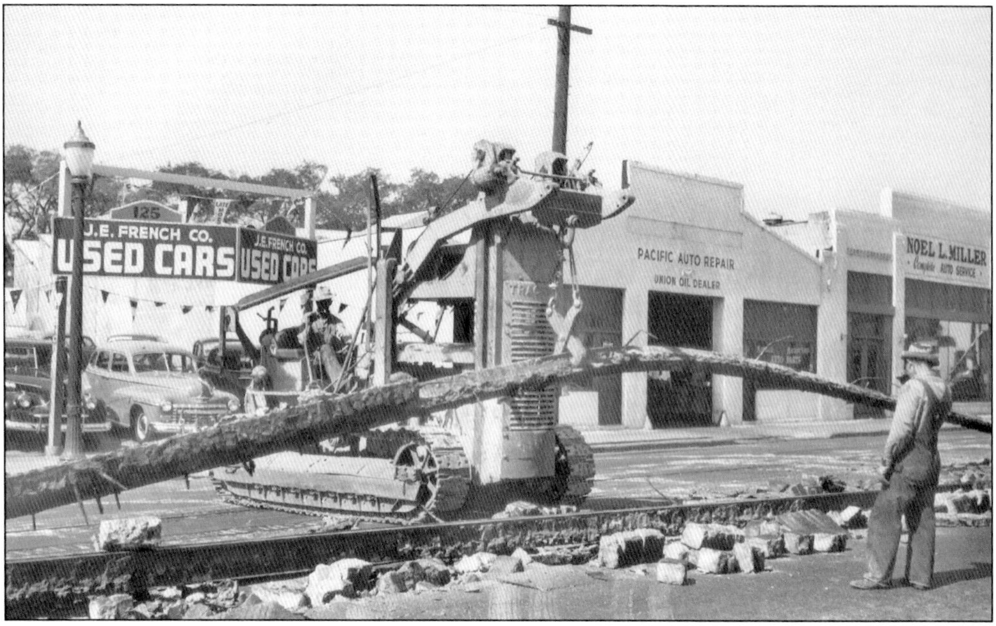

This is how the rail was yanked from the street. Pacific Auto Repair, behind the tractor, is author Walter Vielbaum's family business. The City of San Francisco backed out of their responsibility to remove the track and deeded it to San Mateo and Burlingame to do with as they wanted. (Courtesy Walter Vielbaum.)

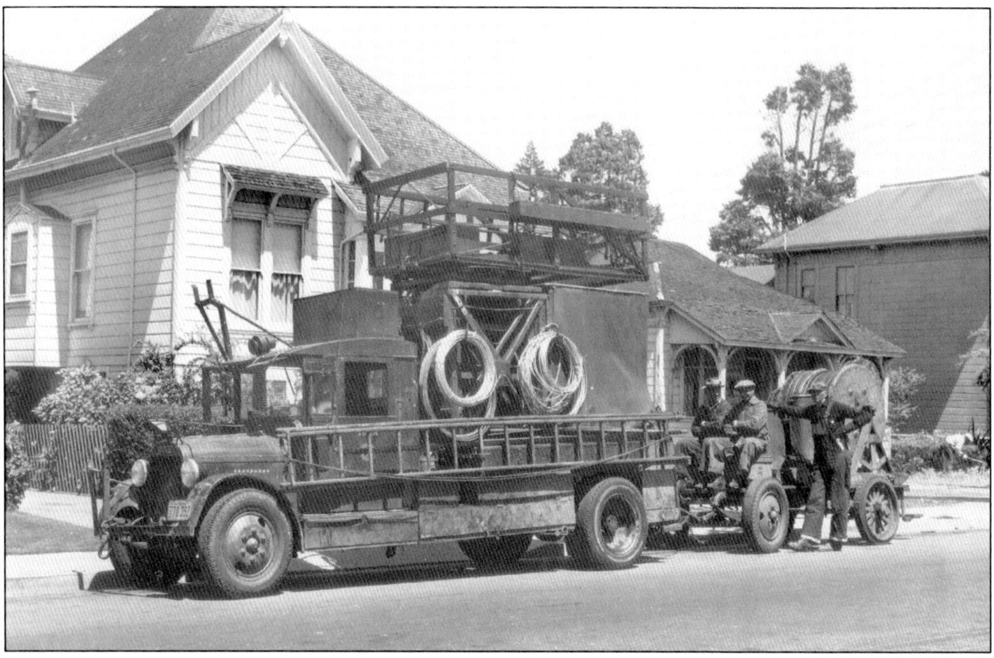

Here the old Fageol line truck and trailer from Municipal Railway of San Francisco takes down the valuable copper feeder cable on Ellsworth Street in San Mateo. The power was turned on and the winch wound up the cable hot. The controller is visible behind the man standing. This was common practice in the old days. Note the wooden-spoke, solid-tire wheel on the trailer's rear axle. (Courtesy Walter Vielbaum.)

CARS OF THE 40 LINE

During the almost 50 years of service to San Mateo, a number of different types of cars operated over the line. The following is a brief description of those cars.

THE SAN FRANCISCO AND SAN MATEO RAILWAY CARS

Car #	Trucks	Builder	Year	Renumbered
1-15	Single	O'Brian and Sons	1891–1892	
16-30	Double	Hammond	1891–1892	
31-40	Single	Carter	1894	URR 621-630
41-50	Double	Hammond	1900	URR 671-680
51	Double	Holman	1900	URR 681
52-70	Double	St. Louis Car Co.	1901	URR 682-698

THE BIG SUBS

Car Numbers	1–12
Builder	St. Louis Car Co.
Date	1906
Seats	56
Length	52' 1"
Trucks	St Louis 61A
Motors	4-GE 73
Controllers	C-6-K
Weight	75,640 lbs.

Car #1 disposed February 26, 1935
Car #2 disposed July 22, 1933
Car #3 disposed July 19, 1933
Car #4 disposed March 15, 1935
Car #5 disposed March 20, 1935
Car #6 disposed July 16, 1933
Car #7 disposed July 26, 1933
Car #8 disposed February 24, 1935
Car #9 disposed July 18, 1933
Car #10 disposed March 25, 1935
Car #11 disposed July 10, 1933
Car #12 disposed February 18, 1935

THE 1225-CLASS CARS

Original Configuration

Car Numbers	1225 to 1244	Seats	48	Motors	4-GE 58
Builder	Laclede Car Co.	Length	45' 9"	Controllers	GE K-14
Date	1903	Trucks	Brill 27E	Weight	54,060 lbs.

These cars were modified several times during their 46-year service life (1903–1949).

URR Interim Rebuilding (1916–1920): The URR modified 18 of the cars in the late 1910s by creating a short three-window open section at one end of the car. Apparently, the 1239 and 1242 were unmodified.

MSRy PAYE Conversion (1921–1922): This rebuilding program included modifications to enable PAYE service and partitions to create a three-compartment car, and upgraded the cars to replace the "Big Subs" on the San Mateo line. After rebuilding, the changes to the configuration of the cars were as follows:

Seats	40	Motors	4-GE 57	Weight	56,138 lbs.
Length	48' 1"	Controller	K-28B		

Subsequent Modifications: A number of additional changes were made to the cars by the Market Street Railway in 1926, including electric heaters under the seats, leather cushioned seats, electric signal bells, air-operated gongs, and route number boxes. In 1930, field taps were added to increase the speed of the cars to 50 miles per hour.

Unique Cars

• Car 1228 was modified as a one-man car, but never used in revenue service as such. It was rebuilt back as a two-man car configuration, but retained its folding steps and door configuration. No photos have ever been found of the car in its one-man configuration.
• At one time, Car 1229 had air horns. The air horns were removed by Muni.
• Cars 1225, 1230, and 1234 retained rub rails on the car sides. All other cars had been rebuilt with straight sides.
• Teddy Roosevelt was reported to have ridden car 1242 in 1903.

Paint Schemes

Market Street Railway Era: All 1225-class cars were repainted in the late 1920s with white fronts, red window sash, and yellow striping on their green sides. None of the 1200s received the "zip stripe" paint scheme that many of the city cars received starting in the late 1930s. In later years, MSRy omitted both the red windows and striping as an economy measure.

Municipal Railway of San Francisco Era:
•The 1225-class cars were the first of the former MSRy streetcars to be repainted by Muni. The following cars received the yellow and blue paint scheme then in use on the system: 1227 to 1230, 1232 to 1236, 1238, 1241, and 1243 to 1244 (note: 1235 was later repainted cream and green with wings as listed below).
•The 1232 received an experimental yellow and blue with a blue "V" on the front and was subsequently repainted to the plain yellow and blue.
•The 1225 was the first car repainted in cream and light green (with no wings).
•The following cars received Muni's cream and green with wings paint scheme: 1228, 1231, 1235, 1237, and 1242 (note: 1237 had a cream front only for a short period of time; cars 1226, 1239, and 1240 were retired by Market Street Railway).

Car #	Date of Disposition
1225	Retired October 5, 1948
1226	1942
1227–1238	Sold January 31, 1949
1239	Car hit a truck in San Mateo in 1940—Retired 1941
1240	Car hit a truck at Mission and New Montgomery in 1939—Retired 1941
1241–1243	Sold January 31, 1949
1244	Car burned at Millbrae in Aug 1947—Retired September 17, 1947

Cars 1715, 1716, and 1722: In the 1910s, three car bodies were built by URR. These cars were designed after the arch roof 200-class cars and used electrical equipment from wreck-damaged cars of the 1550 class (1690, 1722, and 1745). In 1923–1924, they were extensively upgraded for service on the No. 40 line, with interurban type seats, large headlights, whistles, and enclosed platforms. At this time, car 1745 became car 1715, while car 1690 became car 1716.

Car Numbers	1715, 1716, and 1722		Length	46' 6"
Builder	URR		Trucks	McGuire 10A
Date	1915 to 1918		Motors	4-GE 57
Seats	44		Controllers	GE K-28B

One-Man 900-Type Cars: During World War II, one-man service between Daly City and San Mateo was inaugurated using specially equipped 900-type cars. These 900-type cars were distinguished with their large interurban headlights that enabled them to operate at night, including 950, 952, 953, 957, 958, 959, 960 and 962.